W9-ACP-763

The Gospel according to *Star Wars*

Second Edition

The Gospel according to *Star Wars*

Faith, Hope, and the Force

Second Edition

John C. McDowell

WESTMINSTER
JOHN KNOX PRESS
LOUISVILLE · KENTUCKY

© 2007, 2017 John C. McDowell

Second edition
Published by Westminster John Knox Press
Louisville, Kentucky

17 18 19 20 21 22 23 24 25 26—10 9 8 7 6 5 4 3 2 1

All rights reserved. No part of this book may be reproduced or transmitted in any form or by any means, electronic or mechanical, including photocopying, recording, or by any information storage or retrieval system, without permission in writing from the publisher. For information, address Westminster John Knox Press, 100 Witherspoon Street, Louisville, Kentucky 40202-1396. Or contact us online at www.wjkbooks.com.

This book has not been prepared, approved, or licensed by any person or entity that created, published, or produced the *Star Wars* movies or related properties.

Book design by Sharon Adams
Cover design by designpointinc.com and Allison Taylor

Library of Congress Cataloging-in-Publication Data

Names: McDowell, John C., author.
Title: The Gospel according to Star Wars : faith, hope, and the force / John
    C. McDowell.
Description: Second edition. | Louisville, KY : Westminster John Knox Press,
    2017. | Includes bibliographical references and index. | D
Identifiers: LCCN 2017005505 (print) | LCCN 2017021783 (ebook) | ISBN
    9781611648140 (ebk.) | ISBN 9780664262839 (pbk. : acid-free paper)
Subjects: LCSH: Star Wars films. | Motion pictures--Religious
    aspects--Christianity.
Classification: LCC PN1995.9.S695 (ebook) | LCC PN1995.9.S695 M43 2017
    (print) | DDC 791.43/75--dc23
LC record available at https://lccn.loc.gov/2017005505

♾ The paper used in this publication meets the minimum requirements of the American National Standard for Information Sciences—Permanence of Paper for Printed Library Materials, ANSI Z39.48-1992.

Most Westminster John Knox Press books are available at special quantity discounts when purchased in bulk by corporations, organizations, and special-interest groups. For more information, please e-mail SpecialSales@wjkbooks.com.

GARY PUBLIC LIBRARY

To my father, John D. McDowell,
and to my children, Archie, Jonathan, Joseph, Meg, and Robert
Feel the Force around you!

In memorium of my grandfather Thomas Manson

GARY PUBLIC LIBRARY

I . . . find it very interesting, especially in terms of the academic world, that they will take a work and dissect it in so many different ways. Some of the ways are very profound, and some are very accurate. A lot of it, though, is just the person using their imagination to put things in there that really weren't there, which I don't mind either. I mean, one of the things I like about *Star Wars* is that it stimulates the imagination, and that's why I don't have any qualms about the toys or about any of the things that are going on around *Star Wars*, because it does allow young people to use their imagination and think outside the box.

Star Wars creator George Lucas
to journalist Bill Moyer

Contents

Acknowledgments

A long time ago, in a galaxy far, far away . . ."—well, thirty-nine years ago at the time of writing, and in a small town in Northern Ireland, although I suppose many would claim that that is indeed a galaxy far, far away—I was rushed after dinner to the local cinema by my father. The movie we traveled to watch I had only heard of by observing some peers in the school playground carrying a novel titled *Star Wars*. It was, after all, a time prior to internet available trailers, frequent attendance at cinema multiplexes, and movie advertisements on television or on the side of buses. What happened on that warm early summer evening is a rather unremarkable story. What is noteworthy, though, is the fact that it is one a multitude of children of my generation from across the globe have recounted in similar ways.

The queue outside the theatre was enormous, but the movie was certainly well worth the two-hour wait. From the moment the brass section boomed out the initial notes of John Williams's unforgettable opening theme, I was hooked, captivated, inspired, transported to another galaxy far, far away. *Star Wars* toys, games, clothing, mugs, bedding, posters, collectable display items, school stationery, books, model kits, film soundtracks, multiple film formats (VHS/DVDs/Blu-rays), and so on have ever since cut a huge (and I should really emphasize the word "huge") hole in my family's bank balances of an ion-canon-blast-proportion. I even purchased a data projector specifically to watch the movies on a 180-inch screen on a wall in the house. To say that I have been a "fan" of *Star Wars* is far too tame a word: "fanatic" would probably better describe my passion. I unhesitatingly confess to being one of the so-called "Jedi-generation" and to having spent ("misspent," some would claim) many of the early years of my youth—and every year since the rerelease of the 'classic trilogy' in 1997—deeply engrossed in watching, reading, and talking about the films.

As in the first edition of this book, my family deserves a sympathetic mention. My wife, someone still not imbibed with any great enthusiasm for the saga, continues to express her exasperation with me and the too-regular *Star Wars* conversations that take place at home. (To make matters worse, she enjoyed *The Force Awakens* most out of the seven episodes, which adds a whole other level to the household arguments about the franchise.) I owe her an apology. But she also deserves my gratitude, since one of my inspirational moments came during her frustrated complaint that I talk to our children more about *Star Wars* than I talk about theological matters. It was this, rather than my love of the whole *Star Wars* universe, that directly led me to undertake the project, a study that was and continues to be a labor of love. This book is largely about my wrestling with the theological-educational value of two trilogies of epic material, and it is also a self-justification to my wife that my conversations with our children really can be more theologically profound than she otherwise believes. My children are now at a stage where they can engage with substantial insight, sensitivity, knowledge, and some considerable critical understanding of the saga and the Expanded Universe materials. Last year I even managed to lose for the first time to my eldest, Archie, at *Star Wars* Trivial Pursuit. The wound still smarts. I still reign victorious at *Star Wars* Risk, *Star Wars* Monopoly, and *Star Wars* chess, however, although Archie, Jonathan, and Joseph do show me up in the various versions of *Star Wars* Battlefront. With their Yoda-like skills in wielding lightsabers, they make me look like the laboring Obi-Wan from *A New Hope*.

Those I thanked in the acknowledgments of the 2007 version of this study deserve to be thanked again. My colleagues and friends at New College in the University of Edinburgh, in particular my fellow systematic theologians, covered for me during my sabbatical in the first semester of 2005–6. I had planned to write a different book during that time. But, after watching *The Revenge of the Sith* for the first time with my brother-in-law one May evening, the *Star Wars* bug bit, and I knew I had to take my own revenge on the Sith by writing an article that quickly expanded into a book. Philip Law of Westminster John Knox Press was encouragingly supportive of the project. Most importantly, several people provided especially helpful comments on the final draft of the initial book, taking considerable time out of their own very busy schedules to do so. The exceedingly thorough observations of James Shaw and Dr. John Yates helped make much of my presentation clearer and more careful than it would otherwise have been. Rev. Graham Astles, Dr. Jason Wardley, and Mark Storslee were also instrumental in forcing me to think harder about what I was attempting to argue. Hilary Lenfesty, Brian Adair, Andrew Hayes, Robbie Leigh, and Kate Wilkie provided useful comments at various stages of the drafting process. Dr. Bill Stevens had been kind enough to lend me his DMin thesis, which guided some of my thoughts on Jungian archetypes (*The Quest: Models for Euro-American Male Spirituality Based on the Legends of the Search for the Holy Grail*, unpublished DMin, San Francisco Theological Seminary, 2000).

In the years between 2007 and 2015 I have had published, among numerous other things, some more specialized academic works on the *Star Wars* saga. In particular I would like to thank McFarland Press for doing a fine job with *The Politics of Big Fantasy: The Ideologies of* Star Wars, The Matrix, *and* The Avengers (2014) and *Identity Politics in George Lucas'* Star Wars (2016). These studies have allowed me to engage with publications in cultural and ideological studies and have permitted a level of detail and footnoting that has not been appropriate for *The Gospel according to Star Wars*. My conversations, debates, and academic arguments with two very talented young theologians, Drs. Ashley Moyse and Scott Kirkland, have inspired me over the last few years. I am privileged to have been their doctoral supervisor. I am indebted to them for helping me refrain from compromising my theological interests and stay true to the appropriate academic rigor during, to borrow from Obi-Wan, "the dark times" of "the Empire," albeit an Empire more corporately than militarily focused. I would also like to mention Prof. Mario Minichiello and Drs. Fergus King and Chris Falzon.

I continue to miss those football clubs with which I had been involved for almost six years, Lambton Jaffas and St. Johns Football Clubs, especially the lads of the 14/1s whom I was very much blessed to coach for three unforgettable seasons. Go Invincibles! My boys and I have been able to find a new home with Croydon Ranges.

It is, however, with sorrow that two friends are now to be acknowledged *in memorium*: Drs. Mike Purcell and Jason Wardley. Jason was a source of valuable information when I first turned to writing on popular culture at Edinburgh in 2005, and Mike was instrumental in settling me into my new working environment there some five years earlier. Both are sorely missed and very warmly remembered. I must also mention in the same vein the external examiner of my doctorate, Prof. John Webster. My maternal grandfather, Thomas Manson, passed away late in 2013. He had been a tremendous inspiration to me, a man with a responsible heart, and I hope that in everything I do I will honor the legacy of this self-deprecating man.

Since moving to Melbourne to the University of Divinity early in 2015, I have been refreshed, reawakened to Force-consciousness even, and reenthused by my work in a way that has reinvigorated the theological passion of my time in Edinburgh. I am reminded on a daily basis that good and honest theology matters. Melbourne's verdant land nourishes a sense of adventure all too undernourished by the devouring wilds of Tatooine's desert. Dr. Suman Kashyap has been a skillful and diligent administrative resource in the Research Office, and Prof. Peter Sherlock has been a truly inspiring and hospitable Vice Chancellor. It has been a pleasure to find such support and vision at a time when higher education is losing a humanitarian sense of its purpose and is becoming heavily bureaucratized for largely corporate ends. The Australian government, like so many in the contemporary West, appears to badly lack a sense of the need for a humanizing, and not merely technical, education. I am grateful to the members of the Yarra Institute for Religion and Social Policy for having appointed me to their board and now to the committee of their newest incarnation as the University of Divinity Centre of Research in Religion and Social Policy, and I thank Yarra Theological Union and Catholic Theological College both for accrediting me to teach.

My thanks are due to David Dobson and all at Westminster John Knox Press for not only having done a splendid job with the publication of the 2007 first edition of the book but also for having invited me to produce this second and revised edition.

Prof. John C. McDowell
Director of Research
University of Divinity
Melbourne, Australia

Abbreviations

ANH   *Star Wars Episode IV: A New Hope*
AOTC *Star Wars Episode II: Attack of the Clones*
ESB   *Star Wars Episode V: The Empire Strikes Back*
ROTJ   *Star Wars Episode VI: Return of the Jedi*
ROTS   *Star Wars Episode III: Revenge of the Sith*
SW   *Star Wars*
TFA   *Star Wars Episode VII: The Force Awakens*
TPM   *Star Wars Episode I: The Phantom Menace*

Introduction

*I*t hardly needs to be said that *Star Wars* is the most successful franchise in cinematic history. In fact it is a phenomenon, an extraordinary pop-culture sensation of an unprecedented scale. In its ground-breaking cinematography, monstrous merchandising blitzkrieg, and sheer popularity, the films have been epoch making. According to one commentator, "It was *Star Wars* that jump-started . . . [science fiction] in the 1970s, turning it from a vigorous but fairly small-scale genre into the dominant mode of cinematic discourse."[1] "What *Star Wars* and other similar breakaway hits from 1977 onwards achieved was to bring back many people who had previously given up on the cinema, and also to generate new stories (based on long-standing traditions, of course, but never told before) that were so appealing that they have been extended and retold countless times both in films and in other media ever since."[2] In fact, it is often claimed that the *Star Wars* movies actually saved Twentieth Century Fox from extinction. Of course film-magazine polls largely reflect the general age of their readership, but frequently *ANH* or *ESB* top the lists of "favorite film," and Darth Vader tops the "best screen villain" and even "best screen character" categories. In 1977 *ANH* was voted the year's best film by the Los Angeles Critics Association, was selected as one of the best five English-language films of the year by the National Board of Review, and made it onto the annual "ten best" lists of *Time* and the *New York Times*. It received ten Academy Award nominations (including best picture and screenplay), winning seven (all in the technical and craft categories). This was considerable critical as well as popular acclaim for a supposedly infantile "blockbuster" science-fiction movie.

In fact, the impact of *SW* has famously been felt even in political life (Reagan's Star Wars defense policy of the 1980s). *SW* creator George Lucas made some self-effacing comments in 1983 when claiming that the saga has "given people a certain amount of joy in a certain time of history . . . [and

that ultimately] it will be nothing more than a minor footnote in the pop culture of the 1970s and 1980s."[3] This impression now seems to have been too
unrealistically modest. Instead, as Garry Jenkins more accurately observes,
"*Star Wars* had, in many ways, been the central story of its era." And with the
release of the cinematic special editions of the classic trilogy in 1997, *TPM*
in 1999, the classic trilogy DVDs in 2004 and *ROTS* in 2005, and the first of
Disney's saga outputs in 2015, that cultural legacy has continued and been
considerably deepened. "Twenty years after it began re-writing the record
books," Jenkins observed at the time of the release of the Special Editions,
"it seemed suddenly as if *Star Wars* had never been away."[4] Of course, with
the (albeit controversial) prequel trilogy, the six seasons of the *Clone War*
animations, the *Star Wars Rebels* animations, and the much-hyped *Star Wars
Episode VII: The Force Awakens*, the cultural impact of the franchise continues to grow.

This phenomenal success has been something of a double-edged sword,
however. After *ANH* Martin Scorsese apparently complained: "*Star Wars*
was in. Spielberg was in. We [the makers of intelligent films] were finished."[5]
Apparently in 1997 Lucas's ex-wife confessed: "Right now, I'm disgusted
by the American film industry. There are so few good films, and part of me
thinks *Star Wars* is partly responsible for the direction the industry has gone
in, and I feel badly about that." There may be truth in the claim that *SW*
contributed to the "infantilizing" of the cinema, exaggerating movie-makers'
interest in the money that can be made from producing "children's films conceived and marketed largely for adults."[6] Yet there is also a serious danger
that the saga's ethical richness may be forgotten if we see *SW* simply as a
set of "Hollywood" movies. While Lucas was particularly dependent on the
Hollywood machine for financing *ANH*, we should not forget that *SW*, from
ESB until *ROTS*, can perhaps better be described as the most expensive *independent movies* ever made. Now that the Disney Corporation has purchased
the rights to the franchise and has embarked on a new cinematic trilogy, the
relationship between the stories and the mainstream corporate culture has
shifted markedly.

I am concerned about the common claim that Lucas's *SW* movies are little
more than fantasy "popcorn" fare, "heady, escapist stuff," and purely astonishing entertainment.[7] Lucas's creation undoubtedly is all of these, and originally he had hoped to return to the excitement of early adventure serials.

> I didn't want to make 2001. . . . I wanted to make a space fantasy that was
> more in the genre of Edgar Rice Burroughs; that whole other end of space
> fantasy that was there before science took it over in the Fifties. Once the

atomic bomb came, they forgot the fairy-tales and the dragons and Tolkien and all the real heroes.[8]

The roots of *SW* lie largely in the narrative traditions of folklore, fairy story, and even romantic chivalric tales. There are the magical Force, Jedi Knights with shining swords sworn to defend the good, an archetypal black knight, and so on. Each of the movies even opens with the text "A long time ago in a galaxy far, far away," which provides a clear nod back to the "Once upon a time . . ." of fairy tales. An interesting game is also to try to spot how many different materials Lucas has eclectically drawn together in his vision of the swashbuckling "classic trilogy" (or perhaps "classic thrillology")—the *Flash Gordon* serials, Westerns, Akira Kurosawa's *Hidden Fortress* (1958), the King Arthur and Robin Hood legends, J. R. R. Tolkien's *The Lord of the Rings*, *The Wizard of Oz*, and Joseph Campbell's reflections on mythology, to name but a few.[9] Samuel L. Jackson, who plays the great Jedi Master Mace Windu, sums up the feel of these films: "I look at these as the swashbuckling adventures of the modern era."[10] And this is why Gary Kurtz (producer of *ANH* and *ESB*) reveals that "We decided [with *ANH*] that we were making a *Flash Gordon*–type action adventure, and that we were coming in on Episode Four; at that time there was no thought of a series or prequels."[11] In this sense it is fascinating to observe the carefully created complexity of the back-stories of the various characters, the conditions and natural habitats of these characters, and the engineering details imagined for each and every vehicle.

On the other hand, *SW* is much more than mere entertainment. Many critics and fans alike miss this, perhaps because they do not know how to approach the complex relation of these movies and popular culture. "Because popularity is commonly equated with escapism and triviality, blockbusters have either been shunned or dismissed by most academic film scholars as calculated exercises in profit-making. . . . It is perhaps time to stop condemning the New Hollywood blockbuster and to start, instead, to understand it."[12] We should remember too that, as with any generalization, popular culture should not be spoken of as a monolith and the many differences among pop culture works need to be respected. Even folklore and fairy-story narrative traditions are socially and ethically important and not merely entertaining. *SW* is not an escapist fantasy that encourages us to forget (even if for a moment) our moral responsibilities in our "real" world. In fact, if we read it well, it possesses rich resources to change or transform us as moral subjects by helping us in some measure to encounter the deep mystery of what it means to be truly human.

But is this not to take the films "too seriously" and approach them in a way that distorts their proper meaning? One critic of *ANH* writes: "This picture was made for those (particularly males) who carry a portable shrine with them of their adolescence, a chalice of a self that was better then, before the world's affairs or—in any complex way—sex intruded."[13]

It is crucial to recognize that there is no ethically neutral narrative, no story we tell that does not say something about how we understand and value the world. "A society's mass fantasies," Archbishop of Canterbury Rowan Williams wisely warns, "are anything but trivial."[14] In fact, movies not only can tell us something of how the cultures from which they arise understand themselves, but they can equally and creatively engage with the way their audiences come to understand themselves. Bryan Stone puts it like this: "The cinema may function both as a *mirror* and as a *window*, but primarily as a *lens*. . . . Movies do not merely portray a world; they propagate a worldview. . . . [Cinema] helps us see what we might not otherwise have seen, but it also shapes what and how we see."[15] Lucas, of course, specifically designed *SW* to be broadly educational, so as to remind a morally cynical generation in the mid-1970s of the importance of being morally responsible.

> I wanted it to be a traditional moral study, to have some sort of palpable precepts in it that children could understand. There is always a lesson to be learned. Where do these lessons come from? Traditionally, we get them from church, the family, art, and in the modern world we get them from media—from movies.[16]

This is revealing and indicates that there is something distinctly misleading in the claim too often heard that movies are fun, nothing more. The entertainment-only approach is problematically naive about the formative effects of culture. After all, one should remember that the etymology of the very term *culture* comes from the Latin agricultural term *cultura* and refers to the soil that cultivates, nourishes, and supports the growth of plants. The multitalented Cicero (106–43 BCE) spoke of the "cultivation of the soul." Consequently, understanding people from their cultural expressions, the cultural artefacts that provide the conditions or soil for their self-understanding, becomes a crucial and unavoidable part of appreciating who that people is, how their views are formed, and how they understand themselves in their environment and in the world.[17] Here I would refer the reader elsewhere, particularly to my 2014 volume *The Politics of Big Fantasy*, especially the introduction, and to the ideological critiques of the saga that have emerged in recent years.

Furthermore, this fun-only approach simply distorts or violates some of Lucas's own stated intentions.[18] Lucas acknowledged, in an interview published the month following the theatrical release of *ROTJ* in 1983, that "film and [other] visual entertainment are a pervasively important part of our culture, an extremely significant influence on the way our society operates. . . . But, for better or worse, the influence of the church, which used to be all-powerful, has been usurped by film."[19] He continued by indicating a keen awareness of not only the teaching possibilities available through contemporary forms of media, of having what he later calls "a very large megaphone," but also of the moral responsibilities of filmmakers.[20] This is a notion he mentions on a number of occasions, and he does so particularly by appealing to the possibility of myth-making, something I shall take up in more detail in chapter 1. So, as early as an interview published in April 1977, prior to the release of *SW* (from 1979 known more fully as *Star Wars Episode IV: A New Hope*), Lucas was lamenting that "there was not a lot of mythology in our society—the kind of stories we tell ourselves and our children, which is the way our heritage is passed down. Westerns used to provide that, but there weren't Westerns anymore."[21] He continued by offering the claim cited above concerning his desire to provide a "traditional moral study." On a number of occasions Lucas has connected *SW*, morality tales for children, and mythology. At some point prior to October 1982, he admitted to Dale Pollock, an early biographer, that "I wanted to make a kids' film that would strengthen contemporary mythology and introduce a basic morality."[22] Just prior to the general theatrical release of *TPM* he declared that "somebody has to tell young people what we think is a good person. I mean, we should be doing it all the time. That's what the Iliad and the Odyssey are about—'This is what a good person is; this is who we aspire to be.' You need that in a society. It's the basic job of mythology."[23] So Pollock announces that, for better or worse, "Lucas offers more than just escapist entertainment; he gives us a vision of what should be."[24]

Of course, the notion of "mythology" is not a straightforward one, as will be seen especially in chapter 1, and Lucas has tended to employ it as a reference to Joseph Campbell's work in depicting a decontextualized understanding of the "monomyth" of the heroic journey that underlies and shapes mythic tales. *SW*, he claims, is designed to be "mythological," and through this observed "mythic" template Lucas consciously attempts to provide a form of moral instruction. (Michael Kaminski's challenge to the connection between Lucas and Campbell will be discussed in a major endnote in chapter 1.)

Rohan Gowland recognizes that the classic trilogy "was not just 'entertainment'; like many biblical tales, *Star Wars* was full of lessons about life."[25] Because I am exploring the ethically interesting material of the movies, this book is not particularly interested in the typical cinematographic questions that many voice or the worries many have about "wooden acting" and "stilted dialogue," and so on (although I do realize that bad performances in these areas can affect attitudes to the films that will consequently distract from the more thought-provoking questions about their narrative content).

But is a "theological" reading an appropriate one? This could be asked by someone who engages with these movies precisely at the level of entertainment-value alone. The *effect* of the movies on their audiences can be studied by the academic disciplines of psychology and sociology, perhaps in the guise of cultural studies, but not by theology. Yet as we will see, the mythological structure of *SW* (chapter 1) addresses in relatively profound ways many issues that theology is concerned with, and these we will explore in the following chapters: for instance, questions about God (chapter 2), good and evil (chapter 3), moral decision making, the shape of the organization of public life (chapters 4 and 5), the shape of being human (chapters 6 and 7), and hope and redemption (chapter 8).

But whether a "theological" reading is an appropriate one could be asked differently from a second perspective—that of a Christian worried that *SW* is occultic, perhaps we could say *sin*ematic. From this perspective, the saga is apparently unable, even in some small way, to point helpfully to God. Two examples of this concern were posted on a Web site message board. "A concerned mother" confessed: "We had thrown all of our Star Wars films out after I began a study of gnosticism along with my study of the freemasons. I realized that Star Wars was indeed a gnostic fairy tale—something which sounded just like the philosophy of gnostic Trevor Ravenscroft in his book about Longinus' spear—*The Spear of Destiny*—and Hitler's obsession with it. Well, the devil is the 'god of forces.'"[26] Another "concerned mother" explained what apparently happens when someone comes under the influence of *Star Wars*:

> They may be tempted to fall back into the old, sinful, godless way of thinking that man is his own god, determines the course of his life, and can save himself. . . . When non-Christians see *Star Wars*, they may renew goals which lead away from God. Their denials of God will be strengthened.

This is a damning indictment on the very project of reading *SW* theologically. Or is it? There are several possible ways of responding. For instance, because *SW* expresses something of the consciousness, hopes, and dreams of the culture from which it arose, it is important to know what it can reveal about what is happening in popular culture. Ian Maher sensibly recognizes that "Christians cannot afford to be *out of touch* with popular films if they are to remain *in touch* with the swirling currents of contemporary society" and the ideologies that sustain it.[27] After all, a great many fans even speak of their experiences of these movies with almost religious reverence. For instance, Matt Bielby, editor of *Total Film*, comments: "For anyone whose formative years took place in the late seventies, *Star Wars* is a religious experience";[28] and Ian Nathan, editor of *Empire* magazine, admits, "It changed my life for the better. And I knew millions of others were feeling exactly the same thing at exactly the same moment. *Star Wars* became part of us."[29] Religiosity and spirituality have begun in recent years to take a new shape, and the way that many fans have responded to *SW* illustrates much of what has been happening.[30] According to Peter Krämer, *SW* helped move "spirituality and religion back to the center of American film culture."[31] Moreover, the fact that the saga is aimed "at a particularly impressionable audience" demands that its assumed and portrayed values be carefully scrutinized.[32]

Some Christians have taken another approach to the movies. Even though it is clear from various statements of Lucas that *SW* is not 'Christian' as such (see chapter 2), many have argued that there are a number of 'moments' and even a perspective within *SW* that are broadly compatible with Christianity. Consequently, "Part of my fascination with *Star Wars*," David Wilkinson writes, "has been the way that it resonates with my Christian belief."[33] Of course, such resonances should hardly be surprising since the saga is a creation of a Western imagination—even if it does eclectically draw on non-Western resources—and the West is still colored by its Christian heritage. *SW* has in this way been used for apologetic or proclamatory purposes. Any quick internet search that combines *SW* and *God* or *church* will throw out numerous *SW*- themed or inspired sermon series, bible studies, and so on. Lucas himself announced some years ago that "Quite a number of churches have used *Star Wars* as a way of getting young people into the church. They use it as an example of certain religious ideas, which I think is good. It gives young people something entertaining to relate to and at the same time it can be used as a tool to explain certain religious concepts, more general good and evil concepts."[34] Themes of loving others, resisting evil, having faith in other people, encouraging friendship, the need for community, the importance of moral responsibility for the community, and so on are all illustrated with material from the films. Dick Staub, for instance, likens Luke's Jedi development to Christian discipleship and claims that a proclamatory use of the saga follows Paul's use of "the cultural icons of Greek culture to build a bridge to Christian truth" in his speech on Mars Hill in Athens (Acts 17).[35]

My theological use of the saga, however, is more radical than this strategy. Notice for a moment what is going on in this second possibility: non-Christian culture can provide moments of *illustration* and is helpful *only* as it furnishes images to show *what Christians already know* on the basis of divine revelation. It cannot theologically teach or remind Christians of anything. But we should consider at least two things that justify seeing *SW*—and indeed any non-Christian text—as potentially illuminating and instructive theologically: (1) the range of God's speaking and (2) the partiality of Christian witness to the truth. Theologian Douglas John Hall expresses this first point well:

> To be a Christian theologian is, surely, to open oneself—or more accurately, to find oneself being opened—to everything: every testimony to transcendence, every thought and experience of the species, every wonder of the natural order, every reminiscence of the history of the planet, every work of art or literature, every motion picture, every object of beauty and pathos—everything under the sun, and the sun too! Nothing is excluded a priori, nothing forbidden, nothing foreign.[36]

Timothy Gorringe rightly makes the point that "culture . . . is concerned with the spiritual, ethical and intellectual significance of the material world. It is, therefore, of fundamental theological concern."[37]

The Scriptures themselves provide some examples of what I have in mind here, and two in particular stand out. First, in the New Testament, the faith of the Roman centurion Cornelius enabled the apostle Peter to hear God saying that Gentiles should not be excluded from God's coming kingdom by early Jewish Christians (Acts 10). Second, from the Old Testament, the Assyrian invasion of Israel and the Babylonian annexation of Judah came to be understood as acts of Yahweh's (God's) judgment on the chosen covenant people. On both of these occasions the "cultural resources" (the Gentile Cornelius and the Israelites' pagan neighbors) had an important teaching function to play. But it is a *negative* function as such, in that these instances can remind God's people of things they have forgotten and reveal the bad practices and teachings that have gone under the name of "God's people." After all, Peter had obviously not understood Jesus to be speaking about the universality of the gospel (Jonah's relation to the Ninevites is an Old Testament example of this theme); and the Israelites had not been adequately prepared to properly engage their neighbors. The fact that even Joseph and Daniel could work reasonably well with the non-Israelite governments of their day suggests that all was not dark outside the communities of God's people. In fact, the imperative of Paul to the church at Corinth to "flee from the worship of idols" suggests that all was not well within the life of the Christian communities (1 Cor. 10:14).

It is incumbent on Christians, then, to listen carefully to an opponent's arguments, to understand these articulated perspectives as well as they can, and perhaps even humbly to admit that their conversation partner can identify problems affecting Christianity. This, however, is *not* the same as taking the further step of admitting that the *worldview* of the conversation partner is necessarily legitimate. Nonetheless, Christians have good biblical reason to expect that God can and will speak, even if only faintly discernible, in and through what they might otherwise consider to be strange places.[38]

The second theological layer to my appeal here has to do with the place of sin in Christian thinking. It is strange that a considerable number of Christians speak and act as if sin affects only what they *do* and even how they think about what they should do but not the *very process and content* of their believing itself. And so they imagine that Christian creeds and confessions are handed down in such a way that those who confess them today know what they mean just as clearly as their original framers did, and in this way they become deposits of faith to be protected (at all costs!). Yet Christian believing is intrinsically a complex affair, and what we think are good readings of the Bible are often influenced by many factors and not merely the presence of God's illuminating Holy Spirit. The fact that Paul cautions the Corinthian church against being too sure of itself should be a continual warning to us not prematurely to overstep our limitations: we do not yet see face-to-face but rather see through a glass darkly (1 Cor. 13:12). The real problem with Christian believing arises less from the fact that we know ourselves to be sinful than from our forgetfulness of it. The Christian claim is that Jesus Christ *is* the Truth and Truthfulness themselves enfleshed (John 14:6), and Christians are being led into the Truth that he is (John 16:13). That means that Christian communities have decisive theological reasons to resist any nation, group, church, or people claiming *absoluteness* or *finality* for anything they say or do. Our communities and nations are tempted to identify themselves *unqualifiedly* with God and God's way only when they forget that all perspectives may be flawed, and this mistake then leads them unhesitatingly to oppose all who are not like us in their self-assertion. A little knowledge of church history indicates where this process leads, and it certainly does not make comforting reading. Recognizing this is not to import a political problem into a properly apolitical theology. Rather, it is to call the way we live in absolute finality what it is: idolatry.

This may all seem a long way away from evaluating the *SW* movies, but it is important to indicate what features should guide our reflections and to encourage those who might otherwise reject this book outright to find ways of getting theological insight from these movies as much as is possible. An uncharitable reading of cultural artifacts—and here this means Lucas's creations—is not a legitimate option for Christians. Truthfulness and truth-telling are vital marks of the call to witness to God's healing and hospitable embrace of God's creatures. Albert Mohler complains that "in trying to evoke 'spirituality,' George Lucas turns to myth instead of the Bible." I hope to help the reader understand that the assumptions underlying his view are *theologically* mistaken and not merely *practically* so.[39] Only when the morality of non-Christian materials *clearly contradicts* Christian virtue should the question of the vice of those particular materials even arise. In order to identify the light and darkness within our world, we have to become morally intelligent. In the words of Martin Luther King Jr. (1929–68), we have "a moral responsibility to be intelligent," for only in learning to "read" or understand the so-called world and the gospel together do we learn to become wise or become people who can discern God's presence.[40] Tolkien once admitted that, at its best, fantasy serves as "a far-off gleam or echo of *evangelium* [i.e., gospel] in the real world."[41] While Lucas does not share the Oxford don's particular Christian commitments, and his material should certainly not be squeezed into a Christian framework at the points where it is most resistant, nonetheless his films are rich resources for theological reflection that can encourage some of the unlearning and relearning necessary in Christian life. To miss that is to miss the kind of life-stories that they tell. To miss it is also to fail to develop an appropriately honest and diligent form of media literacy or cultural discernment. We need to be more aware of how cultures are born and how their values are reinforced beyond simply looking for whether there is bad language, realistic violence, sexual references, and so on.

The editors of *Star Wars and Philosophy* observe that "in *Star Wars*, conflict is a constant, but it's not the fighting in the 'wars' of the title that spurs the development of the main characters' personalities. . . . Instead, it's the struggle to understand and overcome deep problems of identity, truth, freedom, and the tragic side of life that defines the rise, fall, and rise again of the Skywalker family and the impact they have on allies and enemies alike. Essentially, the *Star Wars* movies tell a simple story of tragedy, courage, and redemption."[42] The following chapters will turn to these themes once we have asked more fully about how *SW* can be "truthful" (chapter 1).

What Is New to the Revised Edition?

Not only has this introduction been revised, but some new material has been added to the first chapter in order to make it clear what an appeal to *SW* as modern myth properly involves and to contest, in a very long endnote, a recently published but weak reading of the matter by Michael Kaminski. An occasional tweak appears in chapters 2–8 and new material supplements the afterword. This tinkering is itself very Lucas-like. I have added the lengthy chapter 9 in order to critically reflect on *Star Wars: The Force Awakens*. It provokes a series of questions that have arisen in earlier chapters, especially in relation to matters of violence and the good life, and does so in a way that have dissatisfied many commentators about the original 1977 movie. I have also updated the bibliography to include a number of volumes that I have worked with since 2007.

In order to go deeper into many of the issues raised in this book with regard to film and cultural theories as they address matters of ideology, politics, and identity, I would encourage readers to use my recent studies *The Politics of Big Fantasy: The Ideologies of* Star Wars, The Matrix, *and* The Avengers (Jackson: McFarland Press, 2014) and *Identity Politics in George Lucas'* Star Wars (Jackson: McFarland Press, 2016) as companions to this book. They do a number of things differently than *The Gospel according to Star Wars*, including delving into greater critical depth, and they also operate on the assumption that it is ethically important to analyze such a culturally pervasive set of movies.

Over the next few years I plan to revisit and develop the argument of the final chapter once *Episodes VIII* and *IX* are released. I also intend, at some future point, to critically engage with George Lucas's early dystopian movie *THX 1138*.

Notes for Reading

Finally, let me share some of my parameters for this book, which should help the reader anticipate the ethos of what will appear in the various chapters.

I have deliberately written the book as jargon-free as possible, without assuming much or any theological knowledge on the part of the readership. It has been humbling to discover that my general readership academic text has been the subject of numerous discussion forums and blogs, as well as church study groups and nonreligious SW fan groups. I have learned, for instance, that reference to the book has been made in numerous sermons/homilies and in popular culture talks and that American troops in the Middle East have been reading it in groups. I would love to hear what they have made of it.

While I do not assume familiarity of theological matters among my readership, I do anticipate that readers will have at least a basic familiarity with the movies. It might be fair to say that the level of detailed reference to the movies actually requires readers to have more than a passing acquaintance with the movies. A few reviews of the first edition of the book noted the "geek-ishness" of the references. This is, I would argue, necessary in order to try and lay bare the rationale for my reasoning, the attempted validation for my arguments and perspective on the movies. Anything less would treat the movies with little respect and succumb to a practice of me simply asserting my opinion rather than laying out my claim through justified argument. There already is too much weakly researched and quickly written commentary on *SW*.

There is one little detail that I need to explain in case knowledgeable fans of the franchise think I am anachronistically importing a later category into my use of material. The first movie made in the saga was simply entitled *SW*, and at one stage it was slated to be called "The Star Wars." I will, for the sake of ease, refer to it by the title *ANH*. In July 1978, in order to coincide with the impending release of a sequel, *SW* was retroactively retitled *Star Wars Episode IV: A New Hope*. The next movie in the franchise was *ESB*, and it came with the subtitle "Episode V."

I attempt to respect the particularities of the movies themselves and the conditions of their production and distribution. It concerns me when the materials are used in order to justify something that is actually foreign to them. For instance, and I need to make this clear, there is a real problem with studies that make the movies Christian movies, or that try to read them as Taoist or as Buddhist, and so on. This is to impose a Procrustean framework on the movies that is not always illuminating, and it is to operate with a lack of integrity. Hopefully chapter 2 will make it clear that Lucas's own portrayal of the Force is considerably more eclectic. Therefore spiritual readings of the movies are in real danger of flattening out the material and of expressing a considerable naiveté on the part of the writer. They all too rarely do the hard work of familiarizing themselves with matters of the movies' contexts or engaging with different and conflicting readings of the material. As a consequence, they seriously fail to listen carefully to these film texts. Whether intentionally or not, this shows a profound disrespect for this particular body of cinematic work. That is not to say that the writer and reader cannot come to the movies with a particular set of questions or assumptions. It is important to continue to ask whether and how far movies like those in the *SW* series can be appropriated by Christians, Muslims, Buddhists, Jews, political liberals, political neoliberals, and others. One of the dangers with the way these questions are asked in practice, however, is that often the questioners have an insufficiently informed understanding even of their own theological, philosophical, and political traditions.

The study will on occasion engage in some theological argument, and the reader otherwise unfamiliar with this approach will thereby be inducted into traditions of argument and disagreement among Christian theologians. For those who balk at the thought of a theological politics or of Christian non-violence, for instance, I can only direct them to do more theological research in order to appreciate the long and difficult history of theological claims and perspectives.

Similarly, I will often engage in presenting the material in conversation and/or argument with other relevant readings, perspectives, and scholarly discussions. With the increasing ill-tempered style of self-assertion that pervades the blogosphere, in which personal opinion seems to have become a virtue, this too will be something of a novelty to many readers. I make no apology for my discussions of others' studies for a number of reasons. First, even our opinions do not arise in a vacuum but are shaped by the environments we come from and the engagements or relations we have had with others. It would be naive as well as disrespectful to those who have written on the topics addressed in this book not to consider their work. Second, I hope to demonstrate where my claims are new by offering critical observation and reasoning about the claims made by others. Third, my critical engagement aims to reason out my arguments rather than simply assert my opinions or fan theories about the matters at hand. It remains to be seen, of course, whether my attempt to enhance the quality of reasoning, conversation, and argument about *SW* and theological matters is at all successful.

Another matter that is important to indicate at the outset is that I am focusing the book's attention on Christianity. Every study needs to focus on something, but there are numerous reasons for this particular concentration. After all, apart from a handful of Christian devotional texts that attempt to force intersections between *SW* and their understanding of Christianity, there are very few in-depth discussions of the overlaps. Of course, there is good reason for this, as chapter 2 will endeavor to make clear. The influence of a variety of Eastern traditions is particularly evident in Lucas's movies. He himself admits that Yoda "is kind of like a little Dalai Lama."[43] However, it is important to recognize that *SW* was largely a product of a modern Western pluralist perspective on these non-Western traditions. Not only is this a point that chapter 2 specifically hopes to highlight, but it is something that the book as a whole engages with. Moreover, my critical methodological aim is to engage with *SW* from a Christian theological angle, just as Matthew Bortolin's deals with it from a Buddhist perspective and John Porter's tackles it from a Taoist outlook.[44]

Before I move on to the next point, it is worth indicating that because this is a study of *SW* from a theological perspective, I do not explicitly spell out my own theological views. This is a study not a theological autobiography.

On the other hand, the theological angle very much reveals what my particular perspective is, from the theological sources I select to the types of claims that I make to the positions I raise distinctive questions about.

Despite occasionally glancing at the Expanded Universe series when this sheds light on Lucas's movies, my discussion will largely avoid it for three reasons: the materials are not exactly an expression of his own controlled vision; the *ROTJ*'s ethos and end celebration have an apocalyptic ambience or mood of climactic resolution that makes the post-*ROTJ* New Jedi Order material interesting but problematic; and the appearance of *TFA* has rendered this material covering the post-*ROTJ* events redundant.

This last observation, of course, then raises the question of the Disney Corporation's artistic control of *Episodes VII–IX*. Technically these movies have to be counted as canon, but it remains important to recognize the possibility of a significant difference in vision (political, religious, and so on) between Lucas's stories and the more recent ones. Chapter 9 attempts to lay bare certain instances where that becomes morally important.

This book spends little time exploring the culture of *SW*'s fan-base, noting it only when it affects the way these movies are understood. It is of no interest to this study that a number of fans might emotionally react against my use of *Episodes I–III*, or that others might have an emotional investment in some part of the Expanded Universe materials and others not, or that some feel *TFA* is a strong movie while others stridently disagree.

Finally, although Lucas's six movies are all episodes of *SW*, these six films have different emphases and perspectives. This might seem to contrast with the movie maker's own admission: "I see it all as one movie; I don't pay much attention to whether people like individual chapters or not."[45] Of course, he could be referring here instead to the thread underlying the various narratives. Throw in J. J. Abrams's *TFA* (and the more recent *Rogue One*) and the canon of the *SW* franchise becomes more disparate again, albeit not as much as the *Alien* franchise, or at least not yet.

Chapter One

A New Myth

The Truthfulness of *Star Wars*

> *What you get out of it is what you bring to the cinema, and you read*
> *into the thing the things you want to read into it.*
> —Gary Kurtz, cited in John Baxter, *George Lucas:*
> *A Biography* (London: Harper Collins, 1999), 166.

*O*ne of the many reasons for watching SW is the way it relates to and reveals currents in contemporary culture (from 1977 to the present), reflecting that culture's understanding of itself and its inherent value system. Conversely the saga's success reflects a deep cultural resonance with its story that is manifested in a zealous fan base and has further enabled several of the characters to take on a life of their own (Darth Vader advertises a throat lozenge and Mark Hamill plays himself acting the Luke Skywalker character in an episode of *The Simpsons*, for instance).

However, not only does the saga distill something of the ethos of popular culture; it is also significantly culturally generative. Put another way, it can shape and reshape the ways in which many think and feel about themselves and their world. Because of its massive appeal worldwide—particularly at a time characterized by fragmented and professionalized knowledge—SW is enviably well positioned for mass communication. It is well placed to appeal to, generate, and reinforce a certain collective consciousness with a shared stock of images, narratives, and categories. As Orson Scott Card observes, "Hardly anybody can answer the easy Bible questions on Jeopardy anymore, but almost everybody can tell you about Obi-Wan Kenobi, Darth Vader, Yoda, and The Force."[1] James Ford suggests it even carries "more influence among young adults than the traditional religious myths of our culture."[2] In this way the saga seems to fit Conrad Kottak and Kathryn Kozaitis's criteria for "myth": expressing "fundamental cultural values," being "widely and recurrently told among, and . . .

1

[having] special meaning to, people who grow up in a particular culture," and also "at least partly fictionalized."[3] Yet critics such as John Baxter see Lucas's control over the saga as somewhat subverting this sense of *ANH* as popular mythology:

> Although Lucas claimed he had created *Star Wars* to endow mankind with the mythology it lacked, his behaviour became less and less philanthropic with the film's success. Over the next decade, he became obsessively proprietorial of his characters and ideas, ruthlessly pursuing anyone using them without permission and payment. . . . Real mythology, by its very nature, is communal, and open to interpretation by all. But Lucas . . . hadn't given us a mythology; we could only rent it.[4]

Lucas himself is profoundly aware of the teaching possibilities available through the medium of film. He claims to have been presented with "a very large megaphone" in making his films, and he consciously uses this to provide a kind of instruction in moral matters.[5] "Somebody has to tell young people what we think is a good person. . . . You need that in a society."[6]

It is this supposed mythic quality that makes *SW* as myth such rich material for theological and moral reflection. Steven Spielberg claims, "George [has] . . . created a mythology of characters—he touched something that needed touching in everybody."[7] *SW* draws on certain mythic archetypes, a practice that enables it to become a hybrid of *Flash Gordon,* Japanese samurai epics, Carlos Castaneda's *Tales of Power*, and the theologically profound fantasy fiction of Tolkien and C. S. Lewis. *SW* is Lucas's myth, exploring possibilities of struggle, journeying, discovery (particularly self-discovery), good and evil, and so on. In order to understand the performance of these works, we need to turn to the well-known work of Joseph Campbell (1903–87), which attempted to identify and describe the general pattern that mythologies have taken, especially the hero mythologies. In fact, when we speak further about "myth and popular culture," the prominence of Joseph Campbell's PBS interviews,[8] and the popularity of the 1997 Smithsonian Institution's National Air and Space Museum exhibition "*SW* and the Magic of Myth" are the main reasons why "in the public's imagination, the terms 'myth' and '*SW*' are very closely linked."[9] As Liam Neeson, the actor portraying Qui-Gon Jinn in *TPM* declares,

> George's tales, the *Star Wars* tales, have really tapped into the psyche and mood that popular modern culture has never done before. For me that says yes, these films are incredibly well made, but also it's tapping into a void

which we have as human beings that we have kind of lost something. And George provides . . . the great storytelling sense of myth.[10]

It is through acquaintance with Campbell's *The Hero with a Thousand Faces* that *ANH* in particular is shaped, although, as we will see, Lucas goes much further in providing a vision of society that questions the dominant values of modern Western liberal individualism.[11]

Campbell's *Hero* compares the myths of various cultures and concludes, echoing the work of the Swiss psychologist Carl Gustav Jung (1875–1961), that they are all the same "monomyth." In other words, each myth broadly depicts the same hero, even if that is under different culturally specific guises. Consequently, the characters driving every mythic narrative are ancient or "primordial" archetypes. A cardinal problem with this approach, of course, is the fact that it "is interested less in analyzing myths than in using myths to analyze human nature."[12] Campbell unfortunately "cites hundreds of myths and extricates from them hundreds of archetypes . . . [but] he analyzes few whole myths," and deals with even those in insufficient critical depth.[13] Also, his assertion that all mythologies are broadly the same seems too strained, although we will not develop this observation for the moment.

"A Long Time Ago . . ." *Star Wars*, Genre Pastiche, and the Fairy Tale

An early draft summary (May 1973) of what was then tentatively titled *The Star Wars* was set in the thirty-third century. Lucas had in mind a Buck Rogers/ Flash Gordon type action/adventure story, but he failed to procure the rights to remake *Flash Gordon*. So he began to develop an original hero-in-space adventure story. The story gradually was removed from a future-of-this-world setting, and early in 1976 the script for *The Adventure of Luke Starkiller as Taken from the Journal of the Whills: Star Wars* opened with a longer version of the now famous scene-setting line: "A long, long time ago in a galaxy far, far away . . ." Possibly a result of Lucas's familiarity with Bruno Bettelheim's *The Uses of Enchantment*, this introduction provided a distinct conceptual link to fairy tales and legends; in other words, to the stories of our past.

Like Tolkien's *The Hobbit* and *The Lord of the Rings*, Lucas had conceived of *SW* as being part of a grand narrative being recounted many years later, something picked up by Peter Jackson's setting of his Hobbit trilogy. To that end, Lucas developed the idea of the *Journal of the Whills*, echoing the function of Tolkien's ancestral mythology of Middle-Earth in *The Silmarillion*. This, Lucas claims, "was meant to emphasize that whatever story followed came from a book," an inspirational legend of chivalry, heroism, and adventure passed down through the ages in the form of a book, a "holy book."[14] "Originally, I was trying to have the story be told by somebody else," Lucas explains. "[T]here was somebody watching this whole story and recording it, somebody probably wiser than the mortal players in the actual events."[15]

In the opening crawl there is a reference to a princess, but this is an echo not merely of fairy stories but of another influence. Initially, when searching for a story to tie a few visual ideas together (principally, the cantina scene and the space battle), the story became shaped around Akira Kurosawa's sixteenth-century adventure *The Hidden Fortress* (1958). While the narrative developed through subsequent drafts, the influence of this movie remains in several places in the final version: in the perspective on the story offered through the two squabbling peasants, Tahei and Matashichi (in *SW*, C3PO and R2D2); in General Rokurota Makabe (in *SW*, General Obi-Wan Kenobi), who rescues the young Princess Yuki (in *SW*, Princess Leia Organa) to return her to her own people (in *SW*, Leia's family on Alderaan, and then the Rebel Alliance on Yavin IV). Lucas also named his religious order the Jedi after the Japanese term *jidai geki*, meaning period film; and the Jedi were dressed in Buddhist-like monastic robes with kimonos underneath. At one stage Lucas even toyed with the idea of making *SW* a wholly Japanese affair.

The director from Modesto was keen, too, on the swashbuckler movies of old, such as those starring Errol Flynn, and from this comes the notion of the Jedi as knights and of their weapons as sabres (albeit a technologically sophisticated version, lightsabers). The eminently popular Westerns of Lucas's youth had enough of an impact upon him for *SW* to raid that particular genre, with its frontier hero mythology, for some of its inspiration. The saloon scene in John Ford's *The Searchers* (1956) "partially inspired the [Mos Eisley] cantina sequence";[16] Tatooine was a frontier environment, with settlers under constant threat from nomadic indigenous peoples (Tusken Raiders or Sand People); Han Solo is an old-fashioned gunslinger, kitted out in waistcoat, boots, and low-hanging gun belt; Luke's uncle Owen and aunt Beru are farmers living at the edge of civilization; and the gun and the gangs (the Hutts, with their hired hands and bounty hunters) are the "law."

There are also references to, among other things, Isaac Asimov's *Foundation* stories in the term "The Empire"; to the histories of imperial Rome,

Britain, and Nazi Germany; to Fritz Lang's 1926 masterpiece *Metropolis* (Lucas's C3PO); and Carlos Castaneda's *Tales of Power*.

But while *SW* involves something of a pastiche of genres, its eclecticism is not a simple homage. Instead, its referential diversity suggests that here we have something that sums up all others in a single instance. This would consequently entail that it becomes a representative narrative. This, in turn, has much to do with its appeal to myth, and specifically the kind of understanding of myth it is largely predicated on.

According to Lucas, "being a student in the Sixties, I wanted to make socially relevant films. . . . But then I got this great idea for a rock & roll movie, with cars and all the stuff I knew about as a kid."[17] As he was completing *American Graffiti* (1973), he began to slowly design his space adventure. His first foray into theatrical moviemaking with *THX 1138* (1971) had been a financial disaster two years before, and he was having problems selling the idea of Apocalypse Now, which he had spent some of the past four years developing—Vietnam movies were too controversial for film studios and audiences at that stage.

SW was conceived against a backdrop of cultural turmoil in America—the Vietnam War limped to its ignominious end, and many in the nation suffered from traumatic introspection; President Richard Nixon was implicated in the Watergate scandal (1974); and economic misery loomed on the horizon. Francis Ford Coppola had challenged his friend Lucas to make "a happier kind of film" than *THX 1138*.[18] In response, *SW* was supposedly created to encourage wonder, an enjoyment of stories, and a fantasy imagination among the youth in a post-Vietnam era. More specifically, Lucas hoped to reeducate young people.

To many critics, *SW*, and the director's claims concerning it, look like a return to the older American hero myths, and thus view the film as a simple product of escapism that both emotionally comforts the traumatized American psyche and politically mitigates the possibility of learning from the mistakes that resulted in Vietnam in the first place. So Dan Rubey, in a sharply written paper, claims that Lucas's "ingenuous statements about fantasy and kids and the irrational serve to disguise Lucas's conservative ideological bias."[19] For instance, the Empire's Nazi look resonates for American audiences, with its clear reference to less morally complex wars, and thus reromanticizes American involvement in conflict. Influential film critic Pauline Kael even describes *SW* (and Spielberg's *Jaws* [1975]) as infantilizing the cinema, reconstituting the spectator as a child and then overwhelming him with sound and spectacle, obliterating irony, aesthetic self-consciousness, and critical reflection.[20] Andrew Gordon, among others, consequently claims that *SW* responds to the need for Americans to renew faith in themselves as the "good guys" on the world scene.

That reading, however, can and should be contested. First, Lucas's political/ cultural dystopian film *THX 1138*, adapted from his Samuel Warner Memorial Scholarship–winning student film *THX 1138.4EB/Electronic Labyrinth* (1967), is a critical observation on the United States of the late 1960s and early 70s. The film accuses U.S. society of promoting a dehumanizing capitalism that makes its citizens into conformists in the same way their Communist enemies did.

Second, when Lucas's significant involvement in originally conceiving of the politically subversive *Apocalypse Now* ended, he admitted to migrating several of its broad themes into SW.[21] In particular, America, he claims, is acting in ways similar to the "evil Empire"; the Emperor Palpatine is supposedly like Richard Nixon, and Lucas speaks of Palpatine both as Nixon-like and "the classic devil character";[22] and the Rebel Alliance's guerrilla fighters are like the Vietcong (even if they were represented by an all-American cast).[23] So in an early draft of *SW* in 1973, Lucas envisaged "a large technological empire going after a small group of freedom fighters."[24] In pouring his political observations into his notes for his planned space opera, Lucas wrote that the planet of Aquilae is "a small independent country like North Vietnam." Consequently, "The Empire is like America ten years from now after gangsters assassinated the Emperor and were elevated to power in a rigged election. . . . We are at a turning point: fascism or revolution."[25] *ROTJ* takes up this idea again.

> Originally I started writing *Star Wars* because I couldn't get *Apocalypse Now* off the ground. When I was doing *Apocalypse Now* it was about this totally insane giant technological society that was fighting these poor little people. They have little sticks and things, and they completely cow this technological power, because the technological power didn't believe they were any threat. They were just a bunch of peasants. The original draft of *Star Wars* was written during the Vietnam War where a small group of ill-equipped people overcame a mighty power. It was not a new idea. Attila the Hun had overrun the Roman Empire; the American colonies had been able to defeat the British Empire. So the main theme of the film was that the Imperial Empire would be overrun by humanity in the form of these cute little teddy bears.[26]

Third, it is important to observe that *American Graffiti* produced the kind of fan-mail that convinced Lucas that an upbeat mood movie could be more transformative of young people's increasingly fractured lives. "Traditionally we get . . . [moral values] from the church, the family, and in the modern world we get them from the media—from movies."[27] In response, among other things, he lightened the serious tone by introducing more humor into *SW*'s third script draft (Aug. 1, 1975). It consequently makes sense to understand Lucas's claims concerning challenging the post-Vietnam mood as an attempt to encourage a new hope: not a wallowing in self-pity or pacifying introspection but a learning to be moral agents giving of themselves and taking responsibility for one another's well-being.

Archetypally Mythical

As early as 1977 (the month *before SW*'s theatrical release) Lucas declares: "I wanted to do a modern fairy tale, a myth."[28] What does he mean by "myth" and by *SW* as updating "ancient mythological motifs"?[29] What has been discussed above provides several clues.

The first is the connection between moral truths and myths. Most commonly the journalistic use of the term "myth" operates in contrast to the terms "truth" or "fact." This is largely a hangover from late nineteenth-century studies. So for E. B. Tylor (1832–1917), myths are primitive prescientific explorations of the world that have to be read as literal, and accordingly scientifically redundant, explanations of states of affairs. In contrast, Lucas attempts to provide what he considers to be truthful insight into the nature of things and persons and thereby provide a context for moral reflection and education through a particular visual narrative form. In this he builds more on twentieth-century scholarly developments.

The second is Lucas's reference to the updating of "*ancient* mythological motifs."[30] The idea is not to generate a 'new myth', since such a thing is, by the very *cultural* nature of myths, not possible anyway. Myths are stories that *cultures* tell about themselves and expressions of what cultures deem to be valuable and meaningful (morally and spiritually)—not narratives that flow from a single visionary. Accordingly, the young director from Modesto attempts to discern something in myths that he feels has been unfortunately lost in the culture of its time.

The third is Lucas's reference to "ancient mythological *motifs*, suggesting that myths are largely alike and are not embedded within the values and vision of the specific cultures that have generated them. In this approach he had learned from the likes of Joseph Campbell. Even though it was not until after *ROTJ* that Lucas and Campbell became friends, it had largely been through discovering Campbell's *Hero* that the script for *ANH* had been edited, and Lucas could later call him a mentor.[31] Lucas studied anthropology in college for a couple of years, and there he encountered Campbell's

Hero of a Thousand Faces.[32] Campbell's book had provided a much-needed source of inspiration and direction when both *ANH*'s narrative structure and its character forms were being composed. "It's possible that if I had not run across him I would still be writing *Star Wars* today."[33] When writing *SW* "I was going along on my own story, I was trying to write whatever I felt. And then I would go back once I'd written a script . . . and check it against the classic model of the hero's journey . . . to see if I had gone off the deep end, and simply by following my own inspiration . . . it was very close to the model."[34] Here Lucas explicitly admits using the hero myth as a touchstone for *SW*, checking his writing against the "classical model" (or, rather, Campbell's version), and discovering that he was already working in these terms. In fact, when Lucas came to show Campbell the movies at his home, the myth critic positively and generously remarked, "I thought real art stopped with Picasso, Joyce, and Mann. Now I know it hasn't."[35] If nothing else, this debt to the Campbellian hero enables *SW* to resist to some degree the most virulent of complaints that modern Hollywood has shifted movies away from character and plot to exhilarating spectacle (however, the complaints that *TPM* has fallen into this trap are legion). It is simply a mistake to lament that *SW* "displaced narrative and moved cinema into a revived realm of spectacular excess."[36] Lucas is able to draw from a well-stocked store of ancient possibilities for the general structure of his plot and personnel, and even for the general ethical framework in the identification and cultivation of human wisdom. Nonetheless, as we will discuss in chapter 2, *ANH*'s indebtedness to Campbell potentially weakens its construal of the Force.

As mentioned earlier, for E. B. Tylor myths are primitive prescientific explorations of the world that have to be read literally, as primitive explanations of states of affairs. Modern science, however, has rendered myth, and the myth-making stage of culture, redundant. This primitive explanatory account of myth *reduces* the mythic forms to a single type, and a very modern one at that. But this is not what either Campbell or Lucas use mythic forms for. Campbell sees things differently, and here he builds on the foundations laid in 1876 by Austrian scholar Johann Georg von Hahn regarding the Aryan hero tales and Lord Raglan's 1936 linking of the myth of the hero (the god) with ritual (following J. G. Frazer) with his patterning of mythic narrative. The shape of Raglan's treatment of mythic narrative considerably overlaps with Campbell's account of the hero's journey, as well as many elements of Lucas's plot: The hero's mother is a royal virgin, the father a king. The circumstances of conception are unusual. The hero is reputed to be the son of a god. At birth there is an attempt to kill him, but the hero is spirited away. The hero is reared by foster parents in a far country and is told nothing of this as he grows up. On reaching adulthood, the hero returns or goes after his future kingdom. He achieves a victory over the king and/or a wild beast/dragon/giant. He marries a princess, often the daughter of his predecessor. He becomes king, and for a time he reigns uneventfully. Later he loses favor with the gods or his subjects. He is driven from his throne and city. The hero comes to a mysterious death, often on the top of a hill. His children, if any, do not succeed him. His body is not buried, but nevertheless he has one or more holy sepulchres.

Most controversially, however, Campbell compares the myths of various cultures and argues, following Carl Jung's theory of archetypes, that they are all the same monomyth. Ignoring cultural specificities, he claims that there is broadly the same hero in each one, only with this essence being displayed under different, and culturally specific, guises.[37] Yet while Campbell "cites hundreds of myths and extricates from them hundreds of archetypes . . . he analyzes few whole myths," and in insufficient critical depth.[38] In fact, "He is interested less in analyzing myths than in using myths to analyze human nature." Hence John Lyden is right to argue that "one of the most striking things one finds in reading Campbell's works is his amazing ability to ignore the points of the individual tales he is telling; all are made to fit the mold of the one 'true' story of the 'Hero with a thousand faces' mapped out in the book of that title."[39] What emerges is not interest in the many creation, fertility, or deliverance myths but rather a fascination with the myth of the hero's journey, particularly the psychological one from childhood to adulthood—a journey of self-discovery.

It is this conspicuously Campbellian motif of the *hero's* journey that dominates the structure of the classic trilogy. These are the adventures of Luke Skywalker. Even so, crucially, the shape of this noticeably fits the spirit of the prequels less well. These present instead "the tragedy of Anakin Skywalker," and thus the *tragic* hero's journey. This shift in focus and mood in the prequel trilogy forces a considerable reevaluation of *Episodes IV–VI*. We can now see that the saga is essentially concerned with Anakin Skywalker/Darth Vader more than with Luke Skywalker. In fact, it becomes even more obvious that in the classic trilogy itself the characterization of Darth Vader is in dynamic and not in static archetypal terms (such as with Darths Sidious and Maul). In *ANH* Vader simply plays the space-serial part of the archetypal "baddie," dressed up for the occasion in armor and a cape of nobility while wielding a sword, evoking memories of sinister medieval black knights crossed with Japanese samurai warriors and Nazi SS troopers. But by *ESB* he is stunningly revealed as Luke's father. He is the one whom Obi-Wan had spoken of in such glowingly heroic terms earlier in *ANH*. And by *ROTJ*

Vader himself becomes instrumental in both defeating the Sith and saving his son from death. Noticeably—and this is important, as chapters 5 and 6 will demonstrate—Lucas comes to critique and reconceive the popular notion of the hero, particularly with respect to issues of heroic violence and the place of the heroic ego. The hero's journey is one into sainthood rather than into warrior heroism, and here Lucas distinctly echoes Campbell, according to whom "the hero is still striving, but for oneness with the cosmos, not for control over it. . . . He is, moreover, acting on behalf of others, not for just himself. He is still heroic, for he must still undertake a daring journey to an unknown land, but his heroism is peaceful rather than hostile."[40]

Despite the theme of solidarity with his fellows expressed in the hero's return "from this mysterious adventure with the power to bestow boons on his fellow man," the hero's journey also evokes images of the Western celebration of the individual and his or her self-made success.[41] Campbell's own work in *Hero* is plagued by a tension at just this point. On the one hand, he claims that the journey is both metaphysical (concerning the nature of the reality of all things) and psychological (concerning the individual's psyche), and that both of these are needed. Yet, on the other hand, he tends to exalt the individual and his or her role in society because of the way he draws on Jung's psychological reading of mythic archetypes. The essence of mythology for Campbell is predominantly the journey of the hero *from childhood to adulthood*. According to him, all myth and religion are little more than metaphors for this interior journey of self-discovery. This encourages in the audience or reader, through identification with the hero's story, the idea that "that old man up there has been blown away. You've got to find the Force inside you."[42] According to John Lyden, Campbell has imposed something of Western liberal philosophy, so that "the individual realizes he himself is the absolute, the creator, the center of his own universe . . . and so is responsible for all that happens in it."[43] Consequently, Campbell summarizes his findings in *The Power of Myth* as "follow your bliss." Several critics have complained that this is, at its worst, a justification for selfishness, and at best, something that will find it difficult to resist rampant self-concern (what we might call "Western *egolatry*"). Moreover, the consequences for matters of justice are pronounced:

> Campbell cannot take the problem of undeserved suffering seriously; we deserve everything that happens to us, for we make our own universe. . . . The only "mystery" is what lurks in my own unconscious, which can be plumbed via depth psychology and interpretation of my myths and dreams.[44]

Crucially Lucas emphasizes more the importance of social relations such as friendship and responsibility for the common good (see chapter 7). In fact the whole spirit of the saga works *against* the individualism that dominates the imagination of the modern Western world. Therefore, Campbell's analysis of mythology is echoed in the saga only very broadly and only up to a point. It is more the detailed dynamic of *ANH*'s writing in particular and not its originally prepared plan that resonates with *Hero*. As Lucas himself admits, "There is a Joseph Campbell connection, but it's just one of many."[45]

As I mentioned above, where *Hero* does make sense of the saga is in several of *ANH*'s characterizations, in particular its "hero," Luke Skywalker. This youth is introduced as a stereotypical teenager—whiny, petulant, self-absorbed, a daydreamer with little taste for mundane chores, and so on. He initially complains about having to clean up the newly purchased droids when requested to do so by his uncle, expressing instead his desire to "play" (by going "into Tosche station [at Anchorhead] to pick up some power-converters"). The portrayal of the desert world of Tatooine is symbolically important in this regard too. According to Campbell, the hero eventually breaks free from the secure everyday world in which he is tempted to stay. But in *ANH* Tatooine represents something a little different. It is "a big hunk of nothing" (Biggs Darklighter to Luke, *ANH* deleted scene) that prompts C3PO to complain, "What a desolate place this is." It represents a drying up of Luke's dreams, the barren setting for the emptiness of his life and the frustration of his longings, the representation of all that he needs to separate himself from in order to gain an independent life. He is, Roy Anker argues, "quite literally, 'down on the farm.'"[46] The youth finds life in this setting stifling and burdensome, which is why he yearns for, in Palpatine's words to Anakin in *ROTS*, "a life of significance." Stimulation comes merely momentarily through the escapist thrills of recklessly racing his T-16 Skyhopper and using it to "bulls-eye wamp-rats." In fact, after an incident in which the youth "busted up the Skyhopper pretty bad," he was "grounded" by a furious Uncle Owen "for the rest of the season" (*ANH* deleted scene). Biggs feels prompted to warn: "You ought to take it a little easy, Luke. You may be the hottest bush pilot this side of Mos Eisley, but those little Skyhoppers are dangerous. Keep it up and one day, whammo! You can end up a dark spot on the damp side of a canyon wall."

So while he dreams of adventure and excitement, this "everyman" character is an unlikely kind of hero. Even his "friends" on Tatooine insult him; Camie, for instance, sneering, "I think Wormie's caught too much sun" (*ANH*, deleted scene), and the novelization revealing that Fixer and Camie chuckle "over Luke's ineptitude."[47] According to Aunt Beru, in Brian Daley's radio play of the period, "Even to the young people over at Anchorhead Luke is an outsider. He's not had a close friend since Biggs went to the Academy." Lucas's hero here has the qualities needed to capture the spirit of Campbell's Jungian mythical psychology, for as he admits, heroes come in all shapes and sizes, which means that a hero is not measured by being "a giant hero" or victorious in battle.

> It's just as important to understand that accepting self-responsibility for the things you do, . . . caring about other people—these are heroic acts. Everybody has the choice of being a hero or not being a hero every day of their lives.[48]

We can also recognize Campbell's so-called "call to adventure" when Luke stumbles on Princess Leia Organa's holographic message. This marks the beginning of his personal and emotional "growing up." Yet the teenager on Tatooine accepts the call only after having refused it initially, and this reluctance is significant. He is duty-bound to stay and help his uncle, Owen Lars, with the harvest: "I can't get involved. I've got work to do. It's not that I like the Empire; I hate it, but there's nothing I can do about it right now." Campbell's individualistic analysis of the hero is unhelpful here. Heroes can either, he claims blandly, voluntarily or involuntarily "accomplish the adventure."[49] The difference, however, is crucial. The fact that Luke refuses "the call to adventure" and the "crossing [of] the threshold" out of a grudging responsibility to his uncle's farm, *adds significant moral depth to his character*. (On saying that, however, perhaps the claim about hating the Empire needs to be handled carefully, since Luke was desperate, by his own admission, to enroll in the Imperial Academy.) There would be considerable moral repercussions should he volunteer himself in obedience to "the call" initially. In the context of *ANH*, Luke's eventual answer, while still flooded with ambiguity (he selfishly desires to gratify his longing for *adventure* as much as help another in trouble), *eventually leads to* what is in effect a weeding out of this lingering egoism and self-interest in the very notion of the "hero" itself. He has to "unlearn" his rather tasteless and self-indulgent longing for excitement and adventure in his encounter with Yoda (*ESB*). The *morality* of the movies is instead rooted in the sense of responsibility, despite one's own desires for self-gratification. At the very least, his very daydreaming does make him dissatisfied with thinking that "this is all there is" and in this way sets him apart from his friends and uncle on Tatooine, who (apart from Biggs) are unreflectively content with "how things are."

In the end, however, Luke's hand is forced—his only tie to Tatooine and his familial responsibilities have been obliterated by the brutal imperial exe-cution of Aunt Beru and Uncle Owen. Subsequently, in his journey along with his droid sidekicks Luke is guided by the supernatural aid of the "magi-cal" and "wise old man" Obi-Wan Kenobi; develops a "love interest" with Princess Leia, whom he helps rescue from his shadow nemesis Darth Vader; escapes from "the belly of the whale" (the Death Star); and brings "boon" to his Rebel friends—and indeed the galaxy itself—against all odds by destroy-ing the Death Star. When the parallels between Campbell's *Hero* and Lucas's *SW* are construed in this fashion, the classic trilogy as a whole, and *ANH* in particular, are mainly studies in the character-development of Luke Sky-walker "from hick to hero." He is "schooled" in the kind of death and rebirth that is involved in the transformation of ego.

This is his journey of self-discovery, quite literally in that he comes to discover his true identity through the fact that his ancestry is radically unlike everything he has been raised to believe. First, his father had not been a navigator on a spice freighter, as Uncle Owen had encouraged him to think, but had been a Jedi Knight and hero in the Clone Wars, murdered and betrayed by Darth Vader (*ANH*). Even more destabilizing for Luke's self-consciousness later is the terrible fact that his father is revealed, in *ESB*, not only to be still alive but to be none other than Darth Vader himself. The young man has to mature through this painful test that trains him in coping with the evil (the dark side) he finds in the world around him. But he does pass all the (moral) tests he encounters in *ANH*, which enables him to become a positive force within society. The fact that this all takes place in the "every-man" kind of character of *Episode IV* draws the audience into the possibili-ties for its own ethical growth and self-discovery. Luke becomes our moral traveling companion and exemplar. He symbolizes all human beings—or better, what we *ought to become*—in and through his own maturation. In this respect *SW* explores dramatically some of the pathologies plaguing the "ego," those things that can distort our relationships with others and our selves. It thereby can become a kind of ethical "therapy of self" that enables us to purge and transform our desires. In and through it we are able to tran-scend our ego-centeredness.

This point about the ethics of mythologies, though, hints at an important problem dogging Campbell's construal of the hero myth. Because his hero is the primary and almost exclusive focus in his reading of mythologies, other characters in the stories are made at worst incidental and at best mere instruments for exploring the psychological growth or maturation of the pro-tagonist. His account of the hero myth can sound as if it trivializes the con-flicts, troubles, struggles, and problems faced by *all* the characters. Others' sufferings are only important in the context of one's own self-realization. In contrast, the public ethics or "politics" of *SW* can resist Campbell's interiorization of the mythic experience for the individual's psyche. *SW* obviously traces Luke's voyage of self-discovery, but the fate of the *galaxy* is at stake in the conflict, a conflict that is bigger than this adolescent himself. A pantheon of characters is vital to the proceedings and the flourishing of galactic life. Leia and Obi-Wan are instumental in issuing the "call to adventure"; and, as we will see later, Han Solo helps save Luke from destruction by his pursuers at the Battle of Yavin. In other words, it is in the very relationships conceived by Lucas that the "redemptive" moments occur and contribute substantively to the development of the so-called "hero." These movies are permeated by the ways in which social and political change, even personal illumination and transformation, require the existence of personal relationships. In the saga, it is the Sith who are the individualists, or at least individualists with regard to their own personal development, since they treat all others as a herd to serve themselves in a hegemonic and totalitarian fashion. Campbell, according to Segal, "winds up at the end of his life, singling out [for approval] myths of American individualism, American self-reliance, in contrast to the more collectivist myths of other people."[50] This would reorder myths for personal transformation rather than social well-being. Here Lucas's creation, as the coming chapters will make clear, is much more ethically liberating.

The Truthfulness of *Star Wars*

Scholars have for some time hotly debated just what myth is. The Greek word *mythos* originally simply had to do with "word" or "story," and in early Greek literature its meaning ranged from "a true story," "an account of facts," and so "fact" itself, to an invented story, such as legend, fairy story, fable, or poetic creation. It was only in later Greek thought that it became contrasted with both *logos* (rational thought) and *historia*, and began to denote "what cannot really exist." This broad type of understanding came to dominate the nineteenth century's fascination with mythology. Myth was understood to be anything that is opposed to reality. Accordingly a popular modern journalistic tendency has been to treat "myth" and "falsity" as somehow synonymous, which is why there is the unashamed titling of books with either-or designations, like *The Bible: Myth or Message?* for instance. "Story" becomes frequently reduced to a vehicle for transmitting truths that are developed and known independently from the story, or increasingly to something private (for example, something *entertaining*).

SW, of course, is *fantasy* and therefore makes no historical claims about "what really happened." Its setting "a long time ago, in a galaxy far, far away . . ." sees to that. But this does not mean that it is purely escapist entertainment for private satisfaction. Jeffrey Grupp, for instance, detects a gritty, "everyday" quality in the saga, and this reflects Lucas's own direction to his production staff to make the vehicles and equipment look dirty and used.[51] Something more substantial than the mere desire to update the old Saturday matinee adventure serials directs *SW*'s spirit. "In fantasy literature, the world is not simply left behind for pleasing visions of wonder. . . . The promise of *Faërie* for Tolkien [for instance] is a return to the world from which we have become estranged."[52] Tolkien's stories are not pure escapisms through which the reader enters another world momentarily and then emerges largely unchanged—at least, not if the reader has read the story well. Consequently, Jonathan Rosenbaum's comment on *ANH*, "Whenever this giddy space opera is taking place, it can't possibly be anywhere quite so disagreeable as the present," misses this insight.[53] Instead, *SW* uses the sci-fi/fantasy genre in such a way that even though its universe is alien to ours, it is not so remote from it as to be purely fantastic, and the genre frees us from having to worry about fidelity to distracting questions of how accurate its depiction is of historical events. But it is also important to notice that the saga's basic shape "was based essentially on the Richard Nixon, Adolf Hitler idea."[54] Like many other science fiction stories, *SW* has something of a parabolic function in that it encourages us to reflect on contemporary moral issues through a fantasy setting and therefore enables us to think in a way we might not otherwise do. As Claude Levi-Strauss observes, "What gives myth an operative value is that the specific pattern it describes is everlasting; it explains the present as well as the future."[55] The following chapters will explore what this means.

Were mythologies ever meant to function as "explanations"? At this point it is worth taking a moment to consider the implications of the epochal work of German New Testament scholars D. F. Strauss (1808–74) and Rudolf Bultmann (1884–1976). While Strauss has a tendency to speak of the truths that myths tell in unhistorical terms—they are eternally true ideas—he nonetheless encourages readers of myths to focus on the story, respect its author's purpose(s), and worry less about the historical events lying behind the narratives. Bultmann himself comes close to psychologizing myths and he occasionally also seems to present them as the primitive expressions of prescientific communities. In this he largely follows the work of late nineteenth-century and early twentieth-century anthropologists (for example, Edward D. Tylor, James G. Frazer, and Campbell later), who imagine that mythologies were primitive attempts to *explain*, and thus tame fears about,

the heavens, the annual cycle of nature and fertility, and death. And Bultmann also importantly realized that texts should be read according to their
subject matter (*die Sache*). The message or truth is expressed *through* myth
and not alongside it or inside it, and so the purpose of myths is "not to present
an objective picture of the world as it is, but to express man's understanding
of himself in the world in which he lives."[56] For all Bultmann's particular
faults, he at least indicated on occasions that the mythological covering cannot be easily stripped away and disposed of so that their bare essentials and
teaching of a few basic facts can be seen. Where he was particularly weak,
however, was in paying too little attention to the contexts of, and the differences between, mythological stories. He therefore did too little to subvert
the commonly held understanding that myths depict and express timeless
spiritual truths.[57] Likewise, Dan Rubey complains that "Lucas ignores the
ideological character of these views by claiming that he is working inside an
eternal tradition of fairy tales and myths stretching from Homer's *Odyssey* to
John Ford's Westerns."[58] Therefore, Rubey continues, "Lucas's picture of an
unbroken tradition of adventure mythology stretching from Homer to John
Ford ignores both the specific meanings these stories had for the societies
that created them and the important differences between them." Instead, one
has to recognize in a way Lucas, through Campbell, did not that "myths and
fantasies are not eternal: they are historical."

Reading mythic texts historically or scientifically treats the texts as inert
matter that yields up treasures to the well-armed archaeologist digging
through the dirt that covers their "meaning," or as cadavers to be explored by
trained anatomists. But complex living human beings are not well understood
by the dissection of their corpses, the dead body being unable to challenge
us or speak up for itself. To expect myths to mean the same thing as other
types of literature (e.g., history or science) is a terrible mistake and damages
the "truth" of mythologies and our reading of them (since we are never truly
"encountered" by the text). Quite simply, the narrative form of stories (the
relations that the characters have, the problems they encounter, and the situations they find themselves in) is integral to their potential "truthfulness."
To imagine that their "truth" can be stripped out from them is to make these
stories less than human. Instead, the whole performance, the story and its telling, is essential to the ability of myth to be truthful. This very *storied* form
possesses something that rings more true than abstract theory, for instance.

The fact is that we always live in specific times and places and are caught
up in the complex webs of stories that people, communities, and nations tell
of the world and their place in it. Out of these stories, we and our identities
are formed. All in all, as Mark Allan Powell claims, "Strictly speaking, the

dichotomy between 'history' and 'fiction' in literature is a false one. It is better to speak of referential and poetic functions that can be attributed to all literature."[59] The poet, for instance, can help to make the world significant, displaying aspects of it in imaginative ways that would be otherwise missed or obscured by dominant scientific modes of "reading." Accordingly, for Tolkien for instance, myths can be so true that they shed light on people's lives and situations more effectively than a simple recital of facts can. Some lessons cannot easily be taught; they must be lived and felt. Consequently myths' "truthfulness" is less about prescriptive *didactic* instruction and more about recreating the ethical and psychological imagination, thereby providing new ways of dreaming of possibilities for our own (or our world's) action. They are "paradigms of possibility," and reducing them to the level of pure entertainment is a mistake that prescientific communities would never have made about their identity-generating stories.[60]

But what kind of truthfulness do myths exhibit? What do myths do? Another common definition sees myths as stories that express the senses of the sacred, or the sense of what life is and how it is to be valued, of those communities that created and retell them. In that respect, *SW* can perhaps suggest something of the way in which the culture that formed Lucas's imagination—and (because of its popularity) the way *SW* fans worldwide—understands life, the world, and what is to be valued. But myths do more than express the values of their author and that author's culture; according to Lucas, they also help create and shape the way their retellers and listeners respond to their "truth telling," and they do so in a psychologically beneficial way: "Sometimes the truths are so painful that stories are the only way you can get through to them psychologically."[61] They are told in ways that continue meaningfully to shape the way their retellers and listeners themselves encounter the world, provide a horizon for their moral and psychological imaginations, and determine and regulate possibilities for responsibility to the world, to others, or to oneself. This is particularly done through telling and retelling them in an almost ritualized form. Of course, the very act of retelling the mythic stories is no guarantee that this retelling is continuous with their original meaningful telling, since different generations can hear and interpret the stories in ways subtly (or radically) different from those who originally "performed" them. Nonetheless, through repetition the readers or hearers of the story are drawn imaginatively into the "fictional" drama, so to speak (a "participative reading"). This demands that they be more than mere readers or spectators. Instead, they are to become imaginatively and emotionally involved so that the story told becomes their story and the narrated world becomes their world. This is not so that they can escape from their world and lose themselves in another one but rather so that they learn to identify possibilities for thinking and feeling differently about and in their own. Campbell argues that "the ubiquitous myth of the hero's passage . . . shall serve as a general pattern for men and women."[62] "What myths revealed to Lucas, among other things," one of Lucas's biographers claims, "was the capacity of the human imagination to conceive alternate realities to cope with reality: figures and places and events that were before now or beyond now but were rich with meaning to our present."[63] There is, as Tolkien believed, a kind of "sacramental quality" in myth in that the narrated world becomes to us a means of transformation by enabling us creatively to reimagine our ways in our own world.

This is true not merely of mythic stories but of all good or complex fiction. Indeed, the richer the text, the more complex the relationship to the culture that reads and remembers it and the more varied the cultures that can find "life" meaning in and through that narrated world. So Clarence Walhout argues, "In this way fiction illuminates life and life illuminates fiction."[64] Mythological stories, though, largely because of their own relationship to their cultures, have a particularly rich symbolic expressiveness or signification—they express something about the "truth" of the world, or what its original host culture understands that to be, without being carbon copies or mirrors of it.

Of course that is not an easy process, since many stories are too thin helpfully to encourage the skills of living in a complex world (as I feel is the case with, for instance, a considerable amount of Christian devotional literature); or are ideologically skewed (as, for instance, Hitler's *Mein Kampf*). Opening oneself to the truth of any story is a risk, and yet the gamble is worth making. Moreover, identifying the nature of the particular mythic form in any mythic text is far from being the end of the process of myth study. Yet "much myth criticism ignores the complicity of myth in establishing and maintaining social dominance and power structures," or how myths can "explain why those in power are in power and why those who are oppressed or dominated are (and should be) oppressed and dominated."[65] There are morally significant questions about the largely hidden and otherwise unquestioned cultural assumptions/myths that shape *SW* as well as provide it with an audience. These need to be exposed in order to be morally tested and possibly contested. So, for instance, does it express, assume, and reinforce 1970s' American patriarchalism, racism, homophobia, individualism, consumerism, or American supremacism? "To dismiss the *Star Wars* films out of hand as lowbrow adventure-romance films that cannot support any meaningful analysis . . . is erroneous and perhaps irresponsible. Given the saga's immense popularity, its potential cultural and psychological impact upon millions of viewers . . . should not be underestimated."[66]

Carl Silvio and Tony M. Vinci claim that Lucas's cinematic "textual universe serves as one of our society's richest repositories of contemporary myth and social meaning, a galaxy where collective hopes and anxieties are both revealed and imaginarily resolved."[67] The fact that so many imagine *SW* to be pure escapist entertainment reveals that Lucas has obviously not always succeeded in making known his myth-making intentions, despite his feeling that he has clearly spelled out his message.[68] Many would see the substance of *SW* as too thin for the kind of theological work I am suggesting it can do in illuminating the human condition. They claim that it expresses a pop spirituality, an eclectic mishmash of largely American virtues and values. In particular, the saga apparently presents a morally unambiguous and childish approach to themes of good and evil that also resonates with strong pragmatic and patriotic sentiments and exudes a nostalgia that climaxes in a typically glib and quite utopian happy ending. Its fairy tale provides a bland, pop spirituality that makes only the briefest of demands on its audience. After all, Bruno Bettelheim notes, "the fairy-tale simplifies all situations. Its figures are clearly drawn and its details, unless very important, are eliminated. All characters are typical rather than unique," and all moral dilemmas are clichés.[69] If these claims are true, *SW* would belong to a class of movies that "will not 'free' us from . . . structures of control. But it is not so important for mass culture to show us how to attain liberation, release, and the rest of it. . . . Science fiction films, simulators, and unframed cinemas are not revolutionary; they are *playful*."[70]

We now turn to some of its life-illuminating potential, to the characterization of "the Force" (chapter 2), to the destructive identity of evil (chapters 3–5), and to the making of good relations (chapters 6–7) and hope for our world (chapter 8).

Chapter Two

The Force of the Divine

God and the Good

*I*n SW's list of main characters a name that does not appear is that of God, although the worship originally accorded to C3PO by the Ewoks is worth a mention (ROTJ). In contrast, the Old and New Testament Scriptures portray God as an agent of sorts who walks, speaks, sorrows, warns, blesses, commands, promises, sees, hears, touches, and so on. Instead of God, Lucas's SW controversially speaks of "the Force," a term taken from "the life force" in Carlos Castaneda's *Tales of Power* and Arthur Lipsett's short movie *21-87*, and the connection between these is clear. For instance, the blessing "May the Force be with you" echoes an old Christian one, "May God be with you." In addition, at the end of the climactic Battle of Yavin (ANH) the spectral Obi-Wan's voice proclaims to Luke, "Remember, the Force will be with you always," reflecting Jesus' comforting of his disciples: "And remember, I am with you always, to the end of the age" (Matt. 28:20). Staub's reference, then, to God as "the Lord of the Force" misses the point entirely. Lucas's Force is the movies' "God" and not something over which God is Lord.[1] Many Christians express intense disquiet over this. The Force is too Eastern, they complain, and cannot therefore teach Christians anything theologically. Mohler, however, believes that it is even more directly hostile to Christianity than that.[2] It is, he argues, a "mythology . . . perfectly adapted to the spiritual confusion of postmodern America" and therefore constitutes an advertisement for a "paganism [that] is quick to fill the void" left by Christianity's removal from being the "dominant worldview of . . . culture. . . . In the years since 1977 Americans have become primary consumers of Eastern philosophies and ancient mythologies—dumbed down for popular consumption and dressed up for a media age. . . . Conspicuously absent from Mr. Lucas's cosmology is anything connected to biblical Christianity."

In my introduction I have already suggested why a failure to listen to non-Christian philosophies is a *theological* mistake. There is no good reason instinctively to reject Lucas's Force *before* we assess its place and role in the movies. But there is something else worth mentioning. The Force is in fact more Western than many realize and even importantly parallels some theological matters that Christians would do well to think harder about. These we will discuss in relation to questions of secularism, oneness, divine presence and transcendence, and the personality and impersonality of God.

Forcing in the Divine: No Dramatic Force Acting Up

The Force Is Not with Secularism

Lucas claims that the Force is *not an alternative religious option*, and certainly not *the* religious option, but is something of a plot device that enables certain aspects of the story to occur. It is a kind of mental and psychic energy amplifier that enables the Force-conscious characters to perform certain superhuman feats. In the light of this it seems somewhat odd to ask whether the Force is God. As Lucas himself explains, "When I wrote the first *Star Wars*, I had to come up with a whole cosmology."[3] Even if it did have some theological significance, that would be quite modest since Lucas intended merely to encourage thinking about "spiritual" matters. He claims that he "put the Force in the movie to try to awaken a certain kind of spirituality in young people—more a belief in God than a belief in any particular religious system." Therefore, he intends to encourage a generation of youth that has too little "interest in the mysteries of life" to begin asking questions about their existence. The vitality of a healthy human life requires, he declares, "a belief system and . . . faith. . . . I see *Star Wars* as taking all the issues that religion represents and trying to distill them down into a more modern and easily accessible construct."

In this regard, just like Lucas's later scripts for *Raiders of the Lost Ark* and *Indiana Jones and the Temple of Doom*, *SW* is concerned with the secular dismissal of the religious. The second occasion *ANH*'s audience hears of the Force is in a Death Star briefing room. Admiral Motti commends the Empire's newfound ability to control the galaxy through the construction of what he calls "the ultimate power in the universe." A menacing Darth Vader bitingly advises, "Don't be too proud of this technological terror you have constructed. The ability to destroy a planet is insignificant next to the power of the Force." There has been little in the film so far to prepare the audience for this bombshell, although Obi-Wan's earlier talk of Darth Vader's having turned to "the dark-side of the Force" might have provided some kind of warning. It is significant that the response is made by the character who has already been identified by his dark knight/samurai costume and by his position as an opponent of the characters the audience has already been led to sympathize with. In particular, his comparison of the Force and power is significant, especially when power here means the force or might of the world-destroying capacity of the Death Star. The Force is power, and power is control. While we will discuss this a little more later, it is important for now to recognize the point made by the next stage of the discussion. Motti sneeringly dismisses Vader's warning: "Don't try to frighten us with your sorcerer's ways, Lord Vader. Your sad devotion to that ancient religion has not helped you conjure up the stolen data tapes, or given you clairvoyance enough to find the Rebels' hidden fortress." The secularist condescendingly rejects religion, but Vader's reaction of choking Motti with the mere power of his mind indicates that *SW*'s sympathies are not with the secularist. It is Motti, not Vader, who plays the fool. A little later the secular pragmatist Han Solo patronizingly sneers, "Hokey religions and ancient weapons are no match for a good blaster at your side." Luke rhetorically asks, "You don't believe in the Force, do you?" to which Solo revealingly replies, "Kid, I've flown from one side of this galaxy to the other and I've seen a lot of strange stuff, but I've never seen anything to make me think there's one all-powerful Force controlling everything. There's no mystical energy field controls my destiny." As philosophical theologian John D. Caputo explains:

> Far from serving as a vehicle for debunking religion or exposing it as pre-scientific superstition, the enormous popularity of Star Wars over the years derives in no small part from its reproduction of elemental structures and its transcription of classical religious figures into a high-tech world. . . . The advice is ancient but the packaging is new.[4]

There is a second point worth noticing about Lucas's intentions. Even while these movies affirm the importance of a religious understanding of the universe, the way they encourage spiritual reflection is not coercively evangelistic, and they certainly do not intend to create any so-called pop religion. The science of the fantasy offers a parallel here—it would be an absurd *category mistake* to ask whether the movies' technologies are scientifically feasible. In this regard, claims by Christians that Lucas's creations are devilish or a form of New Age propaganda are ridiculous on at least one level. Far from introducing anything new, Lucas aims to distill the essence of the *old* and present it in a new packaging.

The Force Is One

When pressed in his interview with Bill Moyers to say something about the Buddhist influence on *SW*, Lucas admitted, "I guess it's more specific in Buddhism, but it is a notion that's been around before that."[5] "When the film came out, almost every single religion took Star Wars and used it as an example of their religion; they were able to relate it to stories in the Bible, in the Koran and in the Torah."[6] Apparently, "in many ways, the Force combines the basic principles of several different major religions yet it most embodies what all of them have in common: an unerring faith in a spiritual power."[7] So Pollock claims that "Lucas wanted to instill in children a belief in a supreme being—not a religious god, but a universal deity that he named the Force, a cosmic energy source that incorporates and consumes all living things."[8]

This would suggest that *SW* controversially resonates with something of a pluralist ethos, that all the religions share a *common essence* that may be identified *without the guidance of any particular* religious system. The title of Campbell's major four-volume work, *The Masks of God,* tells us much about this perspective—the Absolute referred to as God is perceived through many different masks. This is why religions appear different; all in their own way depict an inexpressible "something that transcends all thinking."[9] It was perhaps through reading Campbell's "monomythic" approach to the world's religions that Lucas felt comfortable mixing and matching elements of different religions and mythologies in the *SW* movies. He defined his own religion as "Buddhist Methodist."[10]

But occasionally Campbell seems caught between this pluralism and a broad understanding of religion in psychological terms. He claims "that God is within you," and indeed "you are God . . . in your deepest being." Echoing the mystical energy of *ANH*'s Force, he proclaims:

> That old man up there has been blown away. You've got to find the Force inside you. [Your life comes] from the ultimate energy that is the life of the universe. . . . You are God, but not in your ego, but in your deepest being, where you are at one with the non-dual transcendent.[11]

Suggestively, Lucas portrays the Force in quasi-pantheistic terms as "an energy-field created by all living things" that "surrounds us and penetrates us" (Obi-Wan to Luke, *ANH*). Pollock sees in this identifying of the divine and all living things an example of Campbell's psychological approach pervading *SW*: "The message of *Star Wars* is religious: God isn't dead, he's there if you want him to be. 'The laws are in yourself,' Lucas is fond of saying; the Force dwells within."[12] In *TPM* this pantheistic imagery takes on something of a quasi-biomechanical (what many critics complain of as a bio-babble) quality in Jedi Master Qui-Gon Jinn's teaching to the young-ster Anakin: "Midi-chlorians are a microscopic life-form that resides within all living cells . . . inside your cells. . . . And we are symbionts with them." Caputo suggests from this that "the Force is . . . a pervasive mythico-scientific power that runs through all things. The basic religious schema of *Star Wars* is rather more Eastern than Judeo-Christian."[13] At this point it is worth recognizing the many Eastern images and themes that pervade these movies: the samurai-like Jedi Knights ("Jedi" coming from *jidaigeki*, or period drama movies about samurai); Obi-Wan's name, which is partly based on the Japanese *Obi* or kimono sash; the Zen-like Jedi Master Yoda; Dagobah's name, which is apparently the same as an Indian and Burmese Buddhist temple (the Dagoba); and Qui-Gon Jinn's name, which is based on the Chinese meditative and energy manipulating martial-arts discipline *Qi-Gong* (*Qi* refers to the energy thought to flow through all living things from the Tao; a Jinn may be an untamable spirit in Arabian mythology).

We should be careful, though, not to overemphasize this Eastern quality, lest we miss the presence of numerous Christian images. For example: Darth Maul is horned and devilish-looking (*TPM*); Vader's and Sidious's tempta-tions echo Satan's temptations of Adam and Christ (*ESB*, *ROTS*, respectively, and together in *ROTJ*); the *Millennium Falcon*'s emergence from the space slug's belly alludes to Jonah's emergence from the belly of the fish (*ESB*); Obi-Wan's guiding presence to Luke sounds a little like the Holy Spirit's presence (*ANH*); Anakin's name may be a reference to the powerful and giant *Anakites* who descended from the renowned *Nephalim* warriors, the latter significantly being the fruit of the union between the "sons of God . . . [and] the daughters of humans" and whose name significantly means "fallen ones" (Gen. 6:4);[14] and finally there is, of course, the virgin birth image used of Anakin (*TPM*).

Moreover, while it is true that the Buddhism of *ESB*'s director Irvin Ker-shner cannot be unimportant to Yoda's characterization, the Jedi Master is designed more as a representative of a universal wisdom, and the deliberate Einstein-like touch in his facial design testifies to that. William Stephens, for instance, sees him as a Stoic archetype.[15] As we will see in chapters 6–7, the cultivation of the virtues of knowledge and peace to oppose ignorance, greed, and aggression is also vital to a life of Christian integrity. In this way Pollock misses the point when he argues that here "Yoda's philosophy is Buddhist."[16]

This all suggests that Lucas's borrowing seems to be *eclectic* and more postmodern than specifically Eastern. Quite simply, the Force is a slippery idea that can sound at times like the personal psyche and at other times like a transcendent and unknowable Absolute One. The driving spirit appears to be a catch-all concept that assumes a hypothetical commonality in all religions underneath their less important differences. Even if he is not intending to produce a new religion, or even proselytize for an old one, the ideas and values that shape Lucas's Force reveal his modern pluralistic mentality.

But we have to ask quite a few questions of these assumptions. For instance, how can anyone know there is a common divine One behind all religious expressions? How can religious pluralism possess a reliable perspective on all religions when it attempts to "cut all the ties that bind me to any moral or linguistic tradition" and in which I grow, learn, and think?[17] Why should the common elements among the religions be more important theologically than their differences? Does taking the commonality as more important than religious differences fail to take seriously those theological differences? Maurice Friedman, for example, claims with respect to Campbell's pluralism that "many modern thinkers . . . [even] when they know something about the world's religions, . . . do not hesitate to ignore all the phenomena that do not fit their personal perception."[18] Is religious pluralism not an *assertion* of a particular understanding of religion, which John Milbank calls a "sort of tyranny"?[19] Many scholars observe that in a crucial sense this kind of pluralism is the reasoning of "liberal, Western subjects."[20] These are all pressing questions, and they demand that religious pluralism justify its comparative evaluations, especially since it seems to know (or assume) rather a lot about a God who supposedly cannot be known.

Ironically, the pluralist approach itself can be damaging to conversations between religions, for as Kenneth Surin argues, "the pluralist . . . speaks well of the other but never to the other, and indeed cannot do otherwise because there really is no intractable other for the pluralist."[21] In this sense, Lucas's *SW* may be less a religious parable and more a manifestation of "liberal, Western subjects." A pluralistic branding of religion is well stocked for a consumerist era, offering a God who can be expressed through whichever type of religion or spirituality we choose, without any significant theological consequence. As theologian Miroslav Volf argues, "An unknowable god is an idle god, exalted . . . high on her throne (or hidden so deep in the foundations of being)."[22] So while John Brosnan thinks that Lucas creates "a safe religion that doesn't step on any theological toes," the Force may well step, not on anyone, but on everyone.[23]

The Shape of the Force

Yet it is vitally important not to leave matters there. Precisely because pluralism attempts to find a common essence of religion, we should expect the Force to have at least some thin lines of similarity with Christian beliefs. In fact, as we will see, Lucas's portrayal of the Force raises some vitally important theological issues that can force Christians into exploring more deeply their own theological traditions.

The Power of the Nonmanipulatable "Force"

According to some commentators, the Force can be manipulated. This seems largely to be a consequence of the plot-device function it has in *ANH* as a magical "energy field" that "gives the Jedi his power" and amplifies its bearers' *power* (Obi-Wan to Luke). So Obi-Wan speaks of the Force as power and later, to Luke's query about whether the Force "controls your actions," responds, "It also obeys your commands." Similarly the Vader-Motti confrontation focuses on the issue of power. The Dark Lord of the Sith seems to wield and control the Force here. Obi-Wan's act of "Force manipulation" seems to be another example of this Force power. Arguably, this Jedi, no less than Vader, manipulates the energy field of the Force in order to control others (although we will discuss this more in a later chapter). On entering Mos Eisley spaceport, Obi-Wan and Luke are momentarily halted by a detachment of Imperial Sandtroopers in search of the droids that had earlier escaped from the captured Alderaanian diplomatic starship (Tantive IV) with the Death Star plans stolen by Rebel spies. With a subtle wave of his hand, Obi-Wan puts words into the interrogating trooper's mouth and thus forces him to pay no more attention to the little company of travelers.[24] The older man then reveals to Luke that "the Force can have a strong influence on the weak-minded."

Because the Force is portrayed as that which is ultimate, if it is power, then *power is the ultimate truth of all things.* Consequently, the battle between good and evil would be little more than a conflict between two ways in which one can choose to shape life. If the heart of the difference can be reduced to a simple matter of *personal choice*, or perhaps personal instinct, then there seems to be no moral or theological reason for preferring the good over the evil, the Rebel Alliance over the Empire. This is precisely the claim made by Gabriel McKee, among others: "The Force itself seems indifferent to the ends to which it is manipulated. . . . God, *Star Wars* argues, takes a role in our experience, but not on one side or the other."[25]

With *ESB*, however, the situation has been immeasurably enriched and the relation of the Force to power is portrayed differently. Although there are Force levitations and so on, the Force is no longer the simple plot device of *ANH* but instead becomes *morally demanding* of its bearers. As we will explore in more detail in chapters 6 and 7, the "inmost character [of the Force] is far more than power for human disposal. What it is really about is radical love for all things. . . . The Force is far more than another weapon for the macho superhero to add to his blaster-belt; rather, it has a very demanding spiritual and moral content. . . . Ultimately, the history of the universe depends not on Luke Skywalker's physical brawn, combat prowess, or strategic wiliness but on the extent to which he has imbibed the lessons of love."[26] That means that the Force demands nonaggression, and understanding this forces Luke to reevaluate his perception not only of the nature of a Jedi but also of the character of the Force. Learning to "be mindful of the living Force" (Qui-Gon, *TPM*) draws the Jedi devotees deeper into the ethical life and the truth that all things are interconnected and responsible—something that the Sith, for all their power in manipulating the Force, destructively fail to appreciate. (Chapter 3 will demonstrate that the Sith manipulate the Force by *inappropriately* using it for what it is not designed for and therein breaking the proper symbiosis of all life-forms in the life-giving Force.)

This makes the Force sound a little more like the Christian understanding of God. Obedience to the will of the Force is not blind acquiescence to a powerful but morally ambiguous god, and it certainly is not a giving absolute significance to one's own desires. On the contrary, it is the journey into becoming responsible for the well-being of the galaxy or, more personally, one's galactic neighbor. This means that the virtues of coresponsibility, compassion, and so on are ultimately the truth of life. The Force is about dependence and creative self-giving, not autonomy and possessiveness. Of course, the immensely rich Christian image of the triune God—the One who as Father, Son, and Spirit (Tri-unity) inexhaustibly and endlessly lives in Self-disposing relationships of Self-giving—is not one Lucas uses in these movies. While this image suggests that communal relations of giving are the fundamental truth of all things, the very undifferentiated oneness of the Force can make its ethical demands potentially more ambiguous.[27]

A singular or Absolute One (the Force) shaped by modern Western pluralism may unwittingly deny the sense of *difference*-in-relation, since it imagines that all things are dependent on a simple *oneness*. Precisely through not having taken sufficiently seriously the implications of the confession of the triune God, Christian history itself has become littered with the unwitting worship of gods of self-protection, personal comfort, and self-aggrandizing aggression against others—for example, against nonmales, nonwhites, non-Protestants, non-Christians, and all others who are not like "us." As Campbell claims:

> The world is full of mutually contending bands: totem-, flag-, and party-worshipers. Even the so-called Christian nations—which are supposed to be following a "World" Redeemer—are better known to history for their colonial barbarity and internecine strife than for any practical display of that unconditioned love, synonymous with the effective conquest of ego, ego's world, and ego's tribal god, which was taught by their supreme Lord [in Luke 6:27–36].[28]

Christians should be the first to resist possessive and self-securing flattery and instead constantly be alert to, and attentively resist, the aspects of their faith and practice that can damage others, and so follow the transforming way of Jesus Christ's own self-dispossession. It is, after all, *churches* that are urged to flee from idols (1 Cor. 10:14; 1 John 5:21), and that is why Christian theology demands that self-examination involve honest confession of sin.

The Force at least interconnects all things in interdependency, and this is a highly suggestive idea for the notion of moral accountability and responsibility in *SW,* as we will see in chapters 6 and 7. Moreover, it is the object of Jedi contemplation so that they are focused on that which is *other than themselves* and not on themselves as such, and which indicates the *interconnection of themselves with all others*. These are features of the Force that provide rich potential for resisting the self-seeking competitiveness that becomes so destructive of others. *SW* is concerned with our place as responsible agents in, with, and for the flourishing of the shared life of all things. This is why the "Force-conscious" Jedi play the role of galactic Guardians and (in theory at least) live in relations of healthy and nonexploitative interdependency. It is they who represent peace and justice in the Republic. In other words, because they are truly dependent on the Force, the Jedi are properly concerned for all things in a way that has to oppose the Sith Lords' demand for a power that *controls* others. When President Ronald Reagan in 1986 claimed that "the Force is with us," he was actually perverting *SW*'s "self-dispossessing" (or other-focused) ethos.[29] *ANH*'s blessing "May the Force be with you" is the expression of a hope *for others* ("May the Force be *with you*"), not *for ourselves* as with Reagan ("The Force is with *us*"). Moreover, the *SW* blessing is precisely a request of *hope* for others ("*May* the Force be with you"), whereas Reagan's claim sounds like a *possessive* assertion ("The Force *is* with us").

The Force is mysterious and transcendent, which is why the Jedi meditate, in Qui-Gon's terms, so as to listen for "the will of the Force." Yet even those who do so cannot guarantee that they will successfully hear it—the Force critically transcends even the Jedi performance. That is why there are, first, tensions between Qui-Gon and the Jedi Council in *TPM*; second, the religious arrogance of "Force-conscious" Jedi that blinds them to evil's rise within the midst of the Republic; and third, the Jedi Order's unwitting contribution to their near annihilation. There is, in the end, no clear access to the Absolute, to the Force. Even Qui-Gon's supposed attentiveness to "the will of the Force" leads to morally ambiguous results, as is the case with his intense faith in the boy who grows up to *fall* and become Darth Vader.

The theme of the transcendence of God is vital to well-ordered Christian thinking and serves practically as a countercultural motif. As Kathryn Tanner argues, "If divinity is transcendent, then descriptions of divinity are most obviously inadequate; descriptions of divinity are brought first and foremost under a relativizing knife. Religious claims are the first human claims that must be recognized to be conditioned, limited, and fallible. . . . Belief in a transcendent God turns back against itself and forms thereby a self-critical cultural tradition."[30] If God is sovereign, for instance, then no other ruler can claim our allegiance absolutely and unquestionably. Any such attempt to do so by any ruler, nation, economic system, and so on is idolatrous in that it claims for itself the absoluteness of the transcendent God, who cannot be inscribed in or possessed by worldly affairs. Realizing this is what prompts the Jedi Council to be concerned about—and eventually collude with rebelling elements against—Palpatine's increasing emergency powers and ultimate claims for his absolutist state (of course, the resistance comes tragically too late). This is a state that has lost its way—it is now focused on securing itself at all costs and not on the making of good, free, and contingent relations. To say no to this kind of governance, even at the expense of one's own security, is to serve the common good that the state supposedly exists to serve, and therefore to choose the rich life of moral integrity over the bare life of personal longevity.

That is not to deny that creaturely action can reflect God's way with us, for that would be to deny God's mediation (God's presence in and through creaturely means and relations). As we will see in later chapters, God's way has to determine or shape human relations—*all* human relations, contrary to those who want to limit the relevance of theology or spirituality to individuals' private beliefs and religious practices. And as Obi-Wan in the novelization of *ROTS* admits, "It is so far beyond our limited understanding that we can only surrender to its mystery," thus implying that the Force is only to be truly lived within and participated in, and to become the source of one's bearings.[31]

There is but one Force, with two ways of living in and through it. That is probably why *SW* refers to "the dark-side of the Force" in contrast to the simpler and more direct talk of the Force itself. The characters use the language of the Force without qualification when speaking specifically of the Good, whereas evil has to be specified. The Force *is* the Good itself, and that is why they do not speak of the good side of the Force. This suggests that there is no simple duality, as if there are two Forces, or as if the Force is a morally ambiguous power with dark and light sides (see chapter 3). Even the Sith themselves do not believe in such a moral duality. Vader informs Luke that "the Emperor will show you the true nature of the Force. He is your Master now" (*ROTJ*). But it is the Siths who are out of kilter, who are unable to truly understand or "be mindful of the living Force" in a way that appropriately listens for its "will" (Qui-Gon, *TPM*). That is why their way is so destructive. While Lucas speaks in 2001's *The Power of the Force* of "the dark side" as "always there" and "experienced daily by people," he explains that the dark side is "like a huge cancer, alive, festering." It is, he claims, both a reminder of a moral state and a "symptom and symbol of a very sick society." *SW* interestingly, then, identifies evil with disordered desire, in other words, with the seeking of that which cannot and should not be what we desire. The demands of the Good are to reorder our desire. But knowing and doing the Good are not themselves easy tasks. Anakin is portrayed as knowing the ways of the Force perhaps more intensely, or at least more powerfully, than any other Jedi living or dead. Yet not only does that fail to prevent him from turning to the dark side and becoming the ill-fated distortion of a human being (Darth Vader), but the knowledge and "Force-power" he has enable him to commit the most destructive deeds.

Pervasive Presence to All Things

In later chapters we will explore the importance of the theme of responsibility for all life. For now it is crucial to recognize that *SW* makes sense of this in terms of the presence of the Force in and to all things and the fact that all things are symbionts with the Force and therefore one another. While this idea is already present in Yoda's instruction of Luke concerning the "energy" of the Force that "surrounds us and binds us" (*ESB*), it is Qui-Gon who speaks most clearly of it to young Anakin (*TPM*): "Midi-chlorians are a microscopic life-form that resides within all living cells . . . inside your cells.

. . . And we are symbionts with them. . . . [Symbionts are] life-forms living together for mutual advantage." All things and events are interconnected in some way in a complex web, and to exploit any aspect of that arrangement for one's own gain is to risk the delicate balance of life. The main consequence of this idea is that the divine (the Force) is *ethically generative*. In other words, the "Force-conscious" who properly understand the nature and will of the Force realize that they are responsible for the well-being of all things and act accordingly.

When we describe the presence of the Force in this way, there appears to be more similarity between it and certain Christian understandings of God's presence to all things than those who call Lucas's Force pantheistic allow. So Obi-Wan's teaching that the Force "surrounds us, it penetrates us, it binds the galaxy together" (*ANH*) strikingly evokes Pauline imagery of "one God and Father of all, who is above all and through all and in all" (Eph. 4:6). When Christians read the agency of God in terms of God's presence in Jesus Christ (John 1:3; Col. 1:16), the will of God is understood to have saving significance for all things. And finally, the Holy Spirit is the ongoing presence of the "cosmic and intimate" Creator, who makes all things new (what theologians call redemption) and, in Stone's words, guides "the destinies of individuals and can be experienced by them."[32] "Clearly," Stone argues, "the Holy Spirit does bear some resemblance to the Force of *Star Wars*."

This important parallel between the Force and God the Creator, between the ethical implications of the life-giving Force and God's creating, is often concealed when Christians imagine the doctrine of creation to be primarily an explanation of the origin or beginning of the cosmos and believe that the Genesis creation narratives provide a scientific account that rivals and excludes all other cosmological explanations of what happened. This view emphasizes the texts in Genesis 1 that mention "In the beginning" and "God made" as the keys to what the chapter is all about. Among other things, this perspective makes the beginning so distant in the past that it seems to be a matter of only scientific curiosity or antiquarian interest. To confess the world was created in this way would in itself have no more bearing on how I live than the statement that "an eighteenth-century ancestor of mine was called Joseph."

But we need to recognize that the Genesis narrative was composed in opposition to the dualistic cosmologies that dominated the many religions of the ancient Hebrews' neighbors. According to Genesis, the act of creation was not the result of a conflict between eternal divinities or between an abstract good and evil. Instead it was wholly the good product of God's good speaking. In this context, it is arguable that the key text in Genesis 1 is not that the world was created ("In the beginning") but "And God saw that it was good" (Gen. 1:10). In other words, the most important question about God's creating is the question about creation's goodness. That is why there are no fewer than seven occasions when God's positive evaluation of creation is mentioned (1:4, 10, 12, 18, 21, 25, 31). The doctrine of creation is not best presented as a case of plugging the gaps in our account of *how* we came to be here. Undoubtedly, that is why the great Nicene Creed (AD 381) of the universal church confesses simply, "We believe in one God the Father Almighty, maker of heaven and earth, of all things visible and invisible." The Christian doctrine of creation has to do with the fact that our existence is dependent for its being, meaning, and value upon God, *absolutely* and *only* upon God. It has to do with appreciating that createdness, our being creatures, is who we properly are, and that therefore bodily physicality, dependency upon others, and so on, are good. In this way, "To be a creature does not mean to be of no account. It means to be related to God. Creature is a title of dignity and consequence."[33]

Moreover, Genesis does not merely tell of the goodness of the creation; perhaps primarily, it witnesses to the goodness of the Creator. Theologians have frequently confessed that creation is not an act of a needy deity who makes creatures from a desire to receive, gain, or dominate. So the influential bishop of Hippo in North Africa, Augustine (AD 354–430), declares that "God did not create under stress of any compulsion, or because he lacked something for his own needs; his only motive was goodness; he created because his creation was good."[34] In a sense, there is nothing in it for God. So while, as Rowan Williams argues, "God creates 'in God's interest' (there could be no other motivation for divine action)," "that 'interest' is not the building-up of the divine life, which simply is what it is, but its giving away. For God to act for God's sake *is* for God to act for our sake."[35] In this regard, God does not create in a way to constrain creaturely freedom and dignity. This divine tyranny, which is how many have imagined God's sovereignty, would not be the rule exercised by the gracious God who creates wholly out of nothing, as Christians came to confess.

Our perceptions of these qualities in the doctrine of creation shape our understanding not merely of the dignity of human creatures but also of the nonhuman creation. The theme of the cosmic and intimate presence of God with *all* things has been importantly retrieved through the so-called "ecological crisis." This crisis has often (and not wholly unfairly) been blamed upon Western Christians who overemphasize the place of human beings in God's saving will, to the detriment of the nonhuman creation (the "humanocentric bias"). This overemphasis has wrought devastation on the nonhuman environment when that setting has been understood *only* in instrumentalist terms—in terms of what it provides for humanity.[36] Of course, ecologically conscious Christians should not tone down the Scriptures' focus on the creation of human beings but instead appreciate the intrinsic value of the nonhuman creation and of the divine presence in and to it. Genesis calls attention to the human's role as *steward* over the nonhuman creation (Gen. 2:15), and this idea sits uneasily with the practice of dominating and exploiting nature.

The doctrine of creation, then, leads to promising questions about the meaning of being human before God, before other human beings, and before the nonhuman creation. It concerns the divine goals of constructing and maintaining associations of interdependent relations among creatures. Consequently, creation is God's act of "bringing different realms of life into fruitful associations of interdependent relations that promote life."[37]

> To be a creature is to recognize, not merely that one's existence is derived from a source other than itself, but that it is not centered in itself; it revolves around a center other than itself; it is (if there were such a word) extracentric. In this respect it is radically opposed to the prevailing modern attitude, which accords the centrality in all thought and action to the self.[38]

If the prevailing philosophies of the Western world emphasize the importance of the individual, the individual's rights, the individual's freedoms, the value of the individual's choices, and so on, it is highly significant that the Christian doctrine of creation should offer a radically liberating alternative. In this Christian account, our being persons (our personhood) is not formed by being isolated from others or purely autonomous selves but by being "formed in multiple webs of relationships."[39] Particularly through the theme of the coexistence and interdependency of all life-forms in the Force, *SW* likewise opposes just such modern individualism. In order to sustain this suggestion further, we will have to discuss in chapter 3 just how the saga resists a cosmic dualism and parallels a Christian understanding of conflict as a distortion of the true meaning and value of *all* life-forms. The Christian doctrine of creation, properly conceived, rings a warning against the abuse of God's care of *any*-thing and *every*-thing. All creatures in some way or another bear the imprint of God's inclusive valuation of them. Christians who unknowingly affirm dualistic cosmologies, and who construe salvation in terms of being saved *from* the world for *another* world, forget this. *SW*'s concept of the permeating presence of the Force may here importantly echo a more appropriate theology of creation. Of course, we have to admit that the mechanics of the presence of the Force groan under the weight of being pressed too hard, particularly since it is meant to perform only a very broad role in the context of the movies. And yet its image of the dependency of all things on the meaning-shaping Force resonates with the Christian doctrine that God's creating makes healthy sets of morally responsible relations.

Beyond Personality and Impersonality

While Stone sees likeness between the Force and God the Holy Spirit, he thinks they differ radically over the issue of the "personality" of the divine because, unlike the Spirit, "the Force . . . is impersonal."[40] This statement, however, is much too simple and misleading.

In the first place, perhaps we may learn something by reflecting on Qui-Gon's personalistic language concerning the Force. He speaks of listening to the Force and of attending to "the *will* of the Force" (*TPM*). Yet he *alone* speaks like this, providing a different perspective on the rich mystery of the Force. Also, it is not altogether clear that his description has to be understood in personalistic terms. After all, the German philosopher Arthur Schopenhauer (1788–1860) in *The World as Will and Idea* (1816) argues for the primacy of will in the world process, yet without suggesting anything remotely theistic by it. This seems to be the way Stover interprets the Force in *ROTS* when he has Obi-Wan proclaim of the Jedi, "We speak of the *will of the Force* as someone ignorant of gravity might say it is the will of the river to flow to the ocean: it is a metaphor that describes our ignorance."[41]

The clue to Stone's mistake is not to be found in *SW* as such, as if the Force is like the God whom Christians confess. Rather, it lies in the Christian traditions themselves and what they understand language about God to be doing when they assert that God is beyond personality (and conversely beyond impersonality). So while a common Christian response contrasts the impersonality of the Force with the personality of God, there is grave potential for idolatry when we forget the metaphorical and anthropomorphic nature of theological language. Augustine importantly claims that one should "model oneself on the object of one's worship."[42] In the act of idolatry God is (consciously or unconsciously) modeled on the worshipers, reflecting or amplifying worshipers' desires and ideas. The critical gap between the Creator and the creature (the Creator is not a creature) implies that all our talk and conceiving of God are inadequate and only ever provisional. But this troublingly recedes in the act of idolatry. Correspondingly, God becomes a thing among all the things, a being among beings (writing God's being a Thing or Being as nouns in uppercase form does not solve the problem).

This takes us back to the question of God's personality. Christian theology has spoken of the Godhead as a unity-in-distinction, one God in three "persons." Indeed, the very notion of human beings as being persons has its pattern or shape in this Trinitarian theology—we are persons precisely because we have been created in the image of God (cf. Gen. 1:26–27). But there is also another sense in which "personhood" is language we use in order to differentiate between persons in relation. I am a person because I can say, "I am I, and I am not you." Personality consists in my knowing that I am distinguishable only insofar as I am one individual among others, albeit with and for others. So, by its very nature, personality is a finite thing that belongs to creatures. That, of course, cannot be true of God, since God, as the Creator of all that is, cannot be a member of any or every thing or of any class of being. God is the source and goal of all created things/beings, the "cause" of all that is. That means that, as the fifth-century pseudonymous Christian writer Dionysius the Areopagite (better known later as Pseudo-Dionysius) claims, God is "supra-existent Being," "beyond being . . . above and beyond speech, mind, or being itself," and "the Superunknowable."[43] "Christians are the only people," C. S. Lewis claims, "who offer any idea of what a being that is beyond personality could be like."[44]

Consequently, it makes little sense to speak of God simply as either "personal," in the way that belongs to human beings who are called persons, or "impersonal," in the way that nonpersons such as stones or molecules are called "impersonal." God is beyond both personality and impersonality, and ascribing personality to God may thus be theologically misleading. Nevertheless, as Herbert McCabe argues, the image of "a personal God . . . may be useful" in that, when all the necessary limitations on our God talk are remembered, "it seems absurd to call God impersonal. . . . We have to remember that great forces don't really get anything done unless they are wielded in a context . . . and since whatever else we mean by God we mean what gets something done or made or existing, it seems that we cannot think of him as merely impersonal."[45] In other words, and this is what "gets done" by God, the very ability to claim ignorance of God's infinite essence comes through God's self-revelation. Thus in the act of revelation God is revealed as the infinite richness that cannot be seen, plumbed, or adequately spoken of by creatures. In the giving of God's self to us, we learn of our ignorance. So Christian knowledge involves a knowing that is simultaneously a kind of unknowing. But this ignorance or "luminous darkness" is not the same as the blindness of those, in the words of St. John of the Cross (1542–91), who "do not walk in God, [and] . . . are unable to perceive that which hinders them from approaching Him."[46] The "excessive light" of God appears as "thick darkness" to creaturely vision.[47] That is why 1 Timothy describes God as dwelling "in unapproachable light, whom no one has ever seen or can see" (1 Tim. 6:16). Yet this Light itself nonetheless illuminates all things.[48] All creation, all being, is therefore properly known in the light of God's self-revelation, and this act continually purifies and makes holy our sight and hearing (cf. 1 John 1:7). Christian knowing and unknowing can be likened in these terms to a "luminous darkness," in that it is a patiently schooled or educated ignorance of the infinitely rich One that is performed in praise and charity.

Just how far all this can be said of the Force in *SW* is difficult to tell for certain. The Force does not *act* in this way, and the fact that Lucas conceives it out of the kind of ignorance of God that characterizes a modern Western pluralism of religions makes the notion of the agency of the Force a particularly difficult one to conceive of. Perhaps Qui-Gon's anthropomorphic description of the Force may still be of some help, but only if we also remember that the Force is beyond both personality and impersonality. If nothing else, though, the Force does play an illuminative role for living well, as we will now see.

Conclusion: First Steps into a Larger World

After the success of *ESB*, Lucas revealed that "this is the kind of movie we need. There needs to be a kind of film that expresses the mythological realities of life—the deeper psychological movements of the way we conduct our lives."[49] But *SW* never intended to offer a ready-made religion, which is why the Force is a rather vague "amalgamation of lots of different things:"[50] "All I was trying to say in a very simple and straightforward way is that there is a God and there is a good and bad side."[51] Perhaps its popular reception reveals more about some search for moral absolutes and about the migration of the spiritual quest from more traditional forms into something more diffuse, abstract, and individualistic. (In the 2001 census there was a partially tongue-in-cheek attempt to register Jedi as an official religion in New Zealand [53,000], Australia [70,000], Canada [20,000], and the UK [390,000].)

SW itself is, according to Robert Bowman, "a complex, rather than a simple, parable," and Lucas himself admits that it is "made up of many themes."[52] Ultimately, then, it does not offer a systematically coherent philosophy of life or a sustained theology or spirituality. Yet it does keep drawing us back to the ethical questions, what are we to do with evil, and how do we identify it? That was Lucas's intention at least from 1975 onward: "There was no modern mythology to give kids a sense of values, to give them a strong mythological fantasy life. Westerns were the last of that genre for Americans. Nothing was being done for young people that has real psychological underpinnings and was aimed at intelligent beings."[53] The worry that many have with this and with its reflection in *ANH* is that westerns tended to be largely morally simplistic. As Pollock observes somewhat uncharitably, Lucas wants to "pontificate on the differences between right and wrong."[54] Yet Lucas's prequel films in particular, and possibly even *ESB* before them, demonstrate the difficulty of moral intuition, and here they are theologically at their most interesting. (In juxtaposing the spirit of *Episode IV* and its sequels, it may be significant that Han Solo in *Episode V* discards the saloon-shootout-style waistcoat of his cowboy costume, and by *Episode VI* he dons a full-length combat trench coat.) Despite the vastness of the galactic landscape, and the grand scope of a pluralistic approach to the Ultimate of the religions, this vast cinematic canvas encourages us to think hard about the most intimate and personal of topics—the idea of the human itself.

"The major theme in *Star Wars*, as in every Lucas film, is the acceptance of personal responsibility."[55] This means that Orson Scott Card's claim that *SW* makes "no rules other than a vague insistence on unselfishness and oath-keeping" is odd.[56] But can the Good ever appropriately be a nonreligious idea, and nonspecific if it is religious? Lucas's pluralistic tendencies problematically suggest it can—the Good can be known and lived apart from belief in God, and here the movies draw on a general stock of ideas and perspectives in this regard. They offer rousing storytelling driven by themes of moral struggle and transcendence. The origins of *SW*'s Force are clearly not specifically Christian as such, and certainly not without their philosophical problems. Yet the movies give a kind of imaginative shape to certain human insights, and like classical Greek and Roman myths, *SW*'s pop myth has become a part of the cultural landscape. Overstreet declares that it, "like any great myth, gives us glimpses 'through a glass darkly' of things essential and true. Virtue, courage, patience, peace, self-control, love . . . the Good Side are they."[57]

SW then does have some quite profound ethical implications, so that even if it is "religion lite," there are, in any case, quite a number of strings attached. The *SW* religion becomes quite demanding indeed:

- The transcendence of the Force undermines any account of the divine that echoes and legitimates any particular human thought or performance. The divine is not readily identifiable with what is.
- The pervasiveness of the Force in all things denies that our responsibilities can only be for our family, tribe, nation, and so on. Instead, responsibility is borne for all things.
- The life givingness of the Force resists the life-denying or life-suppressing modes of living that dominate, oppress, or deny others their personhood.

- The "will of the Force" seems to have a sense of the equity of being—all come into the world through the Force, are pervaded by the Force, and have life together.

These points resist the idea that the divine is so much the Wholly Other, and therefore so different from the world's life, that we can be indifferent to it and that it makes no difference in practice. In fact, the delicate balance of language of transcendence and immanence makes it possible to imagine ways of human living together (and living with the nonhuman) that resist all that distorts and destroys a proper *making* of all things *one* together.

Chapter Three

Evil Strikes Back

As chapter 1 argued, while myths are produced by the cultures in which they are born and they express their cultures' self-understandings, they are also culturally productive, in that, if taken seriously, they can in turn shape our experience and impression of the world around us. This chapter begins the exploration of the way these movies depict their world by exploring the evil that pervades it. Chapter 5 will describe the political implications of the presence of that evil. The ethos of Lucas's imagination is supposed to reflect certain trends in modern Western culture. Yet the saga works with a quite sophisticated series of images that should ask questions of how Western cultures commonly understand good and evil and contribute to the projects of human flourishing. To explain why this is significant, we should listen to Augustine's claim that "we ought to know the causes of good and evil as far as man may in this life know them, in order to avoid the mistakes and troubles of which this life is so full."[1]

Dualism of the Fates

According to Campbell's reading of mythology, "The source of all existence . . . yields the world's plenitude of both good and evil."[2] Does this mean that good and evil belong to one another as darkness and light? In this approach, evil is the projected personification of all we fear: the dark figure, the shadow, the threatening other that usually takes the form in stories of wild animals, werewolves, vampires, the demonic, aliens, and even the less-than-human foreigner. Lucas's ancient and distantly situated galaxy seems to be quite different from this approach, however. He tells the mythical story of the conflict *between* good and evil, but he does not offer a creation theme that posits the Good in the beginning such as Tolkien's *The Silmarillion.* Consequently many see *SW* as a dualistic philosophy presenting the *conflict between two eternal principles*, and Lucas himself seems to suggest as much: "The idea of a positive and negative, that there are two sides to an entity, a push and pull, a yin and a yang, and the struggle between the two sides are issues of nature that I wanted to include in the film."[3]

Is this why the Force is spoken of as having a "dark side"? Mary Henderson, curator of the *Star Wars: The Magic of Myth* Smithsonian exhibition, makes an interesting observation: "There is no crossover between the two forces; when the Death Star is destroyed along with everyone on it, it is a clear-cut victory of good over irredeemable evil."[4] Arguably Emperor Palpatine (the Lord of the Sith, Darth Sidious) is less a person than a metaphysical principle, evil incarnate, wholly lacking moral depths. His actor, Ian McDiarmid, describes him as "the blackest of the black. . . . He's a solid block of evil [with] no redeeming features."[5] And according to Mark Rowlands, *SW* is unsubtly shaded in terms of "black and white," making it similar to Manicheism and therefore putting it firmly outside the pale of Christian faith.[6] (Just to explain, Manicheism takes its name from the Persian Mani [AD 216–77], who believed, among other things, that the world is the battleground between two cosmic forces—light and darkness. I will discuss later why it was rejected by the mainline Christian traditions.)

Significantly in *ROTS*'s novelization, Jedi Master Mace Windu admits to Yoda and Obi-Wan in 19 BBY that the "Jedi create the light, but the Lords of the Sith do not create darkness. They merely use the darkness that is always there."[7] This sounds dualistic, but his following comment suggests what might be called an "evolutionary ethic" instead: "Greed and jealousy, aggression and lust and fear—these are all natural to sentient beings. The legacy of the jungle. Our inheritance from the dark." There is an ethical problem here, though; if evil and the traits we might call vices are natural to the jungle of life, as well as crucial to developing who we now are, then why should it be only part of our past heritage and not something we utilize now? Mace will find it philosophically difficult not to reduce evil's evilness, or to make evil something that helps the Good develop, rather than as something *wholly resistant to and destructive of* the Good. At least Manichean dualism has a pronounced sense of *conflict* and can say something more meaningful of the *evilness* of evil.

A Manichean approach, however, also has troubling ethical consequences. For instance, a balancing of light and dark or good and evil drastically weakens our ethical resolve to act wholly and utterly *against* evil (leaving aside for a moment what balance means here—although, ironically, the "balance" brought to the Force by "the chosen one" had left the Jedi for several years as an order of two: Yoda and Obi-Wan in *ROTS*, Obi-Wan and Luke in *ANH*, Yoda and Luke in *ESB–ROTJ*). That is far from all. Again leaving aside the complex question of how to identify the Good, if good and evil or light and darkness exist together eternally, then it becomes more difficult to sustain honest reflection on how so-called evil people and evil deeds are complexly made. Michael Gelven reflects on the implications of this in the context of the Holocaust: "The Nazis were not immoral [a dualist might say], they were far worse than that. They were insane. Mad. Cosmically vile. But of course if they are mad they are not responsible; . . . it seems to eclipse responsibility, appealing again to dark forces greater than our comprehension."[8] As a result of this projection of evil onto others, borne out of a "narcissism and fear of the Other," frequently Western cultures become cultures of blame.[9] Evil is *out there*. It is among, in, or even identifiable as "them," vampiristically attempting to feed off "us." Nazi anti-Semitism was itself one particularly horrific manifestation of this "blame" sensibility, blaming the Jewish people for most of Germany's ills since at least 1918. To draw this discussion back to *SW*, Card sarcastically asks, "Isn't it grand to be on the side of Truth and Justice? Especially when we never have to explore exactly what is true and who is just."[10]

Because many read *SW* in dualistic terms, there have been complaints about the portrayal of Anakin in *TPM* (this is a more substantive complaint than that over Jake Lloyd's acting). This nine-year-old boy is depicted in the brightest and least morally suspect of terms. He embodies a quite remarkable ethical virtue: "He [always] gives without any thought of reward" (Qui-Gon), "he knows nothing of greed" (Shmi). The audience is well aware that he is going to become Darth Vader, and critics have found it particularly difficult to connect the two. This, though, may reveal more about readers' expectations, assumptions, and understandings of evil than of the quality of Lucas's storytelling. After all, the classical form of one kind of tragic drama portrays the fall of a good, if flawed and therefore imperfect, protagonist (see chapter 4). Certainly *ANH* does often sound quite Manichean, but *Episodes V–VI* sound much less so. Indeed, the tragic structure of Lucas's story indicates that a dualistic reading of *SW* is misleadingly simplistic. Admittedly Lucas himself made a dualistic-type comment on one occasion: "The overriding philosophy in *Episode I*—and in all the Star Wars movies, for that matter—is the balance between good and evil. The Force itself breaks into two sides: the living Force and a greater cosmic Force."[11] What I am suggesting is that Lucas's practice (his movies) is theologically much better than his theory (his theological understanding).

Evil's "Backstory"

Every Saga Has a Beginning, but Evil Comes from Nowhere!

SW nowhere explains the origin of evil, at least not in terms of offering a cosmology and providing a creation or fall story. Instead we are taken into the midst (Latin, *in medias res*) of the realities of the conflict of good and evil. This may strike many as a kind of Manicheism, but significantly, the refusal to explain evil is quite natural to the determinedly anti-Manichean Augustine. Although the great bishop of Hippo, himself a Manichee devotee (AD 373–82) before his Christian conversion (386), speaks of creation and fall, he does not offer these as ways of *explaining* evil. Instead, these theologically explain what evil *is not*. It is neither something caused by God, even if God does *subsequently* work good out of evil, nor an aspect of creation as God creates it; thus it is not necessary to creation. The only reason God *permits* it to exist is because God can and does bring good out of it, but that is categorically not the same thing as saying that God *actively wills* evil to exist because without it the Good would not be good or would be less of a good.[12]

There are suggestive echoes of this particular Augustinian approach in *SW*, which entails that Christopher Brown makes a terrible theological mistake when he claims, in his exploration of *SW* through Augustine, that "evil is a necessary part of reality—the 'flipside' of goodness . . . that the fall of good and the rise of evil is something inevitable."[13] According to Obi-Wan, "For over a thousand generations the Jedi Knights were the guardians of peace and justice in the Old Republic, before the dark times, before the Empire" (*ANH*). The allusion here is to the thousand years of peace spoken of in the Revelation to John, after which come tribulation and the freeing of Satan (Rev. 20:2). The suggestion is of a paradisal setting into which evil *subsequently* comes. It is also clear that Darth Sidious has a certain satanic quality about him—so in the terrible "Order 66" there is an echo of the number of the beast recorded in 13:18, and it is his ascension to power that destroys the golden millennial age of peace and order in the Republic. As Lucas has recently commented, "Palpatine represents the devil, he represents the pure evil, the dark Lord of the Sith who is purely out to get more power in his greed."[14]

McDiarmid, on the other hand, suggestively declares that Sidious "is more evil than the devil. At least Satan fell—he has a history."[15] In the Augustinian account, there is no dualism in the natural order *as created*, but evil is introduced into the story through a *fall*, and thus Satan is portrayed as an angelic figure who himself becomes satiated with the rebelliousness that follows from his pride. Yet *SW* does immerse us *in medias res*, and its image of the paradisal conditions that become *subsequently* disrupted by evil suggest a Manichean reading is inappropriate. The prequels deepen this by portraying not only an already existent evil intruding into paradise but also a corruption that comes *from within the midst* of the Republic's paradise itself. The backstory of the Sith Lords is equally significant in this regard. Their order itself comes from within the midst of the Good. The Siths are *fallen* Jedi.

According to the ancient legends in the Expanded Universe materials, from around 25,000 BBY the newly formed Jedi Order agreed to pool its knowledge of the Force, continue to study it, and educate and regulate those who possessed its power.[16] However, a fierce debate raged, with many arguing that the dark side could be harnessed and controlled, and this eventually ensued in one hundred years of war ("The Great Schism"). After their decimating defeat, the remaining "dark Jedi" were exiled into uncharted space and subsequently discovered what they considered to be a primitive race of Force adepts called Sith on Korriban. The Jedi exiles conquered and enslaved this indigenous people and became known as the Lords of the Sith. (Incidentally, the designation of the Sith Lords as "Darth" may come from the title "Dark Lord of the Sith.") More than forty centuries BBY, two heroic Jedi of the Jedi Civil War, Revan and Malak, stumbled across Korriban and themselves became corrupted both by the knowledge they discovered there and by the brutalities of the war they had just fought in. They renounced the Jedi Order and became Sith. Finally, ten centuries BBY, another Jedi departed his constraining Order, taking forty-nine other disaffected Jedi with him into the new Sith Order.

This motif of *fall* running through *SW* is why there are two such fallen Jedi among the Sith's ranks, Darths Tyranus (Count Dooku) and Vader (Anakin Skywalker). Is it possible to read the archetypal evil Sidious in this way too? He is a character seemingly without complex motivation and with few redeeming qualities (he does, I suppose, commendably exhibit patience, determination, and devotion to his task). The only moment that seems to suggest there is morally more to him than this is when he seems to tenderly and compassionately lay a hand on the horrendously injured young Vader after the Mustafar duel. (It is arguable that he is concerned only with what a living Vader can provide for him and thus is not compassionate at all—but the tenderness of the moment and comments made by McDiarmid himself suggest that there is here the briefest of glimpses into Sidious being driven by something more than pure wickedness.) We should certainly be wary of describing him as evil itself or suggesting that "he *is* evil" without any further qualification, as Hanson and Kay do.[17] After all, he is but one in a long line of Sith and has been trained in wickedness by Darth Plagueis "the Wise" (*ROTS*).[18] In this way he could become more fully a satanic figure with his own story of inglorious fall, like the serpentine figure in the story of Adam and Eve's fall in Genesis 3 who is presented as just being there, without any explanation of his origins. His role as tempter of Anakin and Luke resonates with this. And yet, interestingly, the fact that Vader too becomes satanic tempter (to Padmé Naberrie in *ROTS* and Luke in *ESB*) also indicates that Sidious is not *uniquely* evil, even if he is the evil archetype.

Blessed Are the Proud, for They Will Inherit . . .

"Evil" is a rather general term, and grammatically it, like "sin," is *relational*, given that it is the *antonym* of "good." The Augustinian Christian tradition, for instance, construes sin as primarily the relation of rebellion against God; because it is against the Creator, it necessarily shapes relations with all God's creatures too. Understanding this puts us in a better position to ask just what kinds of *relations* are evil.

Through the narratives of the archetypal figures of Adam and Eve many Christians claim that the paradigmatic form of sin is *pride*. According to Alistair McFadyen:

> Pride involves active referral of all goods to the self, it denotes worship of the self . . . [and the] rebellion of self-assertiveness. . . . Pride is therefore construed in the mainstream of the tradition as overabundant self-assertion: the attempt to live as completely autonomous self, without reference to God or any external realities, values or claims.[19]

"Pride" is the attempt to extricate ourselves from relations of interdependency in order to become wholly "free," independent, or shaped only by "self-governing autonomy."[20] Of course, while the Augustinian tradition understands this pride to be sin, it is actually modern Western societies' good. Freedom of speech, for instance, generally becomes less a *responsible* freedom to speak on behalf of the needs of others and oneself than a *self-assertive* freedom to say what I want (responsibility to others only comes in as an afterthought), and modern liberal political life is bound up with national *self-interest* (responsible interest for other nations likewise arrives only *after* this).

This theme is present in abundance in *SW*'s characterization of Palpatine/Sidious. His good is power, or at least his good presumably when he is not on the receiving end of another's powerful self-assertion. Hanson and Kay simplistically claim that "that is why he is a politician."[21] This, though, could imply the evil of politics and would fundamentally misunderstand Padmé's important symbolic role as the true political conscience of the Republic. Hanson and Kay continue, "He is motivated not by evil, but by the absence of feeling and emotion." As we will see later, they are right that he is not motivated by evil as such (in fact, evil is not a thing to be motivated by), but he is certainly not emotionless. Instead, Palpatine/Sidious is passionately driven; the real questions are, by what and to what end? The answers are revealed in his greedy ambitions. He conceives life through inventing his own values, which *serve only his well-being*. The logic of this is in fact little different from a Han Solo greedily driven by financial ambitions (*ANH*); or even a Luke greedily desiring the self-pleasure of adventure and excitement (*ANH* and much of *ESB*). As Lucas admits, the Sith Lords "were greedy and self-centered and they all wanted to take over, so they killed each other. . . . [T]hat is the antithesis of a symbiotic relationship,"[22] and is instead a "cancer" that eventually kills the host. In the end, only one Sith survived the Sith War, and he adopted an apprentice. Due to the threat of self-destructive conflict, never again were there to be any more than two of them at any one time. But even here the greed of unhealthy ambition remains a powerful motivating factor in the Sith Lord–apprentice relationship—for example, Darth Plagueis's pupil assassinated his master (*ROTS*), Vader briefly attempts to overthrow the Emperor (*ESB*), and the Emperor attempts to replace Vader with Luke (*ROTJ*).

The Lucas-inspired Expanded Universe backstories here are richly suggestive. The first thing we should recognize is that the Siths' self-centeredness is expressed in terms of the menacing *power and control over others*. They construe power in terms of that which serves them, with all the connotations of domination, control, and oppression that that has. So the Empire seeks to control its star systems through the use of military coercion and the regional control of the Grand Moffs (governors). The contrast between this governmental style of centralized rule imposing uniformity and that of the Republic's space for partial regional federalist autonomy is important. So too is the difference between Palpatine/Sidious and Luke, and to a lesser degree Han, in that the Emperor possesses absolutely no sense of loyalty to, or respect for, anyone other than himself (for all their faults, Luke and Han are not that shamelessly self-promoting). All without any exception are there to serve him, and even his name is a symbolic play on imperial Rome's original settlement and subsequent seating of power on the Palatine hill. Similarly Dooku, who at one point seems to have more moral ambiguity as an elegant idealist who had departed the Jedi Order in disillusionment over Senate corruption (*AOTC*), is revealed as greatly desiring power. He appears at heart more a self-serving pragmatist than political idealist (his name is possibly adapted from *doku*, a Japanese Buddhist term meaning "to control/govern" or "poison").

Sidious's rise to political power in the guise of Senator (and then Chancellor and, finally, Emperor) Palpatine is made particularly possible because he is able to manufacture situations beneficial to himself by exploiting others' *self-concern*. Most obviously, that is why Darth Maul becomes such a willing assassin and Darths Tyranus and later Vader become such effective accomplices. Secondly, Sidious is able to utilize the economic insatiableness of the Neimoidian rulers and their Trade Federation, a greed that seems to be written into their very evolutionary biology: "Raised as grubs until the age of seven, young Neimoidians are kept in communal hives and given limited amounts of food. The less acquisitive ones are allowed to die as others hoard more than they can eat. This practice makes Neimoidians greedy and fearful of death."[23] (This, of course, should raise all kinds of ethically significant 'nature-nurture' questions.) Thirdly, Palpatine's ascendancy and political governance would not have been possible without the personal self-indulgence of numerous senators and eventually the ambitions of countless military commanders who recognize that they can benefit from "keeping on side" with the powers that be. As Senator Mon Mothma declares, "The Chancellor has played the Senate as well. They know where the power lies, and they will do whatever it takes to share in it" (*ROTS*, deleted scene). Finally, and crucially, in a totalitarian regime run through dominating control, Palpatine/Sidious instills a fear that he can shape and direct to his own ends (what is later called "the Tarkin Doctrine" in the Expanded Universe series). So in the guise of Palpatine he initiates and sustains the Republic's Civil War by playing on the Republican citizens' fears for their own existence at the hands of a threatening enemy (the Confederacy of Independent Systems, or the "Separatists"). In the emergency situation that ensues, Palpatine is granted emergency powers for the duration of the conflict. However, through careful management of the conflict (as Palpatine he micromanages the Republic's forces and strategy, and through Dooku he directs the Separatists' military machine), that moment drags on into a protracted war. His apparent military successes considerably enhance his reputation among the Coruscanti; his abduction by "the fiendish droid leader, General Grievous" (which he had also carefully staged), further gains him sympathetic concern; and the Clone Wars' cessation slips into the new emergency situation brought on by the Rebellion's "terrorism" against Palpatine's renamed Galactic Empire.[24] In these ways the fear of the other is exploited to good effect by his protectorate. But the fear *of Palpatine* himself also secures his position. As chancellor he introduces a way of checking much of the potential for political dissension by using intrusive Hovercams and deactivating the Privacy Screens in the Senate. Dissenting mischief that cannot be managed and kept safely at bay can be crushed, and this is enough to dissuade much potential sedition from threatening his carefully designed political arrangement. He will brutally demonstrate "the peril of [others'] independent thinking . . . the refusal to obey orders."[25]

However, Christian considerations of sin helpfully encourage a second line of inquiry—into the victims of Sidious's wickedness. Pride and all that is associated with it is not the only type of sin in the Christian tradition, even if all others derive from it. For example, many feminist theologians have observed that traditionally women oppressed in patriarchal societies have suffered what is called "sloth," the sin of being forced to suffer self-abasement. This is the condition that the sinful proud oppressively tarnish their victims with. (The fact that sloth can still be called *sin* at least suggests that in some way victims remain participants in their being oppressed, even if we have to be careful not simply to blame the victim.)

In this regard Sidious's aggressive will to power negatively determines the identities of others and creates victims among those who have been forced to yield to his dominating lordship. These oppressed peoples (the later enslaved Wookiees, for instance) are caught in the vicious circle of his wickedness, are forced to become purely passive puppets of his violent control, and are denied the ability to become free and creatively self-determining agents in their own right. In this Palpatine is closer to Western liberal values than many would like to admit, following—in Walter Wink's words—the idea that "life is combat. . . . It is a theatre of perpetual conflict in which the prize goes to the strong. Peace through war; security through strength."[26] Moreover, these violent values are endlessly perpetuated when victims become inverted mirror images of their oppressors, as when the tables are turned, they come to play the role of oppressor. "Change" in this sense does not transform; it merely alters the names of those acting wickedly against others and thus retains the rules of the game itself. Luke eventually refuses to play this game, and that action makes him a saving figure (chapter 6).

The Sith take this self-interested and self-assertive individualism to its logical conclusion, which is why they cannot make peaceful relations. In fact, the only peace available to them is that which comes from the silence those who live in fear of them provide. Because they relate to others only by desiring dominating power, their relations are ultimately unstable. Unless secured in some way, they are necessarily self-devouring, since in their essential self-promotion they can create no loyalty or cooperative friendship but suffer always under mutual suspicion, jealousy, and betrayal. "Powered

by treachery, the Sith Master–apprentice relationship was always a dangerous game. Trust was encouraged even while being sabotaged; loyalty was
demanded even while betrayal was prized; suspicion was nourished even
while honesty was praised."[27]

Significantly, as mentioned earlier, the backstory emphasizes their numerous near self-annihilating power struggles. It was only in the aftermath of
"the New Sith War" (c. 1032 BBY) that the sole Sith survivor, Darth Bane,
himself betrayed at the end by Darth Kaan, instituted the rule of two—"a
Master and an apprentice" (Yoda, *TPM*), "one to embody" power, "the other
to crave it."[28] This line of pedagogic pairing successfully prevented strife in
the modern era of the Sith and better hid their existence from the Jedi. Yet
this Rule of Two fails to prevent Sidious's betrayal of his master Plagueis and
of his *disposable* apprentices, whom he *uses* for his ends. For instance, the
Zabrak renamed Darth Maul had been kidnapped from Iridonia as an infant
in order to be trained in the ways of the dark side of the Force but existed for
no other reason than to assassinate early political enemies of Palpatine. It is
this instrumentalized quality that renders him such a flat monodimensional
character and presents him physically as a rather obvious and unsophisticated
incarnation of evil reminiscent of the most simple demonic and bestial, in
contrast to the more complex Sidious (*TPM*).

Count Dooku seems to forget that the Sith way is a way of betrayal, which
is why he looks genuinely surprised by Palpatine's/Sidious's order for his
execution by Anakin aboard the Confederacy flagship the *Invisible Hand*
(*ROTS*). In fact Palpatine's abduction by Grievous and the Magna Guards
and Dooku's duel with both Obi-Wan and Anakin are all carefully and elabo-
rately staged so that Palpatine/Sidious can investigate whether Anakin can be
turned to the dark side. The executing of the defeated and literally disarmed
Dooku is Anakin's primary test. According to James Luceno, "Sidious had
promised to intervene in the duel, in the unlikely event that Anakin gained
the upper hand. But intervention . . . was never part of the real plan."[29] So
Sidious informs Grievous on Utapau of his plans via hologram: Dooku's
"death was a necessary loss. Soon I will have a new apprentice, one far
younger and more powerful." "Like Darth Maul before him, . . . [Dooku] is
little more than a placeholder for the apprentice Sidious has sought from the
beginning: Skywalker himself."[30] That is why Obi-Wan is soon after ordered
to Separatist-occupied Utapau to confront Grievous, since, with him absent,
Anakin would be more susceptible to Palpatine's wiles. In fact, "Sidious may
have even feigned losing to Windu at the right moment [later] to cast a difficult impression on Anakin when he arrives at the Chancellor's office."[31]

This theme of the instrumentalization of others' lives indicates the main ethical problem behind both the creation of the Grand (Clone) Army of the Republic and the monstrous biotechnological recreation of Grievous as a cybernetic organism (and even more so of Darth Vader, as we will see later).

The cloning template was the Mandalorian warrior Jango Fett, but unlike Fett, the Kaminoan cloners genetically manipulated the clones in order to diminish their autonomy (*AOTC*). Intriguingly Richard Hanley argues that this does not deny the worthwhileness of the clones' lives, especially when the process is undertaken for a greater goal—the Republic's self-defense.[32] Hanley has, however, badly missed the larger symbolic point of the cloning process. Sentient life is created in order to do another's bidding, and *only* another's bidding, and accordingly is of value only for this purpose. That approach, of course, is the *way of the Sith*, and the striking parallels between the Imperial and Clone armies are therefore symbolic: the clones' uniforms link them directly to the later Imperial Stormtroopers; their starships are direct precursors to Imperial Star Destroyers; and *AOTC*'s Clone troopers depart for war with the "Imperial March" leitmotiv being performed. Moreover, while the order for their creation came in mysterious circumstances, the backstory reveals it to have been *Sith directed*. Either Sidious commissioned the process via Dooku directly through Jedi Master Sifo-Dyas,[33] or Sidious himself placed the order using the Jedi's identity and subsequently assassinated him in order to conceal the truth.[34] (This second reading may possibly be supported by the fact that in early scripts for *AOTC* the name Sifo-Dyas was originally Sido-Dyas, and a cover name for Darth Sidious.)

These clones are life-forms denied any semblance of independent life. That is why they are known only by numbers (the Imperial stormtrooper known as TK421 in *ANH* is an example of this purely numerical identification). Later on in the Clone Wars many Senators and Jedi Councillors believe the clone commanders, and *only* the commanders, are human enough to have names. These commanders *alone* have been given some sense of human personality through enhanced cloning programming—but those modifications are made in the cloning process only so that they can develop better strategic initiative and battle leadership ability. The clones are, then, little more than biological versions of the Separatists' battle-droids, as the Kaminoan Prime Minister Lama Su implies to Obi-Wan: "They are totally obedient, taking any order without question. We modified their genetic structure to make them less independent than their original host." They are *manufactured* to be docile. Is there then not a perverse kind of cosmic justice in the fact that the Jedi contribute to this process and yet this becomes the principal means of their own destruction?

At this point it is worth pausing with a note of acknowledgment that *AOTC*'s presentation and the significance of it in developing the tragic narrative of the fall of the Republic differs markedly from the sensibility of some of the Expanded Universe materials. In *Star Wars: Clone Wars* and in Disney's more recent *Star Wars Rebels*, several clones are depicted as having rebelled against their former constructed lives and have left the imposed drone-conditioning in order to make independent lives for themselves. Commander Rex is one such trooper, and in the recent animated series, he and two colleagues are even seen taking up arms against the Empire. While there is something noble in this theme, it conflicts quite noticeably with Lama Su's claim about the clones being bred to be docile and to conform to orders. The imagery of *AOTC* owes much to the disturbing image of the hatchery, the predestination factory for human construction and socializing in Aldous Huxley's *Brave New World*. This is life reduced, reduced to its bare core of being *useful* to those in power. Lucas develops Huxley's image of the manufacture of persons in conditions of industrial capitalism, a theme picked up in Lucas's *THX 1138*, and then redevelops this notion in the context of the expendability of life in war for the sake of the self-serving politics of self-aggrandizement.

The Supreme Commander of the CIS's droid forces, General Grievous, is a further symbol of this brutal instrumentalization. The backstory is that the former Kaleesh warlord Qymaen jai Sheelal had been a brilliant strategist and fighter who came to the attention of San Hill, leader of the Banking Clan. On refusing the offer of leading the Separatist troops, Hill and Dooku arranged for a bomb to be planted on Sheelal's shuttle (a more recent *SW* magazine suggests it was a troop carrier, *Martyr*), with the subsequently near fatal incident being blamed on the Republic.[35] The warrior's smashed and dying body was rebuilt by Geonosian biotechnicians with state-of-the-art technology, with his own brain, eyes, spinal column, and internal organs being successfully implanted into an armored droid skeletal form. Not only does this cybernetic organism possess a distinctly skeletal and sinister, inhuman look; in addition, his memories are altered in order to make him a more compliant and ruthless enhanced biomechanical killing machine, a proficient slayer of even several Jedi Knights in lightsaber combat. In some ways he represents an early type of Vader, a reconstructed cybernetic life-form who is perversely resurrected, through the indirect will of the Sith Lord Darth Tyranus (Dooku), and becomes the undead, efficiently dealing out death to his identified enemies as the sole purpose of an existence devoted solely to Sidious's self-aggrandizing tasks.

Wood observes of Tolkien's literary creation that "since evil lives always as a parasite off the Good, the demonic Melkor was unable to produce any original or free creatures. He could manufacture only parodies and counterfeits."[36] In its distorted and destructive form, what we see in Palpatine's/Sidious's career is that the lives of others become the means to the end of his power. They are denied their own potential to become free and equal subjects in their own right but are *manufactured* (and with Grievous and Vader, *recreated*) as Sidious's callous *machines* of death.

. . . Nothing!

Evil, then, is a quality of relations. It has to do with relating to others and oneself in ways that further one's own flourishing at the expense of others'. This kind of relating is dominating, creating empires of deathly order. In this sense, then, wickedness cannot *create* anything or contribute to the goodness of things. Instead, it lives off that which has life and provides only chaos or the chaos of a false order of death and decay. Consequently, according to theologian Robert Jenson, "To sin is to achieve precisely . . . nothing."[37]

Evil—or better, wickedness—is a disease the effects of which are necessarily fatal. But those engaged in wickedness against others invariably fail to recognize that this harmful malady affects and damages them too. Palpatine/Sidious, for instance, understands himself to be a moral creator, the maker of his own fate. One implication of this is that he does not as such understand himself to be evil and so *does not pursue evil for its own sake*. Indeed, even Hitler's "willing executioners" spoke of their acts positively in terms of promoting racial health, German well-being, and the flourishing of humanity.[38] That is why Hannah Arendt, reflecting on the trial of mass murderer Adolf Eichmann, suggests that evil is usually done from neither some sinister satanic will to evil nor a lust for violence. "The horror of Auschwitz . . . is not the revelation of evil perpetrated for its own sake, but rather a demonstration that even the most seemingly absolute evil tends to be carried out by people who imagine, albeit reluctantly, that they are fulfilling the goods of order, obedience, political stability and social peace."[39]

Palpatine/Sidious thus acts not for the sake of evil but for a greater good. Even though his true ambitions are to exalt himself so as to *be served*, he construes this as his truth (and presumably he has no reason to doubt that power is the ultimate truth of the universe). So when in the opera house he educates Anakin that "good is a point of view" and suggests that there is no truth, only power (*ROTS*), he is, in effect, not denying truth at all but only certain versions of it. The desire for power determines his disposition, as Luceno reveals in a promise of the newly self-proclaimed Emperor to the young Vader: "In due time, power will fill the vacuum created by the decisions you made, the acts you carried out. . . . Eventually you will come to see that power *is* joy. The path to the dark side is not without terrible risk, but it is the only path worth following."[40] "Unlimited power" (*ROTS*), he believes, is worth having for its or his own sake—it becomes his *ultimate* life purpose, his good, his god. In imposing his "point of view" on all others he resembles the realpolitik of the Judean governor Pontius Pilate of the Fourth Gospel who asks, "What is truth?" (John 18:38) in a way that asserts legal authority over Jesus and associates truth with the forceful assertion of his/Rome's will. By subtly turning the interrogation around on his imperial judge, Jesus exposes and denies Pilate's claims about the truth of power. *SW* also attempts to do precisely that (see chapters 5–8), thereby resisting the Sith values and disclosing the *deception* of Palpatine's self-promoting claims about truth.

There are two types of masking involved with Palpatine. Most obvious, of course, is the fact that until he is revealed to be Sidious (*ROTS*), Senator and then Chancellor Palpatine actively and in*sidious*ly hides his true Sith identity and ambitions "beneath a façade of wan smiles and smooth political speeches" (Sidious's cowl gives the impression less of Jedi humility than of the shrouding of his identifiable face).[41] In this way the satanic figure masquerades as an angel of light (2 Cor. 11:14). The second type of masking is suggested by another biblical image: our dwelling in the darkness that renders us unable to recognize the true Light when it comes into the world (John 1:5, 10–11). In other words, the truth is hidden or masked from the darkness dweller, for as Augustine admits, "My sin was all the more incurable because I did not think myself a sinner."[42] Campbell observes that

> one may invent a false, finally justified, image of oneself as an exceptional phenomenon in the world, not guilty as others are, but justified in one's inevitable sinning because one represents the good. Such self-righteousness leads to a misunderstanding, not only of oneself but of the nature of man and the cosmos.[43]

Palpatine/Sidious "takes up what is false and holds it as true," worshiping what should be seen as evil as the Good.[44] In his self-interested individualism, utterly divorced from the *common* pursuit of the Good, he is confused about the social nature of the Real, the Natural, the Good, and the True. Palpatine "is himself [incurably] deceived" and blind to the Good of the Force just as much as he is deceiving and blinding of others to the truth of who they are and could be.[45]

Why has he become so blind to the light of the Force? Perhaps because, as Sith, he was probably abducted as a Force-sensitive child and inculcated in the Sith way. In other words, he has *become* Sith through having been trained in a false ideology and its habits. This echoes the Augustinian idea of original sin when understood well. The term "original" primarily refers to the situation or condition that preexists us (*all* of us),[46] into which we are all born, an inheritance through which we learn to feel and think about ourselves and our world, that helps direct and shape our own way in the world, and that we pass on to others. "We do not therefore enter the stage of personal action with a clean slate, morally in neutral as it were."[47] The term "sin" here has to do with the fact that the situation or condition from which we develop our identities is ultimately *distorted* and *distorting*, a pathological and infecting alienation *from the true Good*. As Lucas claims, "The dark side . . . is like a *huge* cancer, alive, festering—both a reminder of a moral state and, at the same time, symptom and symbol of a very sick society." Augustine speaks of this sin as *concupiscentia*, a distortion of desire, or desiring the wrong things in the wrong way, which has serious implications for the way sinners act to fulfill their desires.

Such an inheritance assumes that its own way of seeing the world and acting in it is not only *legitimate* but *natural*—its contingency and arbitrariness are accordingly *masked*. That is why those inculcated into the various forms of racism, patriarchalism, consumerism, and imperialism, for instance, both fail to see through their identity-determining beliefs and find all manner of ways to justify them. In the movie *Mississippi Burning*, Mrs. Pell explains to FBI agent Anderson something of this:

> People look at us and only see bigots and racists. Hatred isn't something you're born with, it gets taught. At school they said segregation's what it said in the Bible, Genesis 9:27. At seven years of age you get told it you believe it. You believe the hatred. You live it. You breathe it. You marry it.[48]

Even the victims of these ideologies learn to understand themselves through the systems. This process of "ideology internalization" is one reason why, for instance, many *women* have willingly opposed the various versions of feminism.

This leads us back to Arendt's notion of the ordinariness or banality of evil, and a scene in the brutal movie *Se7en* helpfully unpacks the sense of this.[49] When the two detectives (William Somerset and David Mills) travel with the serial killer (John Doe), Mills asks Doe, whom he considers to be a "freak": "When a person is insane, as you clearly are, do you know that you're insane?" Mills represents a culture that imagines evil to be extraordinary, almost supernatural, certainly not everyday and ordinary. The evil are mad, demonic, and so on, but *not us* and *not even like us*. But this perspective cannot handle the "work" of someone like John Doe. He is an articulate, highly intelligent, and utterly dispassionate killer who can meticulously plan the most horrific of murders and patiently execute them over an extended period of time. In fact, within his moral perspective his killings are less murders than sermonic lessons about the seven deadly sins given as wake-up calls for the good of society. He does not see himself as a moral degenerate in an otherwise morally intelligent culture: "It's more comfortable for you to label me insane." When Mills refers to Doe's killing "innocent people," Doe's moral anger boils over, causing him to unleash a diatribe about his first five victims:

> Innocent! Is that supposed to be funny? An obese man [gluttony], a disgusting man who could barely stand up. . . . And after him I picked the lawyer [greed], and you both must have secretly been thanking me for that one. This is a man who has dedicated his life to making money by lying with every breath that he could muster to keeping murderers and rapists on the streets. . . . A woman [pride] so ugly on the inside that she couldn't go on living if she couldn't be beautiful on the outside. A drug dealer [sloth], a drug dealing pederast actually. And let's not forget the disease spreading whore [lust].

Only in a world this messed up "could you even try to say these were innocent people and keep a straight face. But that's the point. We see a deadly sin on every street corner, in every home, and we tolerate it. We tolerate it because it is common, it's trivial. We tolerate it morning, noon, and night."

The difficulty with Doe the "preacher's" perspective, of course, is that while he "is setting the example" he has to assume that sin is something others do (all others, perhaps given his comments), and hence *he* is well positioned to reveal its presence in the most violently vicious of ways. Thus he too seems to be largely blinded by the popular assumption that evil is something utterly alien and strange, a virus that most of us (in Doe's case, himself only) are immunized against—and ironically this is precisely the conception of sin that he has been working to undo.

A second example of Palpatine's/Sidious's being deceived can be traced briefly through another illustration. Lady Philosophy, the teacher of Boethius (c. AD 475/480–524), announces that the legendary character Damocles is a paradigm of "a man who must be at the mercy of those that serve him, in order that he may seem to have power."[50] Palpatine/Sidious imagines that he controls his own fate and that dependency upon others is a terrible limitation. Consequently, he attempts to reeducate Luke by encouraging him to feel that his faith in his friends is actually his weakness. Nonetheless, he himself is significantly at the mercy of two groups: those who can positively aid him in this process and those who are presently disempowered and thus can pose no threat to him. In this way, he is a man enslaved to others, as well as to his own wicked desires (from which he could not simply extricate himself by sheer act of will, should he even choose to do so, since it is so much a part of who he is). Not only does he inflict fear of himself on others, but, as with his Sith Master Darth Plagueis, he too obviously lives in fear of being betrayed and overthrown. That is why he constantly has to secure his position. For instance, he manufactures a galactic war (*AOTC*); he even possibly constrains the rebuilt Vader's power by according him only inferior mechanical implants; and he commissions the technology of terror, the Death Star superweapon (*AOTC–ROTS*), in order to sweep away the final vestiges of the power of the old Senate. (There is a profound irony in the image of a constructed *Death* Star, given that stars are sources of light in darkness, and foundations of potential life.) He is an example of his own teaching to Anakin: "All who gain power are afraid to lose it" (*ROTS*).

The Faces of Embodied Dehumanization

Augustine's theology demands that we reserve *theological* language of existence and being ultimately for God alone and, derivatively, for those whom the creative God gives existence or being to. By falling from whom we are created to be, we are shaped in a way that makes us something significantly less, a shadow of the human, and thus on the way to nonbeing. In this sense, then, evil is an *unmaking* of being and existence and thereby has no *substantive* existence of its own. It is simply a perversion or an absence or a privation of the Good (*privatio boni*), an absurd quality determining human relations. Lady Philosophy explains that

> those who abandon the common end of all who exist, must equally cease to exist. And this may seem strange, that we should say that evil men, though the majority of mankind, do not exist at all; but it is so. For while I do not deny that evil men are evil, I do deny that they "are," in the sense of absolute existence. . . . A thing exists which keeps its proper place and preserves its nature; but when anything falls away from its nature, its existence too ceases, for that lies in its nature. . . . For if, as we have agreed, evil is nothing, then, since they are only capable of evil, they are capable of nothing.[51]

Now this does *not* diminish the seriousness of the threat posed by evil to creatures. If anything, it makes wickedness something more threatening: it may be absurd in that it has no *theological* reason for determining our being and action (since God created the world good), but it nonetheless both takes our excuses away from us and distorts all that God has created while drawing it perilously into nonbeing. "Thus then a man who loses his goodness, ceases to be a man, and since he cannot change his condition for that of a god, he turns into a beast."[52]

That means that wickedness cannot *create* but can only destroy. It is wholly destructive of the Good that true life together is created to enjoy. But according to Augustine, evil destroys the one committing it as well as the one to whom it is done, and this double sense of damage suggests that evil makes us less than we should be. Evil is not only immorality; since it distorts the Good, it aesthetically has an ugly quality that exposes it as revolting, perverting, and deforming. Accordingly, Gelven argues, "it is more than a mere violation of the 'natural'—i.e., prohibiting the purpose to be fulfilled—it is a betrayal of it."[53]

While Augustine perhaps exaggerates when he claims that "every sin is more hurtful to the sinner than to the sinned against,"[54] his sense of the injury done to the wicked illuminates evil's texture in *SW*. The idea is symbolized in the most graphic of ways, in that wickedness is inscribed onto the very physical features of those who are most pathologically enslaved to it: Sidious, Maul, Vader, and the skeletal cyborg Grievous. Roald Dahl's *The Twits* expresses this *bio-graphology of wickedness*: "If a person has ugly thoughts, it begins to show on the face. And when that person has ugly thoughts every day, every week, every year, the face gets uglier and uglier until it gets so ugly you can hardly bear to look at it."[55] The Emperor's and Maul's facial deformities express the utter warping caused by evil.[56] Their habituation to wickedness has completely altered them, stripping them of much that defines them as human. Palpatine also has no name, no address, no history—or at least not one that can be traced easily, since all his records had disappeared. Tolkien's Sauron and the Voldemort of J. K. Rowling's *Harry Potter* books had even lost their bodies.

An important scene in *ROTS* focuses on the techno-bodybuilding of Vader. This mechanization serves to further dehumanize him, and there is a visual reference to the monstrous creation of the early *Frankenstein* movies. The care lavished on his reconstruction by the godlike Sidious results in his being raised to "new life." But it is a mechanized life that is half dead, maintained in its bare life only by fragile and exceedingly constraining mechanical life-support systems. This is why a prominent image of his conversion to the dark side is that of the *death* of Anakin Skywalker and the *birth* of Darth Vader. Importantly, this perverse resurrection is symbolically intershot with the perfect new lives of Padmé's twins. The dying Senator from Naboo produces human lives that flourish, whereas Sidious, styled in the look of Hollywood's Death figure, produces with Vader only the coming from death of an inhuman living death. "Sidious and a host of medical droids had merely restored

Anakin to life, which—while no small feat—was a far cry from returning someone from death."[57]

Vader's garb, like that of *The Lord of the Rings* Ring-wraiths or Black Riders, reveals the way *SW* presents evil by hiding his humanness. His darkness depicts a loss of self, and his helmet hides his identifiable face, preventing proper human, face-to-face relations. That is why one of Vader's last requests of Luke, trading symbolically on the contrast between true and distorted vision, is to "help me take this mask off. . . . Just for once let me look on you with my own eyes" (*ROTJ*). According to Jerold J. Abrams, "His being-in-the-world is so artificially mediated . . . [he is no] longer human, he has entirely lost touch with himself. . . . He has, at the very least, forgotten the man he used to be . . . indeed he has even forgotten his own name."[58] So when he is addressed as Anakin, he admits to Luke that "that name no longer has any meaning for me" (*ROTJ*). But Luke reminds him, "It is the name of your true self. You've only forgotten." Vader's evil has become so ingrained, so habituated, that his old, true self as Anakin has been lost in the darkening mists of memory. In this way, as with Tolkien's Gollum, his fall involves a dehumanizing loss of memory of who he truly is. Consequently, Mark Rowlands clearly misunderstands Augustine's idea of evil as *privatio boni* when he claims that when Anakin succumbed

> to the dark side, and became Darth Vader, he not only became less perfect, he also became less real. . . . [Yet Vader] is the most real character in [SW]. . . . His presence, and his evil, is palpable. He is not simply an absence or hiatus in the films. . . . Evil exists, and not simply as an allusion or absence of what is good.[59]

Vader's life has died to (and fallen from) its Jedi collegiality and been raised instead (and exalted) into a bare life of servitude to the one he forever after addresses as Master. The promotion of Anakin from Jedi Padawan to Knight in *Star Wars: Clone Wars* that had marked his coming of age is now lost by his becoming Sidious's *permanent* Padawan. He is "merely a minion, an errand boy, allegedly an apprentice, the public face of the dark side of the Force."[60] This former poster boy of the Clone Wars is even subordinated on the Death Star to an Imperial bureaucrat, Grand Moff Wilhuff Tarkin (*ANH*). "Where Darth Sidious had gained everything, Vader had lost everything. . . . *This is not living.* . . . He was nothing more than wreckage. Power without clear purpose   [a]nd now newly enslaved!"[61] This has indeed *tragically* been an immense *fall*.

Chapter Four

Beware the Dark Side Within

The Tragedy of Anakin Skywalker

The Tragic Adventures of the Skywalkers

ANH is presented as The Adventures of Luke Skywalker, and the classic trilogy follows his journey from everyman farmboy, through Rebel hero, and into self-aware Jedi Knight. The mood in *Episodes IV* and *VI* is largely a triumphant one, of gain in spite of the losses. But the characterization of Vader is particularly interesting, and *ESB* and *ROTJ* enrich his character beyond his initial iconic appearance as *ANH*'s screen "baddie." This development is intensified further in the prequels, which, taken together, feel distinctly more reserved and darker than the classic trilogy. As the credits opening *TPM* ominously announce, "Turmoil has engulfed the Republic," and that darkness casts its sinister shadow back over *Episodes IV–VI*. This new emphasis transforms *SW* from the heroic adventures of Luke Skywalker into the catastrophic tragedy of Anakin Skywalker, which is probably why Lucas was reluctant to develop his originally very broad plans for *Episodes VII–IX*. In fact, this rehabilitation of Darth Vader is "really what the story was all about," Lucas declares, and in the early 1980s Lucas had already worked out in quite detailed ways the direction his later movies would eventually take:

> Darth Vader became such an icon in the first film, *Episode IV*, that that icon of evil sort of took over everything, more than I intended. If it had been one movie that wouldn't have happened. . . . But now by adding *Episodes I, II*, and *III* people begin to see the tragedy of Darth Vader as what it was originally intended to be.[1]

Lucas's claim is probably a bit of an exaggeration as far as the classic trilogy goes at least. This narrative arc follows Luke more closely and not Vader. In fact, in *ANH* Vader was even something of a rather incidental character, spending very little time on screen. This changes with the prominence

Vader takes from *ESB* onward. Certainly by the time of the prequels, Lucas was beginning to reconstruct the series more and more around Anakin and specifically around Anakin as the tragic hero.

This tragic perspective should, of course, hardly surprise viewers of *Episodes V* and *VI*, given the shocking revelation of his having once been Anakin. The stage had been set in the classic trilogy for revealing *SW* as a kind of tragic drama. Pollock, however, misses this when he asserts that "Lucas displayed in *Star Wars* a wholesome, naïve faith in the essential goodness of people."[2] Tragic dramas do not have such a naïve faith.

The marked difference in mood between the two sets of trilogies has to do with the fact that the prequels have a more Oedipal feel than the classic trilogy, which instead revolves around core Jungian archetypes, as we saw in chapter 1. In an echo of the Oedipus tragedy, immortalized by the Greek tragedian Sophocles (c. 496–406 BC), Anakin becomes a tragic figure who attempts to escape destiny by taking his future into his own hands but who nonetheless is fated to kill (here his surrogate father when he is a Padawan) Obi-Wan (although it would be going too far to suggest that Padmé functions in the same way as Oedipus's mother). This removes the *SW* universe from any simple good-overcoming-evil scheme, although it is also questionable whether *ESB* and *ROTJ* were as simple as this, either. The nature of existence is particularly messy, and no obviously neat and untragic story can be told about it.

Tragic dramas come in many shapes and forms, but one type in particular has been especially well known, a type identified by the Greek philosopher Aristotle (384–322 BC): a good but flawed protagonist falls into calamity by a *hamartia* (Greek, "error"), often taking the form of *hubris* (Greek, "excessive pride"), and falls into his catastrophe (*nemesis*—Greek, "retribution").[3] It is precisely this form of tragic drama, executed most clearly in Sophocles' *Oedipus the King* and William Shakespeare's (1564–1616) *King Lear*, that shapes the presentation of Anakin.

Until the thought of Italian philosopher Pico della Mirandola (1463–94), in this classical form of tragic drama the tragic protagonist was no ordinary personage but an eminent person, frequently a royal or some high noble. Thus the consequence of the fall affected more than the protagonist, and even her closest relations, but drew in an entire region and its people. Anakin is no ordinary character, and film critic Peter T. Chattaway entirely misses this point when he complains, "For all the talk of 'democracy', . . . [*ROTS*] is actually less interested than any of the others in the lives of ordinary people."[4] Nor is Anakin merely one of the Force-conscious minority from the ranks of which the revered icons of peace and justice are selected and trained;

but his very conception and birth play a vital symbolic function in the narrative. This is revealed in a conversation between Jedi Master Qui-Gon Jinn and Anakin's mother Shmi Skywalker. "The Force is unusually strong with him," observes the Jedi, "that much is clear. Who was his father?" (*TPM*). According to Shmi, however, "There was no father, that I know of. I carried him, I gave him birth. I can't explain what happened." A little later Qui-Gon wonders whether the slave boy had been birthed in the Force: he detects around the boy "a vergence in the Force" and observes that "his cells have the highest concentration of midi-chlorians I have seen in a life form. It is possible he was conceived by the midi-chlorians." The hero, in Jung's word, is a "greater man . . . semi-divine by nature."[5] Thus *SW* echoes not only the heroic monomyth broadly but, more strikingly, also the New Testament's messianic materials. So Qui-Gon believes that Anakin is "the Chosen One" whose coming to bring balance to the Force has been prophesied long before. The nobility required for the fall of the tragic hero type is secured in the grandest of terms. Given the immense power at his disposal, Anakin's fall cannot but have the most catastrophic consequences for the entire galaxy.

Just by way of an aside, but an important one nonetheless, there is some ambiguity in the relation of Anakin's forthcoming tragedy and this virginal conception, one that Lucas suggests but claims to have deliberately left open to interpretation. The point at issue arises when Palpatine tells Anakin the Sith legend of "the Tragedy of Darth Plagueis the Wise" (*ROTS*): Plagueis became so powerful that he could even manipulate the midi-chlorians in order to create life. This is a reference not only to the godlike desires of the Sith but also to Anakin's apparent birth in the Force. Is this a coincidental overlap of stories? Palpatine's subsequent claim suggests not, whatever Lucas's hesitancy on the matter. The Chancellor reveals that Plagueis's pupil learned all that his Sith Master knew and then betrayed and murdered the teacher. In other words, the knowledge of how to manipulate the midi-chlorians to create life was possessed by another. Was Palpatine in fact Plagueis's pupil? There may well be more of the hand of the gods in Anakin's fall than might otherwise have been thought. This would give new, and even more sinister, significance to Palpatine's friendly remark to young Anakin after the Battle of Naboo: "We will watch your career with great interest." Even the reference by Yoda that "clouded this boy's future is" may be a metaphor for the covering, shrouding, or masking of the Sith over Anakin's future development. Importantly Stover interprets the situation in this way. He has Palpatine/Sidious urge, "Understand who you truly are, and your true place in the history of the galaxy. . . . You *are* the chosen one. . . . Chosen by *me*."

Anakin's Tragic Flaws

Rightly or wrongly, Aristotle argues that a wicked person's fall fails to evoke the fear and pity characteristic of a tragedy, and an innocent's fall is merely shocking but not tragic. Rather, the tragic hero is a basically good person who is flawed. But, as mentioned earlier, numerous critics feel that *TPM* presents the nine year-old slave boy in terms that are too unambiguously good for him to be a believable Vader-in-the-making. But the critics' shock probably has more to do with untested popular assumptions about evil and with an ignorance of classic tragic dramas than with the quality of Lucas's characterization in *TPM*. The nature of the fall in Christian traditions, for example, implies that what may seem like real innocence can eventually cause the most horrendous of evils—what Lucas describes as "an evolution from this very good person, very kind person, very loving person into something that one would describe as evil."

> [The] Phantom Menace was done really to determine that Anakin was a good person, good heart, nice kid. We're not talking here about an evil little monster child—we're talking about this great kid just like we all start out as, or [we] think we start out as. . . . The whole reason for going back and doing the back story on "Star Wars" is that there is an evolution from this very good person, very kind person, very loving person into something that one would describe as evil.[6]

Evil is not something that just *happens to* us or, worse, to so-called evil people. It arises amid the nature of our relations and complex choices, amid the pressures that "conspire" to make us into something less than we are and should be as God's creatures. The question of why some of us become as dark as Vader while others do not has no simple answer. Suggestively Lucas comments, "Most of . . . [those who are wicked] think they're good people doing what they do for a good reason." This, of course, reminds us of the theme of "the banality of evil," which tragic dramas disturbingly display.

Anakin conforms to Aristotle's description of the tragic hero: despite his technical excellence, evident Jedi potential, distinct moral qualities, and relative innocence, his flaws are not far from the surface. They are noticeably rather "normal" looking flaws, as Lucas admits: "He's cursed by the same flaws, and issues that he has to overcome, that all humans are cursed with" and "everybody struggles with."[7] The childhood trauma of Bruce Wayne, for instance, creates the shadowy, but nonetheless heroic, alter ego Batman. Anakin's traumas, in contrast, lead him on to a path toward "the dark side" and a life of ordered or governmentally sanctioned crime. The difference in their pathways lies, in large measure, in the guidance they receive in making the choices that shape the moral characters they become. And that is the point: Anakin becomes wicked because of the cumulative effects of the particular choices he makes in the particular situations he faces, the momentum of which spirals out of his control. Lucas comments: "The issue that he's confronting is that a good Jedi overcomes those flaws."[8] Anakin, however, evidently fails to develop an appropriate capacity for self-restraint and good judgment, and this is what causes his fall.

The Haunting of the Past at the "Expense of the Moment"

Thus while Anakin's fall into the "dark side" (his Sithing, so to speak) may seem abrupt to many viewers of *ROTS*, it has been a long time in the making. *TPM* provides only the briefest identification of Anakin's tragic flaws. It does not, though, suggest that one of those is a psychological effect of being a slave—he is later haunted by visions of his mother's sufferings rather than his own. Nonetheless, there may still be some significance in the young boy's asking if Qui-Gon has come to Tatooine to "free" the slaves. This could possibly be a hint of his desire for the kind of freedom that will later feed his adolescent resentment of authority while Padawan to Obi-Wan (*AOTC*).

TPM focuses on a particularly identifiable anxiety that intensifies as he grows older—his separation from his mother. When he is first brought before the Jedi Council, to Jedi Master Ki-Adi-Mundi's observation that the boy's "thoughts dwell on your mother," Yoda announces, "Afraid to lose her, I think." After all, when departing his home, Anakin poignantly and symbolically looks back at his mother and runs toward her, embracing her with the admission, "I can't do it, Mom, I just can't do it!" His mother's advice signals a warning of what is to come in the saga: "Don't look back. Don't look back." Dwelling on the past, or inordinately looking back, is what Qui-Gon's counsel to his own Padawan at the opening of this movie would rule out: "Don't center on your anxieties, Obi-Wan. Keep your concentration on the here and now where it belongs . . . [and] not at the expense of the moment." (The occasion was over talk of mindfulness of the future rather than the past, but the logic works in this case too.) Later to Anakin he enjoins, "Always remember, your focus determines your reality."

Before the Council, though, Anakin puzzles over the relevance of Mundi and Yoda's insight: "What's that got to do with anything?" Yoda admonishes in response: "Everything! Fear is the path to the dark side. Fear leads to anger, anger leads to hate, hate leads to suffering." In *AOTC* Padmé consoles an

Anakin grieving over the death of his mother, "To be angry is to be human." But her adolescent hearer rightly recognizes that it is vital for him to control this properly: "I'm a Jedi—I know I'm better than this." Attachments to people and things induce fear over their loss, and this in turn moves us to attempt to secure their possession—this is what Jedi training constantly reveals to be the path to the dark side. As the sagacious Master Yoda later declares to the emotionally troubled young man, "The fear of loss is a path to the dark side. . . . Attachment leads to jealousy. The shadow of greed, that is, . . . Train to let go of everything you fear to lose" (*ROTS*). Elsewhere *SW*'s creator reveals that an unhealthy form of attachment "makes you greedy. And when you're greedy, you are on the path to the dark side, because you fear you're going to lose things, that you're not going to have the power you need."[9]

For that reason Yoda's concluding declaration in the Jedi Council Chambers in *TPM*—"I sense much fear in you"—is another portentous warning that reverberates like a death knell through the succeeding two episodes. Precisely because of the potential for disaster, the Jedi Council initially forbids Anakin from training as a Jedi, and even when it does eventually yield (largely out of respect for the slain Qui-Gon's faith in Anakin as "the chosen one"), Yoda remains strongly opposed: "The chosen one the boy may be. Nevertheless, grave danger I fear in his training" (*TPM*). Anakin insufficiently learns how to practice this wisdom, and his reality-determining focus wanders off in harmful directions.

So was Qui-Gon wrong in his judgment concerning the young man? Did he by sheer blind faith force a terrible tragedy on Obi-Wan, the Jedi Order, and ultimately the galaxy, by insisting with his dying breath that his own former Padawan (during the Clone Wars he is promoted to Knight) train the boy? Does wisdom here not lie instead with the iconic sage Yoda? Lucas certainly thinks so in one sense:

> I think it is obvious that [Qui-Gon] was wrong in Episode 1 and made a dangerous decision, but ultimately this decision may be correct. . . . The tale meanders and both the prediction, and Qui-Gon are correct—Anakin is the chosen one, and he did bring peace at last with his own sacrifice.[10]

This trivializes the situation, though. The evil inflicted on the galaxy by Vader, and the dreadful carnage and waste that occurred, cannot and should not be covered over by a thin netting of rhetoric such as "Oh, well, it all worked out all right in the end." The very ability to decide whose belief about Anakin was eventually shown to be true is only something that can be said *after the event*. At the time, of course, this hindsight is not available to the saga's characters. Also, unless we want lazily to promote a cosmic determinism in which all events are fated to occur, we should not miss the important contingent factors that contribute to Anakin's fall. These are factors that—had they been arranged differently, been absent, or even been handled differently by Anakin—would have produced markedly different results. As Qui-Gon argues against a skeptical Obi-Wan, "His fate is uncertain, but he's *not* dangerous." That faith seems to be borne out in Anakin's morally commendable and selfless apology: "Qui-Gon, sir, I don't wanna be a problem." It is intriguing that Yoda refers to the danger in Anakin's "training." As will be explored below, with hindsight we can see that the processes and activities involved in Anakin's training by his trainers, just as much as in the boy's being trained, contribute to the looming tragedy.

By the time of *AOTC* (22 BBY) Anakin has become a more complex figure than the boy of ten years earlier and is the neurotically intensified product of the loves and desires of that child. The flaws lie deep within his person-forming soul. Significantly, he now rather ominously wears darker-colored robes than his Jedi kin. Speaking of the nineteen-year-old Anakin, Lucas summarizes: "In this film, you begin to see that he has a fear of losing things, a fear of losing his mother, and as a result, he wants to begin to control things, he wants to become powerful, and these are not Jedi traits. And part of these are because he was starting to be trained so late in life, that he'd already formed these attachments. And for a Jedi, attachment is forbidden."[11]

Understandably, the young man bears deeply the scars of leaving his mother, and he is tortured by nightmares of her suffering severe pain. When he initially left her a decade earlier, he promised, "I will come back and free you, Mom." He was, however, unable to keep this pledge, and he felt guilty as a result. This feeling no doubt was intensified by his mother's having put the burden of responsibility on his very young shoulders: "Anakin, this path has been placed before you. The choice is yours alone" (*TPM*). Also, rightly or wrongly, he had come to blame and gradually resent the Jedi Order itself for preventing him from rescuing her. Hence, when he finally discovers a tortured Shmi only to watch her die in his arms, the Padawan's guilt in having abandoned her and his bitterness against the Jedi are considerably deepened.

Added to this emotional mess is the remorse he comes to feel over his actions in the immediate aftermath of Shmi's death. Losing emotional self-control, he unleashes his seething fury destructively against her captors, the Tusken Raiders. As he remorsefully admits to Padmé a little later, he massacred not merely the men but the women and children as well. He has become, in that moment, as primitively savage as those sand-dwelling nomads are archetypally presented as being. (Cliegg Lars claims, "Those Tuskens walk like men but they're vicious, mindless monsters.") "They're like animals, and I slaughtered them like animals." And, of course, it is precisely anger and this shame that Palpatine exploits for his own ends later on the *Invisible Hand* (*ROTS*).

What we see in this scene with Padmé in *AOTC* is the way Anakin's anger, guilt, resentment, and sorrow, all growing out of his attachment to his mother, take on a new form. In his grief he begins to desire the power over life and death, the power to be able to "fix" life in the same way that he can exercise technical expertise over machinery. He simply refuses to listen to Padmé's claim that "sometimes there are things that no one can fix." Here is an early indication that Anakin sometimes reduces others' lives mechanistically to the status of *things*, and this notably echoes the Siths' instrumentalization of others. In emotional turmoil Anakin verbalizes that he "should be" all-powerful and threateningly states a newfound determination "that someday I will be. I will be the most powerful Jedi ever. I promise you. I will even learn to stop people from dying." This is not merely his grief talking, since, in a calmer frame of mind, he resolves at his mother's graveside, "I wasn't strong enough to save you, Mom. I wasn't strong enough. But I promise I won't fail again." He imagines that the solution to salvation is one of sheer power and brute force, and he acts on this Sithlike attitude later when—after dreaming of Padmé dying in childbirth—he moves to secure the power he thinks is necessary for her safety from the scheming Palpatine/Sidious (*ROTS*). He proclaims to his wife that "love won't save you, Padmé, only my new powers can do that." She despairingly asks, "But at what cost?" Anakin has not given much consideration to that. Instead, his response displays his possessive assertion of brute power: "I won't lose you the way I lost my mother. I am becoming more powerful than any Jedi has ever dreamed of, and I'm doing it for you, to protect you."

Rejecting the Father

The grief scene in *AOTC* reveals something else: Anakin intensely resents his Jedi tutor. "It's all Obi-Wan's fault!" the young man accuses. "He's holding me back!" This sounds like the ill-tempered reaction of a headstrong adolescent to authority, particularly parental authority. Their regular bickering sounds like that between a father and son, which makes sense of the paternal language Anakin often uses of Obi-Wan in *AOTC*. (By *ROTS* their relationship has matured into more of a fraternal one, with Obi-Wan poignantly asserting by the lava lake on Mustafar, "You were my brother, Anakin. I loved you.") On one occasion the older Jedi has to assert that his petulant student "will pay attention to my lead. . . . And you will learn your place, young one." Anakin is nineteen and exhibits all the arrogance and sullen peevishness of the stereotypical teenager. Critics who comment that Anakin has become an unlikable character in *AOTC* and *ROTS* miss the intent of this development and fail to notice the link with the sullen Luke of the first half of *ANH*.

This is but part of the story, though. Not only does Anakin's behavior express an unhealthy dispositional instinct, but Obi-Wan himself has substantially contributed to the way their relationship has developed. The older man in his own way resents Anakin too and even seems occasionally to regret the promise to train the boy that the dying Qui-Gon pressured him into making. Revealingly he affirms to Yoda: "Qui-Gon believed in him. . . . Master Yoda, I gave Qui-Gon my word. I will train Anakin." In *TPM* Obi-Wan confronts his Master in a rare moment of dissent over Qui-Gon's blind faith in the chosenness of the youngster from Tatooine. Later, of course, he acknowledges to a seemingly dying young Vader in the hell of Mustafar, "I have failed you, Anakin, I have failed you"; and in *ROTJ* he again admits his failings in training Anakin: "I thought I could instruct him just as well as Yoda. I was wrong." The Padawan laments his Master's shortcomings to Padmé: "He feels I'm too unpredictable. He won't let me move on. . . . He's overly critical; he never listens; he, he doesn't understand. It's not fair!" Quite simply, Obi-Wan is perhaps not the best person to guide someone like Anakin, and this gives both potency and poignancy to Qui-Gon's demand of the nine-year-old: "Stay close to me and you'll be safe" (*TPM*).

These two themes (vicious rage at his failures and resentment of his mentor, both fueled by guilt and grief) combine thematically in two musical motifs, as the grief-filled Anakin spits out his fury-filled diatribe—those associated with both Sidious and Vader.

Pride Comes before a Fall

But there is more to the Anakin–Obi-Wan tension than even this. In the Padawan's unleashed torrent of spiteful abuse he alleges that his Master "is jealous" and this is why he is holding the young man back from realizing his full potential. According to Aristotle, the cardinal flaw the tragic hero suffers from is *hubris*, and usually this is translated as "pride" or "arrogance." This form of *hubris* certainly contributes to Anakin's fall, although Henry Sheehan, president of the Los Angeles Film Critics Association, oversimplifies Anakin's teenage rebelliousness as "simple adolescent moral narcissism" and claims that "the whole Star Wars project begins to seem like a study of adolescent narcissism."[12]

Despite the Jedi code, Yoda admits that arrogance is "a flaw more and more common among Jedi. Too sure of themselves they are, even the older more experienced ones." Over the past decade Anakin has grown up with the memory of Qui-Gon's belief that he is "the one who will bring balance to the Force," whose coming an ancient prophecy had foretold (Mace Windu, *TPM*). He has been led to believe that he "*is* the Chosen One" (Qui-Gon), the key to life, the universe, and all things. In a way not wholly unlike John Connor of *Terminator 2*, Anakin feels the weight of being not just any boy (in fact, not even just any Jedi Padawan). Like the Joseph of Genesis 37, he is the special one. The psychological pressure on training a boy to grow into a humble and wise Jedi under these conditions is incalculable. Anakin has become immensely self-confident, even reckless, as his disastrous lightsaber challenge with Count Dooku demonstrates (*AOTC*). Hayden Christensen, the actor portraying Anakin, comments that he has "this unhealthy sense of grandeur."[13]

Unlike Joseph, however, Anakin's sparks of narcissism are not eventually extinguished but subtly fanned into a great conflagration by a fateful source of guidance—Chancellor Palpatine. This prevents the Jedi from being able to mature properly through his experiences. As a fatherless nine-year-old, Anakin latches briefly onto Qui-Gon, but on the Master's death Obi-Wan takes over this paternal mantel. As mentioned earlier, however, Obi-Wan is evidently not so well equipped for the task as Qui-Gon had been with Obi-Wan. Into this emotional mess insidiously slithers Palpatine. Ian McDiarmid interestingly comments, "If you wanted a subtitle for these movies it could be 'Fathers and Sons.' And while Palpatine isn't, we must assume, Anakin's natural father in this film [viz., *ROTS*] he is certainly a father figure for him."[14] He vitally comes to act where he can as a surrogate father figure, watching, guiding, advising, and supporting this young Jedi, and it is in him rather than Obi-Wan that Anakin wholeheartedly trusts. Anakin has, one might say, "been getting in with the wrong crowd," in this case with the embodiment of wickedness itself.

In a gentle moment reminiscent of a fatherlike conversation with a respectful son, the elder statesman instructs: "You don't need guidance, Anakin. In time you will learn to trust your feelings. Then you will be invincible. I have said it many times, you are the most gifted Jedi I have ever met. . . . I see you are becoming the greatest of all the Jedi, Anakin, even more powerful than Master Yoda." Of course, all this is true—Anakin has indeed a midi-chlorian concentration far surpassing even that of the great Yoda (*TPM*). Moreover, in the next scene in *AOTC*, the highly renowned Jedi Master Mace Windu compliments to the effect that "the boy has exceptional skill." The problem is how this feeds Anakin's ego, and this, possibly more than any other factor, fuels his resentment of Obi-Wan's guidance. As he admits to the wise Padmé, "In some ways, a lot of ways, I'm really ahead of him. I'm ready for the trials." Palpatine significantly feeds and guides this unhealthy consciousness, preeminently encouraging both the rising Jedi star's ultimately detrimental feelings of ego-filled self-importance and his indulgent glorying in the flattery over his war heroism.

The Chancellor's influence becomes particularly noticeable as time progresses; and as Anakin becomes the poster boy hero of the Republic during the Clone Wars, Palpatine at every possible point subtly undermines the Jedi philosophy of the virtuous life. In particular, he fatefully encourages the youth to dwell on his feelings, the fruit of which can also be symbolically seen in chapter 19 of the cartoon series *Star Wars: Clone Wars*. In a vicious duel with Asajj Ventress, the Padawan's fury is unleashed to devastating effect against this dark assassin. Ominously, however, in his eventual victorious rage the images of the dark side are cast upon him. The red glow of both Ventress's lightsaber, with which he destroyed her, and the blood-red sun reflect upon his face and torso; the concerned faces of Qui-Gon, Obi-Wan, and Yoda quickly flash upon the screen as he murderously attacks; and the "Duel of the Fates" music plays portentously just as it did when a few years earlier he angrily sped off in search of his dying mother (*AOTC*).

Palpatine more directly orders the young man to break with the Jedi code at another crucial point. When the voice of the shackled Palpatine demands that Anakin execute the defeated Dooku, the visibly troubled Jedi hesitates but then obeys the Chancellor's persuasively overwhelming voice, announcing afterward, "I shouldn't have done that. It's not the Jedi way" (*ROTS*). The blood of Dooku now weighs as heavily on his mind as does that of the nomadic Tusken Raiders on Tatooine. In the most fateful of all the scenes in *ROTS,* Mace announces that he needs summarily to execute justice on Palpatine, now revealed as the Sith Lord Darth Sidious. Anakin refuses to allow the same moral mistake to be made as with Dooku and brutally intervenes merely to prevent Mace effecting his planned punishment. However, this act allows Palpatine/Sidious to recover (or possibly pretend to recover) his strength and murderously dispatch the Jedi Master from the window of his chambers high in the skyscraper. Anakin has acted out of the best motives on these occasions in *ROTS*, but on both he has momentously made the wrong choice. These mistakes disastrously contribute to his already excessive and morally debilitating sense of shame and guilt, and the distorting influence of

Palpatine is central to his ignorance in moral discernment. The shroud of the dark side has fallen over his eyes, as Mace recognizes moments before his death: "There is much fear that clouds your judgment." Through these events he becomes particularly impressionable and malleable to Palpatine/Sidious's wiles, and in the wake of Windu's murder he is reborn as Darth Vader.

"Lost the Trust of the Public, We Have Already"

We need to see that Anakin's action against Mace and eventual backing of Palpatine/Sidious against the Jedi have been heavily influenced by complex events. By the time of *ROTS* the Jedi Order itself has become generally feared and distrusted, suspected in many circles of plotting to seize political power and manipulating the military hostilities for their own ends. Mon Mothma's worrying over Padmé's desire to tell a Jedi of the Loyalist's plot and of the Petition of the Two Thousand expresses this distrust: "We don't know where the Jedi fit into all this" (*ROTS* deleted scene). And in Stover's novelization Yoda reveals: "Lost the trust of the public, we have already."[15] Palpatine successfully plays on these fears, and Anakin's respect for him, as well as his own growing distrust of the Order, make him an attentive, if not wholly uncritical, listener. In the first place, Anakin is appointed by Palpatine to the Jedi Council in a move that both intensifies the Council's suspicions of the young Jedi and, in turn, magnifies the youth's already burgeoning paranoia and feeling of personal insult (there are suggestions that Anakin is also deeply wary of Mace).[16]

It is useful to explain this from the backstory. Anakin is distrusted by many senior Jedi because of the prosthetic right arm that has replaced his limb lost in combat with Dooku on Geonosis (*AOTC*)—they feel that he has lost something of his humanity. In *ROTS* his feeling of insult explodes in a rash outburst against Mace. To the experienced Master's announcement, "You are on this Council, but we do not grant you the rank of Master," Anakin rages, "What! How can you do this? This is outrageous. It's unfair. How can you be on the Council and not be a Master?" At this point several of the seated Council members look distinctly embarrassed, and Obi-Wan shakes his head disappointedly at the evident lack of maturity displayed by his former Padawan. The statement "it's unfair" is a deliberate reference by Lucas to Anakin's bemoaning Obi-Wan's restrictive tutelage—a scene in which the seeds of darkness are seen to be firmly flourishing in the young man's soul (*AOTC*)—and to Luke's similar outburst against Uncle Owen's restricting him to chores before pleasure (*ANH*).

Again, Palpatine has carefully calculated this appointment. He fully antic-ipates just such a clash of mutual suspicions while playing upon Anakin's own desires for promotion, and by flattering him with such a promotion, he augments the young Jedi's trust of him further. Therefore when the Jedi Council asks Skywalker to spy on Palpatine, a man it is now suspicious of, the youth's worst fears about the Order are seemingly being realized—the Jedi are morally duplicitous. At this request Anakin admits his unqualified loyalty to Palpatine: "The Chancellor is not a bad man, Obi-Wan. He befriended me, he's watched over me ever since I arrived here. . . . You're asking me to do something against the Jedi code, against the Republic, against a mentor and a friend, that's what's out of place here." Stover suggests that Obi-Wan real-izes the magnitude of this request to his former student. He begins by reveal-ing to Yoda and Mace "that abstractions like *peace* don't mean much to him. He's loyal to *people*, not to principles. And he expects loyalty in return." Then he bewails the task itself: "I am firmly convinced that Anakin can do anything. Except betray a friend. What we have done to him today. . . . That's why I don't think he will ever trust us again. . . . And I am not entirely sure he should."[17] (Two examples of Anakin's loyalty to *people* are seen early on in *ROTS:* his refusing to rescue Palpatine without first ensuring Obi-Wan's safety and his refusing Palpatine's order to leave an unconscious Obi-Wan behind so as to escape the impending destruction of the *Invisible Hand*.) The Jedi youth consequently feels *morally bound* to assert himself *against* the Council, as he reveals to Padmé: "Obi-Wan and the Council don't trust me. . . . Something's happening—I'm not the Jedi I should be. I want more. And I know I shouldn't."

The crucial scene in this regard takes place at the opera. Here Palpatine exerts all his political charm to fuel Anakin's worries about the Jedi Order. By this stage, the Chancellor has found a not wholly inattentive hearing—Anakin's love of the Council and its methods have been ebbing away. Pal-patine, after some mood-disposing flattery of the young man, speaks of a Jedi "plot": "You must sense what I have come to suspect—the Jedi Council want control of the Republic. They're planning to betray me. . . . Search your feelings. You know, don't you. . . . They asked you to do something that made you feel dishonest, didn't they? They asked you to spy on me, didn't they?" Cleverly, the manipulator here taps into the young Jedi's own affected conscience. Spying on the Chancellor, as Anakin had earlier complained to Obi-Wan, is itself treason. But a Jedi plot? Surely even Palpatine is taking things too far! Anakin is unprepared for this charge. Of course, events would conspire to look as if that is exactly what is occurring, and Mace's refusal to let Anakin be present at Palpatine/Sidious's arrest only waters his fledgling concern. For now the politician has to turn his persuasive rhetoric in a more general direction, and this seed of mistrust is well and truly sown: "Remember back to your early teachings. All who gain power are afraid to lose it—even the Jedi." It is significant that Anakin does not turn this principle back on Palpatine and on his achievement of power, even though Obi-Wan has already suggested this politician was deliberatively and manipulatively clinging on to power after his term in office had expired. Anakin argues instead for Jedi altruism: "The Jedi use their power for good."

Palpatine's line of reasoning now takes a slightly different tack, confusing Anakin about the very nature of moral reasoning itself: "Good is a point of view, Anakin." Many think this sounds relativistic, but we must remember our earlier observations concerning Pilate's exaltation of power. Chancellor Palpatine is instead trying to encourage his immature conversation partner to appreciate that everyone associates his or her values with the Good; consequently he attempts to persuade him that the Jedi's definition of good and evil may not be the best (or true) one. Palpatine does this, of course, not to provoke Anakin into imagining that the Sith and Jedi have some *equally valid* moral consciousness but rather to turn him *against* the Jedi. He is ultimately trying to instill the Sith's values in Anakin, which is why he proceeds to undermine Jedi exclusivity by observing their likeness to the Sith in "their quest for greater power." Anakin claims that the Sith "think inwards only about themselves." But Palpatine's response, "And the Jedi don't?" is a chilling deconstruction of moral endeavor, reducing it to power (that which the Sith appreciate and celebrate; the Jedi openly deny this attitude but secretly practice it). Stover makes this clear: the Sith are only evil "from a Jedi's point of view. . . . *Evil* is a label we put on those who threaten us, isn't it? Yet the Sith and the Jedi are similar in almost every way."[18] Later, of course, Anakin as Vader reveals Palpatine's outlook as his own when dreadfully dueling with Obi-Wan: "From my point of view the Jedi are evil." That certainly does not suggest that he has become a moral relativist—on the contrary, his sense of absolute rightness could not be more pronounced. At this point it is Obi-Wan who casts suspicion on anyone's ability to make such absolutist claims for their own perspective: "Only a Sith deals in absolutes." This also is not moral relativism but rather a recognition of the fragility of anyone's knowledge of the Good.

While these observations on power and the exclusion of threatening others by associating them with evil are ethically astute, they nonetheless function simply as a cover for Palpatine's method of persuasion, which is little more than accusation and suggestion. He does not allow Anakin to entertain the possibility that the Sith's way may truly be evil. Instead, he reduces the difference between Sith and Jedi to a sound bite (against the "narrow dogmatic view of the Jedi") and a difference in degree (they differ only in method), rather than admit a qualitative difference (the ends that determine their different methods radically differ).

Likewise, the politician is able to encourage Anakin to be suspicious of his own wife. On one occasion Padmé confronts Palpatine on behalf of the Delegation of Two Thousand, but Anakin stands behind the Chancellor's chair refusing to return her gaze (*ROTS* deleted scene). When alone, the ensuing conversation between Anakin and Palpatine centers on the Chancellor's sinister claim that the Delegation and those they represent have another agenda: "I sense there is more to their request than they're telling us. . . . They are not to be trusted." The obvious protestations are made by the young Jedi over Padmé's trustworthiness. Ominously Palpatine returns a gentle look and alleges, "These are unstable times for the Republic, Anakin. Some see instability as an opportunity. Senator Amidala is hiding something. I can see it in her eyes." Despite the young Jedi's on this occasion concluding with a note of faithfulness to his beloved, again a further seed of suspicion has been sown. To this the politician adds a final challenge to the young man's Jedi ego and to his well-developed sense of honesty: "I'm surprised your Jedi instincts are not more sensitive to such things. . . . You don't seem to want to admit it."

An Anakin overwhelmed by emotional and ideological turmoil soon has cause to doubt Padmé's integrity further. In the privacy of their home they discuss the state of the war and the Republic. The Senator from Naboo reveals her concern that the very "democracy we thought we were serving no longer exists, and that the Republic has become the very evil we've been fighting to destroy." Anakin's political faith is simplistic and unintuitive, precisely because he associates the Republic with the Chancellor, and in him he has enormous faith (later he significantly proclaims, "I will not betray the Republic. My loyalties lie with the Chancellor, and with the Senate, and with you."). Anakin turns on Padmé, spitting, "You're sounding like a Separatist." He is unwilling to hear criticism of his beliefs but instead deflects critical attention with an assertion of patriotic responsibility. The Loyalist attempt to purify what is loved, as Bail Organa depicts his work with Mon Mothma (*ROTS* deleted scene), is no more patriotic to Anakin's mind than Dooku's Separatist rebellion. The now-paranoid Jedi's tumultuous anxieties come to be fixed on the feeling that his wife is betraying him in league with Obi-Wan.[19] His feeling comes to its breaking point: Padmé arrives on Mustafar to confront the recently named Vader only for her husband to see that Obi-Wan had arrived with her (after having stowed away unknown to Padmé). Vader rants, "You're with him! You brought him here to kill me!" And to Obi-Wan he seethes, "You turned her against me! . . . You will not take her from me!"

Clouded Judgment

It is, according to Terry Christensen, invariably the case in American movies that "the bad guys act out of greed or ambition, and the good guys act to stop the bad guys."[20] This is not the case with the Anakin of *ROTS*. Here the archetypal icon of evil from *ANH* is portrayed as falling into the dark side *while trying to pursue lofty ideals*; though the Jedi are not as such portrayed in dark colors, they too are plagued by ignorance just as much as Anakin is.

Throughout the prequels there are suggestions that Anakin is gradually moving closer and closer to the Sith, largely for reasons and through faults and mistakes that he might be *blamed for* only with difficulty. He is bound by what may seem to be an admirable ethic, and therefore he almost constantly acts with a certain moral integrity. Admittedly he desires power, but *not for obviously self-serving reasons*. Instead, he desires peace and Padmé's safety; and he even acts out of a conservative loyalty to the Republic, trusting Palpatine/Sidious to do what is right in all these cases. So when Sidious announces that if the Jedi "are not all destroyed, it will be civil war without end," Anakin enacts a preemptive strike against both the Jedi in the Temple and the Separatist leaders on Mustafar. "Once more the Sith will rule the galaxy, and we shall have peace," Sidious hisses to an attentive young Vader. Anakin does not by this time perceive the dark side as evil but rather (wrongly) as a different and better way of achieving his *good* purposes. And so Lucas directs Hayden Christensen's performance by informing him, "There's always this good in you at this point. The good part is always saying 'what am I doing?' And the bad part is saying 'I'm doing this for Padmé, I'm doing this for us, it'll be better for the universe, it'll be better for everybody."[21] Anakin promises, "I will not betray the Republic," the Republic in which he has profound (blind) faith because of his admiration for its Chancellor. Hayden Christensen testifies that "he's not doing wrong things knowing that it's having a negative impact, so there's that sort of naïveté to him that wasn't there before."[22]

Anakin's fall is caused as much by the confusion borne by ignorance as by the *hubris* for which he is in some sense morally responsible. He acts out of what may well be morally defensible motives, but he is guilty of being *blind to the truth of the situation*, of being a bad judge of the terrible reality being played out behind his back as well as in and through him. He may have "knowledge," but in the distinction made by Dexter Jettster, he does not have "wisdom" (*AOTC*). The tragic conflict bears the scars of a bewildering array of moral antinomies for Anakin—he possesses all the best intentions (to protect another, to bring peace) but without the necessary guidance of appropriate Jedi wisdom. So Obi-Wan can lament to Padmé, "He was deceived by a lie—we all were," and in *Clone Wars* chapter 1 the older Jedi worries, "Your skills have never been in question. It's your maturity." As we saw earlier by the time of *AOTC*, for instance, he has come to think of power in a way that is separated from wisdom, and this is something *ROTS*'s novelization reaffirms when he petulantly announces to his former Master, "I have the power of any five Masters. Any *ten*. You know it, and so do they [viz., the Jedi Council]." With more wisdom Obi-Wan warns, "Power alone is no credit to you."[23] The pathway to the power to save Padmé is tragically the direction that destroys her.

Anakin, More Sinned Against than Sinning

In his study of the cultural icon of the Batman character, Will Brooker notes that in the 1940s the DC Comics editors imposed "an ethical template onto the previously ambiguous figure of the Batman. . . . They sought to relocate Batman within a new discourse of 'positive-effect' comic books. . . . The no-nonsense tone was still there, but from now on Batman's adventures were clearly no longer to be read as exciting yarns but as moral lessons; his war against crime had become not just a personal vendetta but a patriotic duty."[24] There is here in the Dark Knight of this period no sense of moral complexity, the sense required to ask what contributes to or encourages certain types of criminal behavior. This, then, is the kind of simplistic approach that can be seen in many popular readings of *SW*. The Good is obvious and clean, while the evil just drops demonically from nowhere, with no history and no complex causes.

Anakin's tragedy, in contrast, prevents such moral simplicity and the identification of any unambiguous moral purity and righteousness in a fallen world. After all, the scene of his "resurrection" as Vader invites the audience in to see the world through his masked eyes by the symbolic descent onto the up-turned camera under the mask. Certainly he is flawed, but the combination of circumstances and pressures make his self-control more difficult to achieve and sustain. He is engineered by Palpatine/Sidious to become a victim who not only will be unable to control his emotion but will also lack the crucial understanding of the Good that would enable him to discern the insidious wickedness of the politician's machinations. In tragedies, good may be unwittingly produced through evil and may conversely lead to it, as dramatically it does here. Even the Jedi Council, with its initial war support, its blindness to the Sith in its midst, and the way it treated Anakin, is similarly complicit in its own destruction. These disturbing consequences demonstrate the possibility that those who honestly believe themselves to be doing the right thing may in the end be deluded and unwittingly produce destructive effects. Anakin's blindness to where the Good may be found leads him to look in the wrong place and to make a Faustian pact for Padmé's salvation. (This theme of distorted vision is symbolized by the fallen Anakin's eye-color change and his eventual looking through the armored mask.) Perhaps it is even a mistake to search easily for targets to blame for his fall. His is, as Jeffrey Overstreet sympathetically remarks, something of an understandable fall into wickedness:

> We can't help but sympathize with Anakin as he surrenders to the Dark Side. Lo and behold, Darth Vader did not strive to be a heartless villain. He became one by trying to protect the one he loved, going blind to the greater good in the process. The stakes are finally high enough to earn gasps, and the ensuing tragedy is almost Shakespearean. . . . Anakin isn't just arrogant; he's reacting to a seeming lack of trust, care, and compassion from the Jedi Council.[25]

What happens to the tragic hero is often called *nemesis* ("punishment"), and Anakin's punishing *metabole* ("reversal of fortune") has many layers, each taking him deeper in his fall. But it is very clear that this *nemesis* is not the same as the receiving of some "poetic justice." As Lear famously cries out, "I am a man more sinned against than sinning!" In the context of tragic dramas that claim is not an exaggeration.[26] Therefore, while tragedy embodies the notions of moral responsibility and a relation between the tragic hero and his destiny, this relation is usually exceedingly difficult to make out. The sufferings of Oedipus and Lear and Anakin are disproportionately greater in scale than their vices. Their tragic mistakes have unleashed something overwhelmingly calamitous. In that respect Anakin is as much a victim as a villain, as Lucas testifies, and his tragedy allows for no simple and easy moral perspectives on good and evil, the justice of the flow of history, and so on.[27] The fall of the tragic hero involves sheer, brute waste. "Here is a guy who has lost everything."[28] So he helps to destroy Mace in a moment of moral anxiety, an act that finally leads him into the arms of Sidious; thereafter he helps obliterate the Jedi Order, and that in the name of a "greater good"; in so doing he catastrophically contributes to the annihilation of the Republic's freedom, undoing much that he believes about peace; in his paranoid state he finally destroys his long-standing friendship with Obi-Wan; in a bewildered fit of anger he "Force-chokes" Padmé, causing the eventual death of the one he had been tormented by the need to save; in his fall he becomes unable to be father to Luke and Leia; he loses in battle all four of his limbs and the ability to breathe without a life-support ventilator, severe damage he has to live with forever after; his own humanity is destroyed in the turn to the dark side, as symbolized by these biotechnologies required for basic life-support, including the armorlike attire that masks from view both the human and his dehumanization; his great Jedi potential is never realized because of the extent of his injuries (he cannot use Force-Lightning due to his prosthetic arms, and he has roughly 80 percent of the Emperor's power when before his fall he had the potential to have 200 percent of it); and he dies without ever being reconciled with his daughter. The depth of the tragedy is that not only is this profoundly great Jedi potential—and that of the wise senator Padmé in a Romeo and Juliet–type doubling effect—wasted, but in its loss so much that is good in the galaxy is distorted and destroyed as a consequence.

Conclusion

ANH is quintessentially future-making cinematography, yet it expresses a yearning for a "more civilized age" (Obi-Wan to Luke, *ANH*), in particular for moral certainties and simplicities. It is particularly the characterization of Anakin that eventually comes to resist any easy answers to the so-called problem of evil and to the complex question of moral deliberation. Evil has to do with bad relations, with wickedness. In fact, the "evil Empire" significantly arises from within the good old Republic itself. When we add to this the backstory revealing that the Sith Lords were formed from expelled Jedi ("dark Jedi"), we recognize that evil—or better, wickedness—grows in and through the good, distorting it, never preexisting it but feeding off it parasitically. That is what Augustine has in mind when he describes evil as *privatio boni* (the privation or absence of goodness). While light certainly creates shadows, it does not create the darkness. Darkness does not come from the light but rather from the absence or extinguishing of light. Thus the two are not equal and parallel opposites; they are utterly opposed to one another.

SW is well placed to offer something of an insight into the sophisticated Augustinian doctrine of original sin, a doctrine that speaks clearly of the distorted network of relations that we already find determining us at every stage of our lives, even while it is still we who act wickedly. According to John Kekes, in such a world "the best we can do is to plan our lives so as to minimize their [i.e., the conditions that create tragedies] influence," assuming, of course, that we can adequately identify them all.[29] But even while all relations between persons are distorted by evil (chapter 5), Lucas envisages a flourishing of right relations—an *original* and *ultimate* Good that creates active hope for its coming manifestation (chapters 6–8).

Chapter Five

The Politics of Evil

One of several complaints made about the trilogy of prequels is that they are too political, and some fans of the classic trilogy speak of feeling betrayed by Lucas. Even the important romance that generates the twins Luke and Leia is itself subordinated on one occasion to the lovers' political disagreement. In this scene, set in an idyllic spot on Naboo, Anakin appeals to a strong leader, and the visual context here strongly alludes to 1965's *The Sound of Music* (*AOTC*) and so to the coming of Nazism to Austria.[1] The complaint, however, not only assumes that the earlier films were wholly apolitical but also (given the fact that the criticism is that they are too political) indicates that these critics value the classic trilogy as purely private escapism or, at most, as personally inspiring. Yet this assessment both misunderstands the way Lucas designed these stories for moral teaching and misconstrues *SW*'s rich symbolism.

Lucas's epic denies that evil is an abstract quantity, a thing that can be located, identified, and acted against. Instead, it has to do with a *quality of relations*, and because it has to do with relations, it necessitates reflection on politics. The Greek word *polis* simply means "city" and the things concerning it. In other words, politics has to do with the way people relate to one another and with the way any community is managed and ordered. While the order of this city may be difficult and often painful, nonetheless the goal of a politics so conceived has to do with the so-called common good. Further, because politics is the public organizing of human relations, and these relations are properly understood only as relations between God's creatures, the notion of public relations or politics is theologically significant. What is at issue here is not whether there can be one social body that is political and another that is apolitical (perhaps because it is supposedly "spiritual") but rather the nature of the political relations made possible and performed in any social body. After all, apolitical theologies can easily leave people

enslaved to the God-forsaken bondage of crippling poverty, terrifying paranoia generated by totalitarian governments, abusive relations, starvation, and
so on. People suffering under these conditions are denied the space necessary
for even the most basic environment in which God's creatures can flourish; when they deny the means of resisting these evils, apolitical theologies
become complicit in sustaining the bondage of sin.

Because of this we should speak not of the evil of politics in a damnably
evil world but rather of the more demanding *politics of evil* in God's beloved
world that is now distorted and needing to be remade anew. Politics in this
theological context cannot be separated from the life of the Spirit of God (see
Gal. 5:16–26), who makes *all* things new in "the good news that God loves
the world and that in all its errors and confusions it is still the world which is
loved by Him."[2] Consequently, a theological consideration of political relations is the ethical expression of the Gospel's own proper themes.

Whatever one makes of the political significance of the Christian story,
it remains important to recognize that the separation of politics and religion
or spirituality is not a move that Lucas's *SW* makes. Accordingly, *SW* has
nothing in common here with those who privatize religion or relegate it to
something less than public practice. In *SW* movies those whose spirituality is
in the Force are, in fact, the main movers and shakers in the shaping of galactic public relations, and the Force is presented as the universal life-giving
energy that Qui-Gon describes as the symbiosis of all that exists (*TPM*). The
saga does not ask about how we should handle particular religious commitments in pluralist societies, but it can at least remind us that the nature of the
religious is to be publicly engaged (because "privatization" distorts religion)
and that the "public" needs the religious (because "secular" politics has little
capacity for asking or answering questions about the common good).

This chapter will, after assessing the difficulty of reading *SW* in a political
way, discuss the shape of Imperial politics, the political shape wickedness
takes. Rather than impress upon it some apolitical understanding of "religion," it will follow the logic of Lucas's screened saga. The following chapters will address the shape of the relations of the Good, the broad resistance
of oppressed peoples to the Empire. These themes suggest that there is no
blackening of the political qua political, and so "*SW* and the Politics of Evil"
should not be confused with "the evil of politics in *SW*." *SW* witnesses to the
corruption of, or within, politics, precisely because there is not in *SW*, as John
Caputo recognizes,

> a dualistic opposition of body and soul, earth and heaven, this life and the
> next. . . . In the "Gospel according to Lucas" a world is conjured up in

which the intractable oppositions that have tormented religious thinkers for centuries are reconciled, and they are reconciled by being undercut. . . . Lucas simply devised a world in which such oppositions are unknown and would make no sense.[3]

While the saga's suggestion in this regard may not be ideologically radical, we should remember that these are supposedly "popcorn movies" and such a genre is, by nature, generally averse to painting any moral shade of gray. Moreover, these are popcorn movies made in a culture and enjoyed in other cultures that are generally prone to moral simplifications.

A New Conservatism

"Judge Me by My Size [Gender and Species] Do You?"

According to Terry Christensen *ANH* is one of a class of blockbusters that eschew "politics and analysis in favour of superficial entertainment" and is thereby conservative by default.[4] Its "most lasting impact," he argues, has been to generate "the persistent preponderance of young people . . . who were far more interested in entertainment than in serious analytical or political films." Other critics detect a political conservatism that disturbingly runs much deeper than this one and lambast *ANH* in particular for being a fascistic and militaristic movie on account of its apparent hierarchies of sex, class, and species. In other words, *Episode IV* is humanocentric, and androcentric at that.[5] For instance, Chewbacca the Wookiee does not receive a medal for heroism after the Battle of Yavin; the pair of droids occupy the role of servants; and the fighting is predominantly a male activity. According to Peter Lev, *SW* "in no way challenges gender, race, or class relations. White male humans are 'naturally' in positions of authority. . . . Most of the aliens are relegated to the 'freak show' of the spacefarers' bar."[6]

However, when we take *ANH* as an episode in the larger narrative framework of the one symphonic movie, things come to look distinctly different. *ESB* introduces the important characters Lando Calrissian and Yoda; *ROTJ* depicts Ackbar of the Mon Calamari species as Admiral of the Rebel fleet and Mon Mothma as Rebel leader; and *TPM* makes the Gungans integral to the shape of the saga's opening. These are not mere concessions to the racial and gender differences among persons, and they are certainly not isolated figures. Instead, they are symbolically momentous for the sense of the saga, especially when this differentiation within the Rebellion is contrasted with the homogeneity of the Imperial system.

The Jedi Order is similarly of mixed species and gender. For example, in *TPM* the following females are on the Jedi High Council: Depa Billaba, Adi Gallia, and Yaddle (admittedly that is a paltry three of the twelve members); in *AOTC*: Depa Billaba, Adi Gallia, and Shaak Ti. Added to these are the further prominent Jedi Aayla Secura and Luminara Unduli with her Padawan, Barriss Offee. Significant roles in Lucas-endorsed *Clone Wars* are given to Shaak Ti, Luminara Unduli, and Padawan Barriss Offee. The latter two feature in *ROTS* along with Stass Allie. It is significant that the Order's relations are aptitude based: the Padawans themselves among the galaxy's 10,000 or so Jedi, if they perform well what is required of them in their training, are promoted to Jedi Knight and can subsequently themselves train a Padawan learner. With wisdom, insight, experience, and talent they will be promoted to the level of Jedi Master and, possibly, a seat on the ruling Jedi High Council. This Council itself, in order to promote freshness of visionary talent and a kind of equality of opportunity, provides three of its twelve seats to limited or specified-term appointments; but in order to provide continuity with the traditions of the past, it appoints four long-term and five permanent members. While there is no guarantee of preventing complacency (*AOTC*), according to Reynolds, "this balance of membership keeps the Council wise and vigorous."[7] Even the circular seating plan of this Council in the central spire summit chamber of the Jedi Temple on Coruscant symbolizes a non-dominating equality and collegiality in leadership, open thought and speech, mutual respect, and a shared purpose. Moreover, these talents are not once-and-for-all given, but the Jedi have to depend continually upon the Force and thus cannot fall back on possessive claims of what they once were. All in all, the relations among the Jedi Council, and between the Council and the Jedi themselves, are meant to involve a working "together in trust, free from the petty constraints of ego and jealousy."[8] And yet, the Asian design of the Trade Federation in *TPM* has caused particular consternation among commentators, apparently reflecting American fears about Asian economic domination.

But even *ANH* itself contains several potentially cautionary moments that should modify Lev's reading. For instance, the role and character of the aliens and robots deliberately make (however subtly) a point about discrimination. On one occasion Luke's droids are barred from entering Mos Eisley's cantina, and on another Luke tells his newly acquired protocol and translator droid C3PO to address him as "Luke" rather than with the more deferential "Sir Luke" that is instinctive to the droid. These somewhat less obviously dramatically heroic and socially important characters dominate the opening screen-time of *ANH*, and the galaxy's fate rests in large measure on the mission appointed to the astromech droid R2D2.

Crucial in this regard is Jar Jar Binks in the prequels, a highly controversial addition to the *SW* universe among even *SW*'s most hardened fans.[9] This bungling Gungan is important, and not merely as the comic relief or even for the sales of figurines to preadolescents. Not only is he the dimwitted senator who fatefully proposes absolute emergency powers for Chancellor Palpatine 22 BBY (*AOTC*), but his acceptance by Qui-Gon Jinn makes an important moral point (*TPM*). Obi-Wan, Qui-Gon's Padawan at this stage, doubts the Gungan's worth only to have his own lurking elitism (surfacing in comments of seeming disdain) exposed and challenged by his Jedi Master. There is a distinct contrast between Qui-Gon's attitude and that of Vader; the Sith Lord can be seen to judge beings' worth solely on their abilities and performances and disposes of those who prove unworthy of serving him (Admiral Ozzel and Captain Needa being just such casualties in *ESB*). Jar Jar's "value is hidden deep within him. So deep, in fact, that a Jedi such as Obi-Wan cannot see the value in him. Only Qui-Gon and Amidala find his worth."[10] Of course, even Qui-Gon finds him irritating enough to grab his tongue at the dinner table and instruct him to alter his eating habits.

Padmé's own role here is made even more significant by the fact that her acceptance of the Gungan goes against the grain of her natural instincts. Deep within the queen lurks Naboo's humanocentric elitism. Consequently, her bowing in humble submission before Boss Nass of the Gungans makes a symbolic admission of the symbiosis of all life-forms, and Boss Nass heartily approves of this act: "Yousa no tinken yousa greater den da Gungans. Mesa like dis. Maybe wesa bein' friends."[11]

What about the question of gender? While Leia Organa's title of "princess" and medieval garb are something of a nod back to the fairy-story genre, she clearly is not the stereotypical "damsel in distress." In fact she poses something of a challenge to any simple claim that pervading *SW* is a masculinizing gender politics. Admittedly, she does need to be rescued from the Imperials in *ANH*, but the rescuing heroes' very ineptness forces her into codirecting her own liberation at key points. "She is," according to Lucas, "a natural-born leader."[12] The fact that she is obviously a strong character and has a next-to-central role counters Campbell's denial of "the existence of female heroes" in the hero myths.[13] In fact, Leia occupies more the role of the goddess in Campbell's reading of hero mythologies than the fairy-tale princess. Crucially, when her ancestry is revealed (*ROTJ*), she in her own way becomes something of a symbol of redemptive hope. So Obi-Wan claims that Luke alone "is our last hope" (*ESB*). To this Yoda responds, "No, there is another." There seems to be no gender agenda in the fact that she is a spectator of the Battle of Yavin. As a principal Rebel Alliance commander and the surviving member of the Royal House of Alderaan she would not have engaged in a fighter battle. Of course, in Jabba's palace she is reduced to performing as a dancer chained to the Hutt and clad in a gold bikini, degraded to the status of fulfilling male desire (*ROTJ*). The scene depicts the acquisitiveness of the controlling gaze (Jabba's) as dehumanizing when he attempts to reduce the object of the gaze (Leia) to a passive sexual object. Yet even though Luke is her ultimate rescuer, her own role in killing the gangster should not be underplayed, and she is soon after restored to her role among the upper ranks of the Rebel command.

Now we are in a better position to see the significance of the fact that, in contrast to the (racially oppressive) homogeneity of the wholly human and white male Imperial navy, the Rebellion and the earlier Jedi Order represent a gathering of diverse species and both genders. The saga, it would seem then, does portray something of a "politics of difference"—a relating of one to another that is not defined by the exclusivities and subsequent discriminations of race (even species), gender, or wealth. There is something more fundamental to personhood and the way persons should relate to one another than these criteria would allow.

The Good of the Free vs. the Evil Empire

Yet many critics still feel uncomfortable with the classic trilogy, not so much with whether Lucas's conscious intentions are commendable as with whether his product fulfills these. The critics are concerned about the way these three movies create the evil Empire that the Rebels fight to overthrow. This Empire is loosely based on the ancient Roman and the Nazi empires: Palpatine distinctly echoes the Roman Palatine; an Imperial shuttle is called Tyderium; the Imperial troops are referred to as legions; and so on. There is even a suggestion in Lucas's sympathy for the Republic that he is tapping into an American admiration for the pre-Imperial Roman Republic. The movies echo the Nazi empire in the design of the officers' uniforms, in the naming of the shock troops "storm-troopers," in the modeling of the space battles clearly on World War II Japanese-American aerial dogfights, and in the resonance of Leni Riefenstahl's Nazi propaganda film *Triumph of the Will* (1934) in *ANH*'s celebration ceremony. Further, Palpatine directs the Great Jedi Purge through Order 66 as his own Night of the Long Knives; Hitler-like Palpatine declares the need for "a strong Chancellor" who will "bring peace and prosperity back to the Republic" resulting in a call for a vote of no confidence in Chancellor Valorum—cleverly manufactures a crisis that results in popular approval of his seizing of power 32 BBY (*TPM*) and ingeniously assumes absolute power by engineering a war a decade later (*AOTC–ROTS*). So Martin Winkler declares that "in spite of its often strange appearance, Lucas's galactic world is not all that different from an actual and specific era of history—or, more accurately, from the presentation of that history in the cinema."[14]

This connection with Nazism in particular may mold *ANH*'s bad guys into rather one-dimensional icons of evil. They are on screen largely as foils for our celebration of Rebel heroism, and their deaths can be received almost as a moment of cathartic release. According to Ian Nathan, this means that "*Star Wars* was a universe of innocence," an "infantilising [of the] cinema again" that nostalgically pined for a long-lost age (hence the opening "A long time ago . . ." reference) when moral values were thought of as simpler and more obvious.[15] So Pollock argues that in response to the 1970s loss of moral anchorage, "Lucas remembered how protected he had felt growing up in the cocoonlike culture of the 1950s, a feeling he wanted to communicate in Star Wars," as he had done earlier in *American Graffiti* (1973).[16] Lucas admitted to wanting to use *ANH* to teach morality during a time of increasing despair and introspection after Vietnam (added to the oil crisis, ecological concerns, and the aftereffects of Watergate).

The apparent simplicity of what *SW* seemingly taught chimed with the mood of Ronald Reagan's 1980 presidential victory. Reagan's confident political self-presentation was meant to appeal to nostalgia about traditional values. According to Christensen, the American voters "wanted a president who was sure of himself and his nation, unbothered by doubt, and unfazed by the complexities of the nation, the world, or human behaviour."[17] In the Cold War climate of 1983 Reagan rhetorically named the Soviet Union the "Evil Empire." Americans were encouraged to identify themselves with those who are evidently heroic and classify the threatening other as evil. In fact, according to the macho political rhetoric and simplistically clear-cut or black-and-white politics of his "Evil Empire" speech (March 8, 1983), taking the right side in this conflict (crusade, even) against the evil Soviets was nothing less than the holy Christian duty of the American people. Reagan, of course, was drawing on a powerful current in the history of the American imagination, what has frequently been called "American exceptionalism."[18] This self-consciousness has led to the not uncommon American belief that "under God" the destiny of U.S. national self-interest is identical with "civilizing" global altruism. Consequently, "what was good for America was good for the world," and "the salvation of the world depended on" it.[19] After all, a prominent motto of the self-proclaimed "one nation under God" is "in God we trust." (European nations during the First and Second World Wars would similarly assert, "God with us.")

This us-vs.-them rhetoric, which has been prevalent in many nations' politics, simplistically and all too easily sweeps under the carpet all the historical evidence that would otherwise challenge its perspective. The ideology that is hereby created can consequently lead to genuine surprise when others do not recognize just "how good we are."[20] Similarly anything that would reveal and dwell on the brutal episodes and self-interested politics in a nation's history can be played down and even suppressed by the ambitious sense of having a benign national mission. Even when we are aware of such brutal episodes, we tend to see them less in terms of waste and catastrophe and more in a sanitized fashion, as collateral damage, noble sacrifice, or good steps on the way to the Good (just as Palpatine, of course, rationalizes to Anakin the murder of Dooku, *ROTS*).

Therefore, projecting evil onto the other has a purifying effect on how we understand ourselves, since it denies that we disastrously contribute to the existence of evil. On the occasions when we do recognize our frailty, error, and so on, the force of this is drastically mitigated not only by the us-vs.-them, good-vs.-evil scheme but also the fact that we tend to imagine that our successes reveal the promise of salvation to us. (Wink instead suggests that "to the extent that our blessings are incidental byproducts of our citizenship in nations that currently enjoy domination status over others, our well-being may be more a result of our flagrant injustice than divine providence.")[21] Sinisterly this perspective is not far from a muscular totalitarian politics and celebration of an unqualified unilateral action—God is with us, not with them; they have no right to oppose us, because we are good; when they do oppose us, we must not entertain their evil; we must instead extinguish that evil. In this way there is a pronounced difficulty with the notions of cooperative conversation with, or guidance by, or being held accountable by others (which, of course, in a sense is what occurs with the notion of sovereign nations).

As Jewett and Lawrence notice—and their comments are far from limited to the American situation (and here I can speak from my Northern Irish experiences of my own people)—the heart of the spirit of moral and

> personal crusades against evil, so perfectly exemplified in the American monomyth, hardly qualify as standing within the tradition of democratic sentiment. . . . [Instead, careful] deliberation, knowledge of law, and mastery of book learning [as well as diplomatic conversation] are usually

presented in monomythic materials as indicators of impotence or corruption. In the exercise of redemptive power, purity of intention suffices.[22]

Jewett and Lawrence cite Donald McDonald's complaint about the militarization of American foreign policy "when, at critical moments, it is the military who seem to offer the crisp, definite, tangible options—while those who argue for negotiation, diplomacy, and respect for the decent opinion of mankind seem to be offering the unattractive, endlessly prolonged, and inconclusive options."[23] Protracted and unclear journeys are generally much less appealing than quick and easy solutions. The broad roads, though, unwittingly lead to destruction.

Has *SW* been colored by this sensibility? Does it potentially support "the zealous cult of the nation," as Jewett and Lawrence claim?[24] *ANH* arguably works with the American claim to be a freedom-loving nation, originally established by a rebellion of the allied colonies against the oppressive British Empire. Critics also notice the archetypal Americanness of the Rebel heroes Luke (a frontier farm boy) and Han (a space-age gunslinger, with his preference for "a straight fight" to "all this sneakin' around"). Furthermore, *ESB*'s director Irvin Kershner himself admits that the classic trilogy largely plays with the American cinematic convention of providing an all-American cast for the heroic trio, with an all-British cast for the upper echelons of the Imperial order (although Vader is voiced by American James Earl Jones). A fourth American hero arrives in *ESB* (Lando Calrissian), and the role of Englishman Alec Guinness as Obi-Wan is significantly minimized midway through *ANH*. (In the prequels, however, not only is Palpatine British but so too are Qui-Gon and Obi-Wan and the droids, and the tragic hero Anakin is American.) Lev importantly admits that while "Lucas is not responsible for the uses politicians and governments make of his film . . . the ease with which his ideas were put to political and military ends shows something about the Manichean quality of the story."[25]

Lucas once admitted that he offered simple-minded solutions to complex problems, "but if someone would just take one of those simpleminded solutions, the world might be a better place to live."[26] Nevertheless, complex problems, by their very nature, defy simple solutions, and a less than complex approach endangers the usefulness of the proposed solutions. In fact, while its sequels can encourage complex reflection, *ANH*'s nostalgic mood of moral innocence admittedly seems to ignore the proper lessons of Vietnam, for example, and suspicions of "righteous us–vs.–evil them" type hero myths in a complex and morally messy world.

Another Empire: Making a Political Scene

There is a better way of evaluating *SW*'s evil empire, one that makes sense of Lucas's own claims about *ANH*. The empire can be compared to the American government itself, or rather various aspects of the American government at various periods. Lucas, for instance, gives credence to this possibility when he candidly suggests that he designed the Emperor to be a type of Richard Nixon (U.S. president, 1969–74), and Darth Vader to represent a type of Henry Kissinger (U.S. assistant to the president for national security affairs, 1969–75, and secretary of state, 1973–77). Mentioning that they are *types* is important, since the saga's archetypes are simply too broad to be read in straightforwardly allegorical terms. *SW* encourages viewers to pay broad critical attention to even the most self-proclaimed "democratic" and "free" of political environments; so reductionist complaints that *ROTS* is an anti-Bush allegory cannot be taken too seriously.

"Unlearn What You Have Learned" (Yoda, *ESB*)

In 1990 Pollock commented that "the audience for *Star Wars* movies seems to have grown up. . . . Today's movie audiences have also become cynical and jaded; Tim Burton's dark vision of *Batman* is light years from the upbeat morality play Lucas devised for *Star Wars*."[27] Yet the financial success and media hype surrounding the rerelease of the classic trilogy in Special Edition form in 1997, their release in DVD format in 2004, and the filming of the prequels suggest that Pollock's assessment was wildly premature. Nonetheless, there may be an unintended truth in his claim. For all its visual delights and its aspirations to a Campbellian mythic ethos, *ANH* is arguably as morally unsophisticated as vintage Saturday morning adventure serials were. This is not the case with the prequels; they exhibit a greater sense of both the importance of the political system and the complex nature of political interactions, and these facts demand a more morally sophisticated reading. Although there are crucial lines of continuity, this prequel trilogy comes from a different time and arguably from a different mood. *ROTS* in particular represents the series "all grown up" politically. It is flush with a distinctly more modern skeptical (but not cynical) and perspectival (but not relativistic) feel. Nathan's complaint that the "three prequels have added nothing to the original, bar hype and overkill," is a serious misjudgment.[28] These movies begin (although many question their success here) to strip the pantomime-like readings of the classic trilogy from their simplistic, dualistic approach to good and evil and explore more carefully the complex nature of human interaction, desire, and causality than the earlier movies do.

The Rise of the Political

There are certainly continuities between the two sets of trilogies. Rohan Gowland claims that *TPM* retains the simplistic us-vs.-them mood of *ANH*. The "Western-style democracy, the Senate, . . . is portrayed as bureaucratic and intrinsically corrupt. The only hope rests on the religious order of Jedi Knights to intervene and take direct action as the righteous saviours of all that is morally good."[29] This is a morally vulgar vigilantist mythology in which the righteous interventionistic group bypasses "an elected democracy and [takes] justice into their own hands." Gowland sees this as a reflection of the NATO military intervention in the Balkan conflict at the time. "The United Nations, the democratic body, is seen as bureaucratic and ineffective. The ones taking action, in this case NATO, by bypassing the bureaucracy, are seen as 'people of action,' the good guys on a supposedly moral crusade."

This simplistic moral sensibility just does not fit *TPM*, however. First, *Episode I* is concerned with Naboo's self-defense against the preemptive strike of the conquistador-like Trade Federation, which is seeking the gold of a lucrative trade franchise agreement. Second, Chancellor Finis Valorum does not send the Jedi to intervene militarily but to act as the diplomatic ambassadors on behalf of the *Pax Republica*, so to speak. Third, the Hitler Reich resonance in the classic trilogy entails that the Rebellion acts against a *government that has pushed its exercise of power beyond its legitimate level and has become a nearly unchallengeable tyranny*. This could as easily be applied *against* certain Western governments as in support of them, especially when they intervene in the affairs of other nations.

Mark Thornton similarly misses this point when he argues that *TPM* possesses an "underlying classical-liberal politics" and economics that support "smaller" (i.e., less interventionist) government and the economics of free trade.[30] He sees the Trade Federation as one form of monopolizing big business, imposing its will on others via the military hardware of battle droids, droidekas, heavy assault vehicles, and vulture droid fighters.

But does Lucas's imagery portray an individual company that abuses the capitalist system (i.e., is too greedy and uses legally illegitimate means for pursuing that greed) or more radically address the larger governing system as such? The symbolism involved in the roll call of political Separatists warring against the Republic is particularly noteworthy and highly suggestive: the InterGalactic Banking Clan, the Trade Federation, the Commerce Guild, the Corporate Alliance. It is suggestive that Obi-Wan on Geonosis overhears Count Dooku inform the representative heads of those organizations that "signing this treaty will bring you profits beyond your wildest imagination . . . , complete free trade" (*AOTC*). In fact, the movies' sympathies do not lie with these characters or any others involved in business and personal wealth creation—or at least not until their "conversion" (for instance, as with Han Solo and Lando Calrissian). The Trade Federation's mercantilism uses aggressive military force, Han and Lando are both selfish and unscrupulous, the bounty hunters are regarded as "scum" by the Imperials, and Jabba the Hutt is the vilest and most repulsive of gangsters. In contrast, the more attractive characters appear to have less mundane motivations, especially the Jedi with their philosophy of nonattachment. The rather austere garb of both the monastically attired Jedi and the ambassadorial Leia, as well as Luke in his simple functional farm clothing, suggest that the heroes have a limited concern with superficial matters like personal appearance. Only Padmé is beautifully tailored. The desires of the "heroes" are arguably focused in various ways on the Good as far as they understand it. Consequently, the way *SW* celebrates heroism and the relations between persons tends to display the good life as beyond liberal capitalism and the consumerism that sustains it. Lucas actively directs the audience's attention away from the values of acquisitiveness and self-concern.

> The film is ultimately about the dark side and the light side, and those sides are designed around compassion and greed. The issue of greed, of getting things and owning things and having things and not being able to let go of things, is the opposite of compassion—of not thinking of yourself all the time.[31]

Admittedly the films themselves do not suggest a concrete alternative form of commercial interaction between persons and might be seen to be simplistically antibusiness to a certain extent. Yet Qui-Gon's affirmation of the symbiosis of life-forms (to Anakin, *TPM*) suggests the moral need for an economics of nonexploitative cooperation. This is an approach to economic relations that proglobalization economists, with their appeal to "small government" and completely "free trade," cannot entertain, given that the liberal economic system depends on the conflict of competition and the individualistic celebration of private property.[32] According to Lucas, "The United States is a very adversarial society. The government is set up that way, capitalism is basically designed that way and it's just the opposite of symbiotic relationships. And I'm not sure that works very well."[33] Tim Rayment comments on Lucas's remarks here, which while they are rather broad (in that they do not provide a sense of the various forms of public accountability that can and do check corporations' autonomy), at least question the governing purpose of simple profit-making: "The need for people to live together in symbiotic relationships—for natural advantage, rather than competitively—runs through all Lucas' films. . . . He sees danger in corporations that answer to nothing and nobody except the imperative to make money."

In partial response to Thornton's reading of *TPM*, it is difficult to imagine how smaller government alone could serve the flourishing of communities, unless we think of flourishing purely in economic terms, with no reference to moral and spiritual well-being. This, as the quotation above makes clear, is not what Lucas thinks well-being is ultimately about. *SW* imagines that good relations are vitally more than convergences of free association for the sake of personal gain and consumption. In fact, it is arguable that more interventionist government is required in order to help all citizens have basic access to resources (education, public health, financial support, and so on). The image of the Jedi as guardians of peace and justice would be difficult to sustain if truly free markets, those advocated by Thornton, were allowed to have their way with all people without any regulation. They would instead become the guardians of power, privilege, and the economic system.

The *SW* universe has become a complex moral and political space, and *ROTS* is the movie that provides an unresolvably tragic feel to the saga in terms of its morality and politics.

How Liberty Dies: The Self and Evil

The saga's archetypal evil figure, Palpatine, is a Machiavellian character who manipulates events and people, especially as he lurks in the background as Sidious. His assertion to Mace Windu, "I am the Senate," echoes Louis XIV's claim to be the absolute embodiment of the collective will of France (*"l'état est moi,"* the state is me) (*ROTS*). Because the Palpatine of the prequels is a man with an unchanging mission that he coolly and dispassionately accomplishes, in some ways he is an especially chilling figure.

The way he comes to power *from within* a crumbling Republic partly echoes the more personal or psychological themes explored in the classic trilogy with the temptations faced by Luke. The self-recognition scene in the cave on Dagobah can warn against the dualistic or "pantomime politics" we criticized earlier and can caution all relations shaped by the aggressive fear for our own or for our nation-state's existence. After all, Luke is forced to face the possibility that his own journey could itself lead to the dark side (*ESB–ROTJ*), and thus he eventually offers himself as a sacrifice to the one who ultimately seeks to secure his own power, the Emperor (*ROTJ*). In the prequels we are distinctly forced to see that the Empire is not an alien order, an invading force that conquers the "good" Republic by pure self-assertion. Instead, it is a cancerous growth within the Republic's own body, gaining its life by drawing on the tiredness, complacency, vice, and corruption that plague the Senate. This perspective shows Hanson and Kay's comment to be utterly fallacious: "After September 11, 2001, as America comes to grip with the losses of freedom after the tragedy of the terrorist attacks, the . . . archetypal characters . . . help us to sort out mentally who is good and who is bad, and they provide a loose instruction for how to combat fear and oppression. . . . The evil faction is out there, and we need a rebellion."[34] The significance of all this will become more apparent after we deal with the issue of propaganda.

For years before Hitler was able finally to seize unrivaled political control, his National Socialist Party had been distributing preparatory propaganda. With the general mood of much post–World War I Germany and increasing disillusionment with the Weimar government, Hitler was able to tap into the dreams, desires, and despair of a large proportion of German people. A good example of how propaganda works is Nazi Reichsmarschall Hermann Goering's admission of the malleability of the pre-war German citizens at the Nuremburg trials:

> Why, of course the people don't want war. . . . But after all it is the leaders of the country who determine the policy, and it is always a simple matter to drag the people along whether it is a democracy, a fascist dictatorship, or a parliament, or a communist dictatorship. Voice or no voice, the people can always be brought to the bidding of the leaders. That is easy. All you have to do is tell them they are being attacked, and denounce the pacifists for lack of patriotism, and exposing the country to greater danger. It works the same in any country.[35]

Palpatine, as far as we know, has not played the propaganda game in quite the same way. But his control over the progress of the war (over, in fact, both sides as the Republic's Chancellor and the Separatists' guide through their leader Count Dooku), his continual emphasis on himself as a kindly ruler deeply concerned with peace, and his control of war reporting enables him to create a great swell of popular support both for himself personally and for his place in political office. In these ways he is substantially able to control public sentiment and affection. Later, as Emperor, he uses propaganda agencies to maintain his public image as a beneficent old man who works for galactic harmony. During the Clone Wars, he is able to create for himself the position of popular heroic leader, strong and reliable authority, the very embodiment of the Republican's projected hopes and dreams for peace and security. And, of course, he *is* winning the war and thus bringing a peace and stability to the galaxy *just as he promises* (not that he could lose, given his double role in shaping it). In all this he encourages a state of childlike dependence upon his paternal ability to secure the Republic's citizens, which has several significant facets. First, he is trusted by most of Coruscant's citizens and the members of the Galactic Senate in a way that enables him to stimulate a generous appraisal of his attitudes and approval of his actions that may be less than virtuous in other situations—for instance, the initial militarization of the Galaxy; his retention of power long after his political term has expired; his assuming emergency powers; and the further militarization of what is then renamed the "Galactic Empire" with the formation of regional governors to oversee Imperial administration.

Second, in encouraging trust in himself he blinds others to his true intentions and consequently saps people's ability to think in any terms other than those that he has already established and that are reinforced by the propaganda machine he has set in place according to the Clone Wars backstory. The practice of propaganda circumvents the normal processes of deliberating, testing, and thinking. The very possibility for critically interrogating the message either has been sacrificed for the comforting feeling of the propagandist's supposedly protective care or has been largely subverted by the propagandist's convincing and flattering rhetoric. It then becomes particularly difficult for a people or "a nation that sees itself as close to perfection as any human society can come" to hear criticism of itself.[36] Evil becomes projected onto the other in a way that generates, in the words of Jewett and Lawrence, not only a "complacency about the existence of evil among the saints and a petulant impatience with any resistance to their rule" but also a "complacency about the corruption of the nation [or other tribal group] as a whole."[37] This kind of ideology can likewise support the perpetration of what would otherwise be considered horrendous deeds (torture, tactical nuclear strikes), all now justifiable in the name of the supposedly righteous end. So while the audience is encouraged to feel that the destruction of the Jedi Order is an evil, Anakin considers it little more than radical surgery for the health of the body, a piece of collateral damage necessary in the cause of the greater good of peace and stability.

Even if criticism remains possible, the political machinery ensures that it is muffled and unheard, perceived to be only the rantings of the mad, the unpatriotic, and so on. Palpatine, for instance, is able to mute the message of resistance and circumvent the potential for critical opposition by using intimidation tactics, isolating into a minority those who resist, and buying off others with promises of power and prestige. He, moreover, labels his opponents "treasonous" and makes patriotic claims about loving the Republic, claims that have obvious ideological function (*ROTS*). This is a tactic familiar to American audiences, who themselves are frequently accused of being unpatriotic and even treasonous when they critique the values and beliefs that supposedly make America and her government "great." And yet, as Jedi Master Mace Windu explains in the novelized version of *ROTS*, "The *real* treason would be a failure to *act*."[38] This echoes a claim made by President Theodore Roosevelt in 1918: Unquestioning obedience to the president "is not only unpatriotic and servile, but is morally treasonable to the American public."

To blame the violent imperial turn in the Republic's history wholly on the insidious Palpatine, therefore, is an excuse that blinds us to a problem closer to home. The preconditions for Palpatine's rise lie deep within the greed, corruption, and complacency that were beginning to tire the Republic *from inside*, and the Republic is attracted to his use of military force in order to secure its own existence (and that equally involves denying freedom to the systems that want to separate from it). Hence, the evil of Palpatine and his acquisition of absolute rule cannot be considered without understanding the wider factors that enable and support its birth, progression, and maintenance. It is the citizens of the Republic, the Clone War backstory and the position of Palpatine in the movies suggest, who desire to defend their way of life and their prosperity at all costs; they are susceptible to narcissistic flattery and to the self-securing involved in projecting all problems and fears onto the Separatist "others." That is why Padmé, a great supporter of Republic democracy against Anakin, who is desperate to force agreement, admits, "Popular rule is not democracy, Anni. It gives the people what they want, not what they need" (*AOTC* deleted scene). Palpatine, seemingly, has played the typical political game by appealing to the populace's instincts and *perceived* needs while offering that which is ultimately destructive of what they *truly* need, the good of the Republic. "So this is how liberty dies—with thunderous applause," bemoans Padmé as the Galactic Senate enthusiastically cheers dictator-in-waiting Palpatine while he announces his crusade against the Jedi.

The images in *ROTS* that echo post-9/11 American politics have received heated comment. As mentioned earlier, some within the American political right have denounced the movie as an anti-Bush diatribe. The parallels may well be intended by Lucas, but the movies' intentions are also much more general. Campbell once claimed about the classic saga, "The fact that the evil power is not identified with any specific nation on this earth means you've got an abstract power, which represents a principle, not a specific historic situation. The story has to do with an operation of principles not of this nation against that."[39] Similarly, Lucas claims that his story's spirit was conceived in the shadow of the Vietnam War, and he makes this rather general observation:

> All democracies turn into dictatorships—but not by coup. The people give their democracy to a dictator, whether it's Julius Caesar or Napoleon or Adolf Hitler. Ultimately, the general population goes along with the idea. . . . That's the issue that I've been exploring.[40]

The point, then, is that had Bush and Blair become entangled in the principles underlying *SW*'s "evil empire," then so much the worse for them and the peoples under them.

However, it is not wholly surprising to discover a critic asserting that "Lucas confused the good guys with the bad" and that "the Empire is good."[41] Jonathan V. Last supports this contention by saying, first, that the Empire brings peace, stability, and order to the crumbling Republic. Second, it rids the Galaxy of the arrogant, elitist, and inherited guardians of the Force. Third, it comes after the Separatists' demands for smaller government (but is that what the Galactic Empire provides?) and free trade. Fourth, it has "a relatively benign" dictator. Fifth, it establishes academies that rely on a meritocracy, unlike the elitist Jedi Order that depends on the inherited midi-chlorians. Of course we could try to argue that the imperial project is indeed beneficent, just as Michael Ignatieff does when he argues that the United States is "empire-lite."[42] (By this Ignatieff means that it refuses to possess territories directly through annexation, colonization, and direct centralized government, and is to be celebrated and maintained because it is necessary for "bringing order to the barbarian zones.")[43]

Anakin seems to have taken at face value Palpatine's appearance as a wise ruler ultimately interested in peace. The trouble is that he never tests the meaning of "peace" and misjudges the oppressive nature of Palpatine's peace—it is the peace that victors and the powerful impose for their own interests on the defeated and the weak, which actually spells disaster for these groups. This is a peace that makes some more prosperous and freer than others. Christians, those who follow the Jesus who befriended outcasts and was eventually executed on imperial Rome's cross, should be deeply suspicious of political systems, structures, and actions, however good or promising they sound, that exclude others from the overall benefits of the Good.

But aren't our rulers benign in a way Palpatine obviously is not? While the English-speaking world has not had a tyrannical ruler like *SW*'s Emperor, at least in recent years in the case of the United Kingdom, that question nevertheless remains tricky, in that it requires a judgment about peoples' motivations that is always notoriously difficult to make. As Claes G. Ryn maintains, "Desire for power rarely shows itself in its own tawdry voraciousness. . . . They feel the need to dress up their striving in appealing garb. Hence the will to power almost always presents itself as benevolent concern for others, as an unselfish wish to improve society or the world."[44] Anakin, among many others, is convinced by Palpatine. In fact, in an important sense he does not *blindly* follow the Chancellor, as if he does not have reasons for doing so. Instead, as we saw in chapter 4, he is *blind to the truth* of this man. It is only the movies' audience who can make such moral decisions about Palpatine precisely *because* it has a "God's-eye perspective," seeing events that no character in the movies can see. How would we respond if we were in Anakin's position, faced with the choice to trust a seemingly corrupt Jedi Order or the man who had helped us since we were children?

Moreover, even if a ruler like Palpatine is benevolently motivated, can the shape of his rule be wholly free from various distorting influences, since he always has only a partial knowledge of all causes and situations and, even more importantly, depends on those who may be less benevolently motivated? Perhaps that is why *TPM* mentions that the bureaucracy and corruption weighed down Valorum's term as Chancellor, even though—as the backstory makes clear—he is a politician who is wholly motivated by his desire for the common good.[45] The tragic quality of Anakin's story can help us see that we become particularly bad artists when we attempt to portray ourselves, and consequently we desperately need to develop an imagination that admits and traces how we *all* (and that includes all our nations) tend habitually to act under a misrepresentation of the Good and our relation to it.

Even though the Truth and the Good are embodied in Jesus Christ, we must recognize that it is *he* who is the Truth, the Way, and the Life (John 14:6). *The concept of sin, with the concomitant practice of prayer in the form of self-examining confession and repentance, declares that these qualities are not ours to possess.* Our very sense of the Truth and the Good, even when we participate in Jesus Christ's way, has continually to be wary of our disorienting distortions, and we must repent of them. The face of the One raised but still bearing the scars of execution forces us, if we are honest, to face disturbing home truths that prevent us from curling up warmly under national flags, for instance, and letting ourselves wholly off the hook for the evils that plague us. Both the "politics of a pure heart" and the realpolitik of self-interest in a messy world are naive and destructive. *SW* serves as a stark warning that there is something very sinister about imperial projects.

The following chapters will imply that only by becoming a people capable of living a "politics of repentance" and a "politics of interest-in-the-other" can we have any chance of ever authentically changing anything in the structures of our relations. But this requires us to rethink not merely our political orders but also the church, since at their worst churches have theologically legitimated or left unchallenged the politics of self-interest, the "politics of evil." By *ROTS*, Palpatine does not have the option of gaining religious support for his political endeavors—the Jedi are being deliberately eliminated. They and their practices of peace and justice are a threat to Palpatine's power, in striking contrast with culturally domesticated churches in the "real" world that have allowed national flags and market-driven performance to become integral symbols in the shaping of the God worshiped. It is Anakin who actively supports Palpatine, and he "falls" from the truth of the Force. Yet the political significance of the Christian faith should force us to change the way we think about and practice our own politics. As German theologian Jürgen Moltmann indicates, doing this well will not mean that the gospel is "politicized" but rather that politics (and all public relations) are properly "Christianized."[46] "Christian ethics makes everyday life into a feast of God's rule, just as Jesus did."[47]

What would a politics of repentance and a politics of interest-in-the-other look like? While *SW* may not be able to provide a concrete answer, its notion of the well-being of properly ordered interrelations is suggestive. People and the communities they inhabit are trained together in the character of the Good, as far as it can be conceived. Politics, then, cannot worry about locating and claiming for itself pure spaces of innocence or guilt but should instead learn "how to live with integrity and bring healing to a world of inescapable noninnocence that often parades itself as its opposite."[48]

Conclusion: Politics Corrupted

SW is a popcorn movie made in a culture that is itself prone to making moral simplifications, in that American (and to an extent British) consciousness has been frequently directed by the morally rather unambiguous myth of the hero. In *SW*, in contrast, "the 'enemy' is not a political 'other,' but ourselves, or at least the threat that we will lose our humanity to greed and a selfish quest for power—symbolized by the Dark side."[49] Taking this seriously will require quite an upheaval of cultural and political consciousness. What will happen here to our ability to think and speak of others simply as evil; to our propensity to imagine ourselves (us personally, our churches, nation, government, economic system, and so on) as separate in some way from this evil; and to our ability to imagine that we can righteously dispense true justice and freedom? What would international and national political relations look like when it is patient with the laborious and inexhaustible processes of making a civilized life together, and rejects the infantile myths that sustain self-satisfying pantomine politics? By construing evil in the way it does, *SW* can engender the kinds of self-reflection that may thwart our complacency and our temptations to understand ourselves and our nations uncritically and sentimentally.

In the prequels we see the public impact of the distortions, troubles, and tragedies of the Sith way as it brutally and directly impacts lives and relationships to such devastating effect. Lives are wasted, horrendous evils are perpetrated, and those who suffer them seem to be left with little hope. The Sith worship themselves and express this in their domination over others, their fear of loss and death, and their having no real concern for others' well-being. Even so, *SW* is far from being fatalistic or making political dissidents wholly impotent, as Terry Christensen claims *ANH* does.[50] On the contrary, toward the end of the eminently dark *ROTS* we can hear the subtle but critical notes of hope: Luke and Leia's respective musical themes from *ANH* are performed as they are delivered into the care of their respective adopting families.

Chapter Six

Rebelling against Evil

The Violence of *Star Wars*

> *We shall be made truly free, then, when God fashions us, that is, forms and creates us anew, not as men—for He has done that already—but as good men, which His grace is now doing, that we may be a new creation in Christ Jesus.*
>
> —Augustine, *The Enchiridion*, 31

*M*any theological textbooks put a chapter on sin before their chapters on reconciliation and hope. Similarly, many Christian sermons and talks first try to convince us of our sinfulness and only after that talk about salvation. Salvation seems to be reduced to being salvation from sin. It appears to be more difficult to say what salvation is significant for in relation to the world the Creator has blessed. This approach, however, is based on a theological mistake—or, rather, several mistakes.

First, it separates too neatly justification from sanctification and salvation from the Christian life, in a way that misses the purpose that God saves for—to make all things well. Second, it equally forgets that we properly recognize and admit that we are sinful only in and through the traditions that worship the covenant God of Israel. In other words, God reveals to us our disease *in the very act of healing us*; consciousness of sin theologically does not or should not encourage in us a world-weary despair. Instead, consciousness of sin emphasizes our need humbly to learn where sin may be found and creatively to resist it. As Tanner argues, "As the world God creates and guides and redeems in Jesus Christ, the world is forever God's place no matter how distant it seems from the standards of truth and goodness that God represents."[1] The mistake that Christian forms of world despair make reflects the dualism that has afflicted the Christianity at various times and the cultures that have shaped the Western imagination.

Lucas's 1971 movie *THX 1138* explored the notion of salvation and freedom of the main protagonist from his repressive society by having him walk *away from* it into a sunshine infinity. *SW*, however, offers a more concrete, responsible, embodied, and hopeful sense of salvation that is rooted in the Force. This enables his critique of politics and society not to flow from or into skepticism—never mind its close cousin cynicism. As Lucas admits, "You can learn from cynicism, but you can't build on it."[2] Instead, the journey of the Force-driven life is *purposeful*, with a direction and a vision that are socially creative. So while cynicism's "No!" remains a "No!" *SW*'s "No!" derives from and is the flipside of its "Yes!" that is its positive vision of good relations. Consequently, while *ROTS*'s opening rolling text declares, "Evil is everywhere," *SW* is not essentially about evil.

SW presents a vision in which all manner of diverse beings in the galaxy are drawn together in common cause and in the most visible and therefore public of ways. It is animated by the hope for a harmonious diversity in which Christians may recognize something of the fellowship-making rule of the God of peace. By itself this does not prove that *SW* is actually theologically instructive, but it does suggest that asking whether it can be is worth the effort. In fact, the saga can importantly challenge certain understandings of Christianity in the way it portrays the good life and the nature of conflict.

This chapter will begin by exploring the notion of the savior figure in the saga before asking about the "good life" in relation to violence, military hostility, and peace. In other words, we are now concerned with the shape of redemption for human conflict.

A Saving Parallel

There is arguably no single Christ figure in *SW* but many who are in a sense Christlike, meaning they possess the qualities of the human that are fulfilled in Israel's Messiah, Jesus of Nazareth. Obi-Wan is one such figure: he gives his life for the freedom of others; and while his death is mysterious, it is certainly not his end, since he "rises" to a new life and presence to Luke. Even the comment, "Remember, Luke, the Force will be with you, always," distinctly echoes Jesus' promise to his disciples (Matt. 28:20).

Nevertheless, it is Luke who particularly appears most Christlike, especially when his characterization is connected with the Anakin of the prequels. In fact, the virgin birth theme gives Anakin (*TPM*), and consequently his son

Luke also, a Christ-type hue. But this theme has another significance; given that this occurrence is unique in the saga's mythology, it suggests that *SW* does not clearly present some kind of humanistic anthropology in which all people can easily become Christ figures through identifying with the typical everyman hero. After all, the Christian confession that "Jesus is the Christ" is a claim about the irreducible particularity of Jesus, not a claim that a particular individual called Jesus happened to embody a general set of "Christ virtues." Thomas Horn's feeling that Anakin is a New Age messiah, a product of pantheism's making humans members of the divine whole, is distinctly dubious.[3] While they may be ordinary heroes in some sense, this father and son are supernaturally extraordinary in other ways. Anakin, while one with other beings, has a profoundly unique quality that makes his fate momentous for that of the entire galaxy. According to Qui-Gon, "He *is* the Chosen One."

But with his tragic fall (*AOTC* and *ROTS*), Anakin himself ultimately becomes more an *inversion* of the Christ form. Does this mean that he is a failed Christ, "the chosen one" who could not live up to the greatness of his billing? Or is Anakin instead more the fallen figure of Adam (Gen. 3), with Luke the redemptive one? Suggestively Pollock claims that "Lucas . . . wanted his version of the Christ story in *Empire*. Luke beheads Vader in an underground cave, only to find his own head inside Vader's black helmet—it is the equivalent of Jesus' temptation in the desert."[4] So while Lucas distances himself from a specifically Christian version of this by placing the temptation theme in a more general context,[5] the gospel echoes are noticeable, especially in the temptation of Luke with political power (*ESB*; cf. Matt. 4:8ff.).

The way *SW* presents Luke's redemptive relation to Anakin is particularly interesting theologically. The quite deliberate and elaborate *parallelism* between Anakin and Luke resonates with Paul's Adam/Christ typology (Rom. 5:12–21; 1 Cor. 15:21–22, 45). In making *TPM*, Lucas specifically notified his design staff that

> Anakin [is] kind of duplicating . . . the Luke Skywalker role, but you see the echo of where it's all gonna go. Instead of destroying the Death Star he destroys the ship that controls the robots [viz., the Trade Federation battle droids]. Again it's like poetry, they rhyme. Every stanza rhymes with the last one.[6]

The parallels are many, and we can identify the following as examples:[7] both Anakin and Luke spend their earliest years on Tatooine; there is the parallel between their successes in the Battle of Naboo (*TPM*) and the Battle of Yavin (*ANH*)—although Anakin's victory is portrayed as significantly less deliberate, conscious, and even less galactically significant; both are proficient mechanics and own the protocol and astromech droids C3PO and R2D2; both become Obi-Wan's Jedi-students; both dream of excitement and adventure; both are whiny, petulant, and impatient as young men; both become proficient speeder pilots (*AOTC* and *ESB* respectively); both lose their right hands in lightsaber combat with Sith Lords (*AOTC* and *ESB* respectively); both are involved in temptation scenes by the same Satan-like tempter, Palpatine/Sidious, and have to face the same temptations—to kill their respective Sith opponent (Dooku [*ROTS*] and Vader [*ROTJ*]) and join with Palpatine. Even the movies in which these parallels take place are equivalently placed in their particular trilogy.

But after this the parallels cease, and a significant series of reversals takes place. It is Luke who (with his twin, Leia) becomes the "New Hope": most crucially, while Anakin succumbs to temptation and falls, Luke resists and suffers (Vader's messianic role later doubles back in a return that sees him become Luke's savior); despite Anakin's "accidental" victory at the Battle of Naboo, evil nonetheless wins the day, whereas the Empire takes a powerful knock with Luke's action in the Battle of Yavin; Anakin's involvement in the Battle of Naboo begins the spiral of tragedy, ultimately culminating in the formation of the first Galactic Empire and the destruction of the Jedi Order, while Luke's achievement inaugurates a "new hope" and eventually the new Jedi Order.

Luke, in other words, is a recapitulation of his father—his life story covers the same themes, only this time with a significant variation on the original. He is redemptive not merely because of his origin but because he does not fall. Anakin is the Adam figure but becomes faithless to his destiny or calling and consequently never fulfills his glorious potential. Luke is Christlike by ultimately remaining faithful to his destiny or calling, and consequently he fulfills his glorious messianic potential as the New Hope. If Anakin is the divinely chosen one whose own birth is the fruit of the Force (the "son of God" in a sense), then Luke represents the redemptive second coming of the son. Luke overcomes his temptations to act as the obedient servant of the Force for the good of the galaxy, even giving himself up to possible death at the hands of the Satan-like figure of Sidious and self-effacingly inaugurating the restoration of the Jedi Order. And while Padmé (and to an extent even Shmi Skywalker) was involved in complex ways with Anakin's fall, it is through this good woman (and to a lesser degree Leia too) that salvation can come through Luke. Rowlands badly misunderstands this typology when he complains that Padmé's characterization is an echo of Leia's.[8] According to the Adam-Christ logic of Paul, if through Adam/Anakin came disorder and death, through Christ/Luke come new order and life. This is why the end of *ROTJ*'s action has a notable *eschatological* feel (new life arrived).

The implications of this are pronounced, and five are worth observing. First, an Adam-Christ or fall-redemption framework for *SW* finally excludes a dualistic reading of good and evil. To say *SW* is dualistic is like accusing the later Augustine of Manicheism. Second, the Adam-Christ theological scheme negates any lazy optimism about human beings. The catastrophic waste involved in Anakin's fall sabotages sentimental talk about the effective goodness of all people. Third, while *SW* borrows its imagery and themes eclectically, the central driving force may well be christological. Mohler's claim, "Conspicuously absent from Mr. Lucas's cosmology is anything connected to biblical Christianity," is dubious.[9] Fourth, redemption is not world- or body-denying but is the transformation of this cosmic reality. Noticeably, even if the Jedi who have become one with the Force have a kind of nonphysical existence, they nonetheless possess their own type of bodily integrity (*ROTJ*). Fifth, the prequels are not radically different from the classic trilogy but are, instead, profoundly their inverted echo (fall and tragedy/grace and redemption).

The Journey into the Larger World: Self-Discovery

It is one thing to believe in the Force but quite another to understand, embrace, and live well under its demanding guidance. Though many are called by the Force, so to speak, few are chosen (cf. Matt. 22:14). According to the prequels' backstory, there are millions of Force-conscious beings but only a handful who successfully graduate from Padawan to Knight, even fewer to Master, and almost none who become as important and sagelike as Yoda. This is why Qui-Gon warns the boy Anakin, "Training to become a Jedi is not an easy challenge. And even if you do succeed, it's a hard life" (*TPM*).

When we meet Luke, he is a distinctly average young man, lacking in the guidance of the Force provided by the demanding life of Jedi virtue. In fact he seems to possess nothing particularly noteworthy, and the signs of his self-absorbed immaturity are abundant (see chapter 1). For instance, when he surveys the dreadful murderous scene at the Lars homestead, his comment to Obi-Wan (living at this stage under the name of Ben Kenobi) centers not on the injustice of the stormtroopers' assassinations or on his grief for the deaths of those who had raised him but tastelessly on himself: "I want to come with you to Alderaan. There's nothing for me here now. I want to learn the ways of the Force and become a Jedi like my father."[10] While he had made the comment to Obi-Wan earlier, "It's not like I like the Empire—I hate it," the real reasons he takes up the cause have to do with a series of accidents and his longing for adventure. In fact, as Anker perceptively observes, "his dreams stretch no further than the macho ideals that his culture glorifies, and here the filmmaker undertakes a quiet but persistent strain of social criticism. Luke's great ambition in life is to attend fighter-pilot school to become a 'top gun' and then go off to war."[11] All in all, at this stage he is a highly unlikely candidate for heroism, although perhaps one could argue that his reluctance to follow Obi-Wan initially is at least testimony to his commendable sense of duty to his uncle.

The subsequent adventure proves to be more than he had bargained for, however. It becomes a journey not only "into the unknown" that moves him toward becoming a war hero but also into self-realization.[12] He is jolted from his slumbers as a frustrated and reluctant farmer when Obi-Wan reveals, much to the youth's initial disbelief, that his father had been a Jedi Knight, a hero in the Clone Wars many years earlier, and possibly "the best starpilot in the galaxy, and a cunning warrior." Given his (and later we learn Leia's) "Force-filled" heritage, especially with what we learn of Anakin's ancestry in *TPM*, Luke is anything but ordinary. So Wilkinson is wrong to suggest that, through the character of Luke, "*Star Wars* shows that ordinary people, male and female, can become heroes."[13]

Mentioning Obi-Wan here leads us to the important theme of *learning* in *SW*, especially since this takes place in and through the trustworthy guidance of others. This expresses the sense of the interdependence of all things, in that Luke's learning is *dependent* upon the two remaining Jedi. Yet—and this is crucial too—the constant struggle of *both learning and unlearning* is an indication that the *project of the ethical life* in Force-discipleship is an *unfinished* one. Only Yoda does not seem to undergo any further learning in *Episodes V* and *VI*. And yet Luke's success in resisting Vader and becoming a full-fledged Jedi Knight may perhaps confound his pessimism over the young man's progress; and arguably his attitude to Qui-Gon (*TPM*) changes somewhat (*ROTS*). Luke has continually to undergo training *in looking at the world in new ways* and in having his disordered desires purified.

Furthermore, the apprenticeship Luke undergoes places him *freely within a story*, an embodied social narrative or tradition of the community that learns the ways of the Force. He is ultimately to be faithful to the ways of the Force learned through the wisdom of his Jedi *ancestors*, subsequently setting the scrutinizing vision of Jedi wisdom over and against the dominant culture (depending, of course, on the shape and form of the latter). However, it is indispensable to his becoming a Jedi that he is not limited to slavishly repeating past wisdom. Instead he has to use it creatively, as Qui-Gon does when the demands of the Jedi Council contradict his understanding of "the will of the Force." In fact the very shape of the Master-Padawan relationship bespeaks not only the importance of learning and even of scholarship (learning the wisdom of the past) but the good (as opposed to the Sith) Master's selfless and nondominating drawing of the apprentice into his or her own free and creative participation within those traditions.

Significantly, Luke is being trained in the traditions of Jedi *wisdom*. In one of the first mentions of Ben Kenobi (later revealed as Obi-Wan Kenobi) in *ANH,* Uncle Owen denounces him as a "crazy old wizard." The situational irony is that "wizard" derives from *wys* ("wise") in Middle English, and Obi-Wan is the archetypal figure of the intelligently wise and magical guru who becomes Luke's "protective figure."[14] So Owen is blind to where wisdom can be found; yet ironically he perhaps possesses his own wisdom of sorts in being wary of just what Jedi wisdom, Obi-Wan included, had led the Republic and Anakin to.

Luke's learning wisdom takes a highly unexpected direction. He has to learn how to *unlearn* what he has learned. This demand is first forced upon him when in *ANH* he is forced to reevaluate his ancestral heritage (it is not until *ESB* that he learns not only that his supposedly killed father still lives but that he is none other than Darth Vader himself; and in *AOTC* the audience learns that Owen Lars was not Luke's biological uncle after all). A little later, on board the *Millennium Falcon* he is taught by Obi-Wan to reevaluate the process of knowing by not trusting his eyes. This incident involves sight-deprivation training through wearing a helmet with its blast-shield down, symbolically asking Luke to regard the world in a different way from those who associate what can be seen through the mechanics of sight. Ironically, because he cannot see with his eyes, he can have greater insight into the nature of things. This is a radical reimagining of all things that echoes something of what Christians mean by conversion. As Stanley Hauerwas claims concerning Christian "training": "We must be trained to desire rightly—because, bent by sin, we have little sense of what it is that we should rightly want."[15] *SW*'s sense here further echoes Campbell's theme of "The Belly of the Whale," in which the hero is "swallowed into the unknown, and would appear to have died" (metaphorically or spiritually) in a moment of "self-annihilation," only "to be born again."[16] This conversion theme is expressed in another image—becoming like a child (see Matt. 18:3). So Yoda asks a classroom of Jedi Younglings to help solve Obi-Wan's puzzle of how a planet can both exist and be lacking in the supposedly infallible Jedi archives—Librarian Jocasta Nu had informed Obi-Wan, "If an item does not appear in our records it does not exist" (*AOTC*). To young J. K. Burtola's answer, Yoda eulogizes, "Truly wonderful the mind of a child is." "The child's mind, unlike Obi-Wan's, was less clouded by rigid facts, preconceptions, and set beliefs and could [at least on this occasion] more readily see the truth."[17]

Luke's conversion takes a huge leap forward through his encountering Jedi Master Yoda, whom a ghostly Obi-Wan instructs him to seek out in the Dagobah system early in *ESB*. By this time Luke, the heroic destroyer of the Death Star, has become a commander in the Rebel Alliance. Moreover, his Force-consciousness has improved, as is demonstrated by the Force-grabbing of his lightsaber in the wampa's cave on Hoth. Yet his training in the Jedi way has far from ceased. Indeed his faith in the Force still needs to be radically purged of inappropriate conceptions and evaluations; and he has to be forced to become conscious of, confront, and test his assumptions, and then reconstruct the very way he perceives life and the universe around him.

What Luke finds on Dagobah is far from what he had expected, and the mirror held up to him is painfully revealing. The planet itself is a murky and swampy world, wholly uncivilized in a way that makes his former home world, gangster-run Tatooine, look distinctly cultured and sophisticated. It is simply not the kind of world in which he would expect to find a great Jedi Master. Feeling he is being watched, he swings around with blaster drawn, only to see something apparently unthreatening—an unarmed, diminutive green being with protruding ears. This being acts like a scavenger, uses a strange grammatical syntax, is physically unimpressive, and appears more fool or jester than Jedi Master. But later he is unexpectedly revealed to be the one the young man has been seeking. The problem for Luke, with his obviously militaristic notions of power—as for many of Jesus' contemporaries with their own militaristic expectations for the coming Messiah—is that the reality did not fit the expectation of what "a great warrior" should look like (Luke, *ESB*). According to Anker, the Jedi-in-becoming "finds . . . one who seems to be the very antithesis of power."[18] In this event, he has again to reevaluate the world beyond the distorted impressions provided by his senses so as to become truly reordered toward the Good. This is why Yoda later challenges him with the rhetorical question, "Judge me by my size do you?"

Yoda's initial appearance could not be more contrasting with that of Vader. The masked Sith Lord arrives striding over recently slain bodies, exuding a cool and powerful arrogance, distinguished by his menacing warrior dress, with his cape flowing behind him impressively adding to the threat of his presence. His voice and manner reveal that he is one to be obeyed because, imposing in form and character, he is eminently fearsome. Soon after, he is seen holding a Rebel commander by the neck a few feet off the ground before the sound of breaking bones can be heard. *The difference between Yoda and Vader has to do with different conceptions of power and the self.* For Vader, power is the power of force and the right of might; for Yoda, power has to do with the virtues of wisdom, self-control, and just living. For Vader, the self is to be exalted, at others' expense, while Yoda is a servant of the Force and correspondingly a servant of all living things.

"Wars Not Make One Great!"

Martin Luther King once argued, "The ultimate measure of a man is not where he stands in moments of comfort and convenience, but where he stands at times of challenge and controversy."[19] Luke's engagement in the Rebellion reveals much about him and his value system. Luke, the heroic destroyer of the Death Star, Luke the Rebel Commander, Luke the burgeoning Force-conscious man, possesses an understanding of the self that revolves around a certain understanding of duty and heroism. Yet during his training he has to "unlearn" in the most dramatic of ways his whole understanding of what makes a person. His encounter with the Jedi Master is the first step into a larger world that transforms the myth of the hero, the myth of the Jedi as great and awesome warrior. Luke misses the profundity of Yoda's pithy response: "Wars not make one great!"

Earlier we saw that mythology expresses cultural conditions and can in turn create new perspectives. These stories that we tell ourselves in ritualized form significantly help to shape who we are and become and also what we believe. They have a profound socializing effect, and thus we can deal with the relation between screen violence and social crime only superficially through the question of whether there is a *direct* influence—in other words a *conscious* appropriation or repetitious copying of the fictional violence.[20] We come to assume the values and dispositions portrayed in the violent piece to be the way things are or "natural." We learn through repetition, and the sheer amount of screen violence suggests that the repetition has made us all too familiar with these assumptions. In other words, the greatest power of the media lies at the level of the *unconscious*, the forming of people and people's imaginations in ways that create certain possibilities for self-understanding.

Thus one such question of the cultural system *SW* possibly assumes and expresses has to do with matters of militarism and violence, in particular the so-called "myth of redemptive violence" that Wink identifies as "the real religion of America."[21] However, the role of violence, it will be seen, takes several forms in the multipart saga, ranging from something akin to a "holy violence," through more of a sense of just war, to an ethical philosophy approaching a full-blown redemptive nonviolence. In fact, that last theme may possess potential for subverting that very myth of redemptive violence, or talk of a good war, itself.

Holy a Total War!

Predominantly critics have detected a sense of a "good violence," or holy war, operative in *ANH* especially. Consequently, despite the fact that the Jedi Masters Yoda and Obi-Wan both counsel Luke not to succumb to the dark side of "anger, fear . . . aggression . . . hate," the films apparently justify violence, or at least a certain kind of violence—the *redemptive violence* of the Rebel cause. Consciously or unconsciously *SW* is shaped by and reinforces the violent American celebration of the hero who overcomes all odds to dispense true justice, what Jewett and Lawrence call "the Captain America complex."[22] Lucas naturalizes violent conflict and contributes to making the violence of war (unavoidably) part of the (proper) way of life. So we find Rosenbaum, for instance, arguing, "One would probably have to go back to the 40s, as Lucas did, to find such a guiltless celebration of unlimited warfare."[23]

First, the element of guilt is eliminated, since the Empire is *consistently evil*. It commits mass murder on an unprecedented scale by obliterating the "peaceful" planet of Alderaan (Leia, *ANH*), and not resisting such evil would seem to be ethically unthinkable. In this way the Rebels' motives and means of action come to look enlightened and pure. Second, evil is invariably personified in the flatly dark characters of Vader (*ANH*), Sidious (*ROTJ*), and Maul (*TPM*). Third, critics also cite the way in which even the saga's redemptive moment is portrayed. Michelle Kinnucan, for instance, observes that in the climactic battle, the Emperor is slain and the mortally wounded Vader dies just before the Rebel Alliance triumphs by destroying the second Death Star.[24] So Stone argues, for instance, "The ultimate victory of good over evil finally boils down to firing laser-blasters, detonating bombs, or slicing through one's enemies with a light saber."[25] Arguably, then, the audience is treated to a kind of cathartic experience in which any feelings of guilt are expiated by the overwhelming feeling of rightness of action. Does this mean, then, that *SW* is still unwittingly threatened by a "Manichaean quality" that pits "us against them" and that consequently predicates a difficult-to-test assumption of the moral righteousness of the "us" and those aligned with us? Is there a suggestion of a self-congratulatory self-image that could claim to know just "how good we are"?[26] Critics certainly see it as a "universe of innocence" that constitutes an "infantilising [of the] cinema again."[27]

The saga, it would seem, reinforces what Campbell claims to be a "basic idea" in the mythologies of war: "that the enemy is a monster and that in killing him one is protecting the only truly valuable order of human life . . . one's own people."[28] As Kinnucan argues by citing James Gibson's *Warrior Dreams*, this Darwinian survivalist mythology and the larger and longer standing mythologies of redemptive violence keep people chained to war as a way of life; they infuse individuals, national political and military leaders, and societies with a deep attraction to both imaginary and real violence. They demand that "no premium is put on reasoning, persuasion, negotiation, or diplomacy. There can be no compromise with absolute evil. Evil must be totally annihilated."[29] Moreover, the fact that the Jedi are aligned with the Force provides the most ultimate of sanctions for unself-critical moral agency in the conflict against evil. "The righteous," one writer starkly maintains, "are called by God's law to exercise a holy 'violence' against certain of the wicked, thereby manifesting God's wrath."[30] Without repeating the arguments, we have nevertheless had very good reasons to reject the Manichean account that exteriorizes and projects evil, thereby painting a more flattering image of the righteous.

Nonetheless, there is a second version of the criticism of *SW*'s "good violence" that detects problems at the level of form. Violence is presented in such a sterile or hygienically sanitized fashion that it anesthetizes the audience, as arguably Quentin Tarantino's balletic choreography of violence in the *Kill Bill* movies does. The identifiably sanitized and largely bloodless character of the hostilities in the so-called classic trilogy is intensified by the nature of the *simulated violence* in *TPM*. The audience is distanced from the violence and reduced to being voyeurs of the violent spectacle. The machines of war of the Trade Federation's and the Republic's constructed warriors, digitally animated as they are, accentuate this sense of simulated hyperreality, a violence that is gamed rather than fought and bled in. Accordingly, the catastrophic *consequences* of the violence are rarely displayed. So in *ANH* Luke expends little energy in grieving the brutal loss of his aunt and uncle (does their death come as a bit of a relief to him?); Obi-Wan is less slain by Vader than exalted into an eternally universal presence; Luke's best friend Biggs is killed in the Yavin dogfight, yet the young man's own postbattle mood is *wholly* a jubilant one; none of the main characters is the victim of violent death in the classic trilogy; Anakin Skywalker is redeemed by his violent action; even the terrible slaying of Qui-Gon in *TPM* somewhat loses its emotional resonance because of the film's emphasis on a victorious ending.

We are furthermore spared seeing the consequences for ordinary citizens of large-scale warfare and the violent overthrow of the galactic civil authority.

One might suggest that the *SW* movies are designed for children and that portraying the notion that war is hell would be too gruesome and emotionally disturbing for a young age group. But this defense fails for the simple reason that, *unless it is shown to be morally questionable* (and that, presumably, is something most children could relate to on some level), *violence is rendered part of the everyday, "natural" fabric of existence*—at the very least, *not a bad thing*, and, at most, the (only) path to redemption.

Just a Good War?

A second version of the broadly construed "good war" sensibility is most familiar and palatable to many in the West in the form of the just war tradition. Its most common appeal lies in the claim that war is justifiable when performed in self-defense against an aggressor. This underpins much in *SW*. For instance, the Jedi defend the lives of the three due to be executed by Dooku (*AOTC*), the Jedi defend the democratic Republic (*AOTC* and *ROTS*), and the Rebel Alliance defends the Good against the aggressive tyranny of the Empire. So Yoda instructs Luke in the way of the Force: "A Jedi uses the Force for knowledge and defense, never for attack." "Defense" is a key notion here, and soon we will have to ask, "Defense of what?"

This protective disposition is embodied in the character of Obi-Wan, who can declare, "There are alternatives to fighting." Even when he is forced into battle, the weapon he and his Jedi brethren use, and the combat form he in particular practices in wielding it, is essentially defensive—the more deflective and defensive combat-Form III of Ataru and the patient form of Soresu. According to Expanded Universe Clone War literature, only Mace Windu, his former student Depa Billaba, and Sora Bulq have ever mastered Vaapad combat-Form VII, which is dangerously close to the *aggressive stance of a Sith*, and significantly both Depa and Sora fall into the dark side. When handing Anakin's lightsaber to Luke in *ANH,* Obi-Wan describes it as "an elegant weapon for a more civilized age." Of course we should question the identification of civilization with any form of violence and of weaponry with elegance, especially when we compare it to the graceful style of, for example, the landscape and architecture of Naboo's Theed city. Nevertheless, this talk places the Jedi firmly in the context of chivalrous notions of the knightly warrior and thereby enables them and their lightsaber weapons to express a *defensive sensibility*. And this contrasts sharply with the mechanized and aggressive violence of the blaster or the Death Star's cannon, weapons that can deal death at a distance. As Lucas argues, "The lightsaber became the symbol of that humane way of conducting your life even in that worst possible way which is protecting yourself by killing someone."[31] Obi-Wan's, it would seem, is a modest vision of violence—of a most limited, emotionally controlled, and restrained kind. Is this why, despite the three recorded victory celebrations, there is no sense of the good characters reveling in the deaths of the enemy? That reserve, of course, contrasts with Sidious's visible delight when unleashing Force-Lightning on Luke (*ROTJ*) and Mace (*ROTS*) and when informing Vader that this former Jedi had killed his own wife. The Jedi appear to echo the sentiments of the Tao: "Weapons are the tools of fear." Consequently, "a decent man will avoid them" unless compelled to use them out of dire necessity.[32] Even then, the Tao continues, they will be used "only with the utmost restraint" since a person's "enemies are not demons, but human beings like himself." As a result, the person-at-arms will neither "rejoice in victory" nor "delight in the slaughter of men" but be filled with sorrow and compassion.

So Yoda's response to a rather glib sounding Obi-Wan in *AOTC* is unmistakably haunting and prescient: "Victory! Victory you say! Master Obi-Wan, not victory. The shroud of the dark side has fallen. Begun the Clone War has." Even the Luke who *begins* with a macho sense of the hero myth has to be brought up short by Yoda (*ESB*). The fact that he can ask, "Is the dark side stronger?" indicates just how difficult it is for him to move away from thinking in terms of sheer power, echoing Vader's response to Admiral Motti over "the power of the Force" (*ANH*). Luke's whole sensibility requires to be "unlearned" and therefore transformed in a conversion of his moral imagination.

In this perspective, violent conflict can be seen as always a tragic possibility in a morally messy universe. It is a disruption of the prior and original peace of the old Republic, and as such it perverts and destroys the proper possibilities for the true peace. True peace is not the mere absence of conflict but the good and nonpossessive relations that the virtuous Jedi life of service exemplifies. As Mace declares of the Jedi Order, "We are keepers of the peace, not soldiers" (*AOTC*). In this sense, there is even something fundamentally wrong with using language of the "good" or the "just" to depict violence. Such language at the very least rhetorically masks the *tragic catastrophe that war is* and may even lead further to "the satanic doctrine that war is inevitable and therefore justified, good, and even unavoidable. This rhetoric can discourage more strenuous efforts in the search for peace by dulling and constraining the imagination, which then resorts all too quickly to military solutions before all other options have been *honestly* exhausted."[33] In this context, it is significant that until the creation of the Grand Army of Clone Troopers (*AOTC*) the Republic had no professional standing army, nor did the Naboo in *TPM*, relying instead on volunteers and a handful of dedicated security personnel.

Anger, fear, hate, aggression—all those traits that are conducive to generating violence—characterize the dark side (Yoda, *ESB*). This is why the Jedi who resort to such unrestrained belligerence suffer for their actions. Anakin's aggressiveness, for instance, culminates in his losing his right hand to Dooku (*AOTC*), a fate that similarly befalls Luke when he takes the initiative by hastening to battle Vader (*ESB*). In this way the saga can expose the problems of appealing to "necessary violence." After all, in *TPM* and *AOTC* the violence is the product of the self-serving political machinery of the manipulative and dominating Sidious, aided and abetted by the greed-motivated, profit-seeking big business of the Neimoidian Trade Federation. In a profound sense, then, the saga suggests something of a *presumption against war*—or better, given that this is still too negative a way of expressing the Jedi ethic, a *presumption for peace*.

Of course, the fact that Yoda and Obi-Wan act as *combative* generals in the Clone Wars suggests they must have felt that there was no alternative to fighting, that conflict was the last available possibility, once all other possibilities involving nonmilitary intervention had been ruled out. This more prudential path to war as the absolute last resort, the "exceptional case," is nevertheless a very dark and tragic one fraught with all kinds of seen and unseen dangers, and therefore it is to be handled with the greatest care and sensitivity.[34] Yoda admits to Mace the troubling nature of this, when the only options left are to arrest and possibly execute Palpatine/Sidious and consequently assume control of the Senate momentarily in order to secure a peaceful transition. Only with a heavy heart does he reluctantly agree to sanction the coup. Moreover, Anakin intensely struggles when ordered by Palpatine to execute the defeated Dooku, precisely because he recognizes the darkness of assassinating even one so dark (*ROTS*). Just such a sensibility is expressed in Gandalf's warning to Frodo in *The Fellowship of the Ring*: "Be not too eager to deal out death in the name of justice, fearing for your own safety. Even the wise cannot see all ends"—nor, we should add, the beginning or middle of evil.

The saga does not provide any clear-cut suggestions of when a war can be "just," even when the sense of the phrase "just war" is properly qualified. Indeed, if we follow the course of the Jedi Order's annihilation and Anakin's tragic fall, even the picture of what justice means in relation to conflict becomes somewhat complicated, with blindness and bad judgment affecting all those who are involved in various ways. After all, the Jedi Order is unwittingly complicit in its own destruction. Nevertheless, the Jedi ethical code of coresponsibility and interdependency in the Force might suggest that the only justifiable reason for violence is as the last available option for *serving the life of all others*. That would mean that violence has to be *limited*, so as to create space for the restoration of peace and reconciliation. Jedi wisdom is consequently in a position to ask just what kind of society we would have to live in, and what kind of people we would have to become, if we were to relate to each other in peaceful ways. So, given the broader theological context of the Jedi version of just war reflection, in the making of the good symbiotic life together in and through the Force, there is something distinctly perverse about using the criteria to decide flatly on a moment in time without casting our attention back to what has led to the terrible point. The reason war seems to be *inevitable*, or the *only* alternative in certain situations, has largely to do with the kind of society in which we live and the type of people we are.

Had the Jedi taken more seriously this presumption for peace in *AOTC*, the Clone Wars may have been avoided, for as Republic Senator Padmé Amidala from Naboo observes, "This war represents a failure to listen" (*AOTC* deleted scene). To her mind, not all the diplomatic avenues had been exhausted—indeed they could not have been, given Darth Sidious/Palpatine's manipulation of both the Separatist Confederacy and the Republic. Instead the Jedi Council and the majority in the Republic Senate, blind to the truth of the conditions that had taken the galaxy to that terrible point, allow themselves too easily and uncritically to function almost as Palpatine's attack dog by swiftly acting in practical support for the Republic's war cause. And the result? First, a notable falling-out among Jedi who actively resist their call to war (as noted in some Expanded Universe Clone Wars literature) and the near annihilation of the Jedi Order itself. Is maintaining a political structure, and therefore resisting political separatism, a cause worthy of killing and dying for? How does supporting it compare with the commitment to maintaining and, as far as possible, resisting taking the life of any person? The Jedi, even with their more prudential move to war as the seeming last resort, do not really ask these questions, and this failure significantly aids the unfolding tragedy.

In this regard Pollock discovers, through interviewing Randall Kleiser, an actor in Lucas's early student film *Freiheit*, that "Lucas disliked USC students who felt it necessary to die for one's country to defend democracy."[35] After all, despite the hype of the rhetoric, what about democracy in itself is worth killing for? Do most Western appeals to democracy and freedom not have all too little sense of the positive values of human flourishing? Are they not consequently negative and reactionary? As Hauerwas argues, "Freedom [talk] is an abstraction [and distraction]. . . . The crucial question is what kind of freedom and what do we wish to do with it?"[36] When that is the case, do freedom and democracy not become little more than principles abstracted from concrete people and in that way enable nation-states to continue to exist at the expense of many of their citizens? The same goes for talk of "peace." As Augustine astutely recognizes, while "peace is the desired end of war," this is usually little more than the false peace of distorted creatures, not the peace of God.[37] Luceno's novel on *The Rise of Darth Vader* makes the distortion of the Imperial peace clear when Vader asserts to Senator Bail Organa the illegality of anti-Imperial protests on Alderaan: "Harmony is the ideal of the New Order, Senator, not dissension. . . . The Emperor would not be pleased . . . by your willingness to allow others to display their distrust."[38] And the sense of this is further revealed in a declaration made by the newly self-proclaimed Emperor:

> By bringing the entire Galaxy under one law, one language, and the enlightened guidance of one individual, the corruption that plagued the Republic in its later years will never take root. . . . A strong and growing military will ensure the rule of law. . . . Under the Empire's New Order, our most cherished beliefs will be safeguarded. We will defend our ideals by force of arms. We will give no ground to our enemies and will stand together against attacks from within or without. Let the enemies of the Empire take heed: those who challenge Imperial resolve will be destroyed.[39]

The criteria (right intention, just cause, and proper authority) normally drawn out of Augustine's reflections, via Thomas Aquinas (1225–74), for considering what makes a war "just" actually exert heavy theological pressure on the justifiability of any and every particular war. Thus the just war concept in Augustine, when properly understood, becomes more a witness to the good order of God's creating (albeit a good order that in a fallen world may very occasionally require certain forceful methods to restore the way to that reordering). Augustine, in the words of Padmé, "will not condone a course of action that will lead us to war" (*TPM*).

Peace beyond Violence

By the prequels this suspicion of violence in the name of the Force (or the Good) comes to look shrewd. As mentioned in chapter 5, some neoconservatives have expressed dismay that *ROTS* appears to be so antiwar and even anti-Bush in ethos. Firstly, Lucas denies the claim that the movie's content was deliberately shaped with post-9/11 American foreign policy in mind; its story was composed much earlier. And secondly, *SW*'s ethos would remain ethically challenging whether the warring president was George W. Bush or someone else. Whatever the origins of these ideas, the classic trilogy, and perhaps also *TPM*, suggest that it is right to overthrow oppressive government. Yet *ROTS* makes profoundly clear the catastrophic potential for tragedy in even this. It is in this complex political life that we see the diplomatic sensibilities of Padmé preventing her from rushing in with others to commend growing militarism (*AOTC*) and making her worry about the conduct of the subsequent war (*ROTS*). Hers is the voice of reason, of diplomacy, the voice that *ROTS* eventually suggests is not only the most insightful but perhaps the wisest. (However, by the time of *ROTS* there is a feeling among her critics in the Senate that she is turning a blind eye to the increasingly oppressive climate on Coruscant and the growing centralization of power in Palpatine's political office.)

Toward the end of *ROTJ* Luke's journey seems to have moved him closer to a pacifism that is an *active* nonviolence. Properly understood, pacifism is not a negative term indicating an *absence of action*, a *not doing* (cf. Matt. 5:39). The common misunderstanding of pacifism as nonaction parallels the way peace is generally understood in negative terms as the *absence of conflict*, not a purposeful action as such. Luke is not fighting for some abstract peace, freedom, sovereign autonomy, abstract notion of civilization, or even a set of principles abstracted from persons. Instead Luke's peace is a *positive doing of what is just and right* or doing that which makes for *properly peaceful relations*. His is a struggle that always "take[s] sides," resonating with a resistance that has teeth and a sharp bite and therefore cannot trivialize or sentimentalize peace by imagining that all would be well if only we could act a bit nicer to each other.[40]

Wink observes that "violence is simply not radical enough, since it generally changes only the rulers but not the rules."[41] Those people who have been violated and seek restitution often become, when the chance arises, themselves violators of their abusers. Victims here are made in the image of their enemy and perpetuate the violence through an ethos of revenge rather than restitution and reconciliation. And so we hear Padmé urge the Republic's Senators, "Wake up. . . . If you offer the Separatists violence they can only show violence in return. Many will lose their lives, all will lose their freedom" (*AOTC* deleted scene). The Jedi training in virtue aims not so much to change the rulers—unless the situation in the end demands that—but more radically to change the way people relate to one another. In other words, it aims to change the people who act with, toward, and against other people. As Campbell rightly observes using Christian imagery, "The hero of yesterday becomes the tyrant of tomorrow, unless he crucifies *himself* today."[42] This is why Yoda's lessons for knighthood consist not of better swordplay or martial arts but of training in humility, patience, tolerance, calmness, and trustfulness. In this way, the virtues of the good life have the capacity to work for peace at an earlier and more proactive phase rather than merely dealing with the symptoms of conflictual relations (war). The virtues can reveal and subvert the very causes of state and interpersonal conflict.

Lucas comments that Luke "has the capacity to become Darth Vader simply by using hate and fear and using weapons, as opposed to using compassion and caring and kindness."[43] But by refusing to succumb to these values and his earlier mood of "reactive justice," he rejects patterning his way in the world on relations molded by discord. Instead he acts *restoratively* in loving compassion for his most bitter of foes. His is ultimately a radically different mode of conflict resolution from the reactive one of simple retributive justice. What kind of conflict can be fought by one who is beyond greed, who does not give hate free reign to determine action (see Matt. 5:21–22), but who does not weakly capitulate under the temptation to self-aggrandizement?

Finally, he tosses his lightsaber away and refuses to participate any further in the conflict, a conflict that the Emperor has in any case specifically engineered to entice Luke to the dark side. His "way of the cross," so to speak, is his preparation to sacrifice himself rather than do evil. Incidentally, there is a parallel here with his mother (and, to a lesser extent, since he is silent in the scene, his father) in a deleted scene from *AOTC*. On Geonosis Dooku demands that the captured Naboo Senator join the alliance of rebellious Separatist factions or be executed, and the morally upright Padmé self-sacrificially chooses the second option. "In short, Luke chooses to die because he has at last comprehended the heart of Yoda's teachings: that the universe runs by love and that love should pervade all thought and action."[44] Even if the Emperor does succeed in taking his life (which, of course, he cannot, due to Vader's timely intervention), he cannot in the end take away Luke's obedience to the "ways of the Force" (Obi-Wan to Luke, *ANH*). But more than that, significantly the young Jedi's "nonviolent approach" to, and compassion for, Vader actually "so stirs the conscience of the opponent that reconciliation becomes a reality."[45]

Conclusion: The Fullness of Peace

While *SW*, and particularly *ANH*, has frequently been read as glorifying violence, and we have had cause to distinguish between two particular versions of this good war idea, in the end its mood is shaped by a Jedi wisdom that subverts the very sources of violent conflict. Violence comes from somewhere, and the Jedi are trained to resist and deal with the very places from which it comes and to negotiate justly when other Republicans fail to do the same. The parallels developed through the prequel trilogy between Anakin and his son, Luke, are striking, particularly at the point where Anakin chooses the other-violating Sith way of oppressive peace, while Luke, under Yoda's guidance, moves toward deconstructing the very notion of heroism, finally offering himself sacrificially and nonviolently. Seen in this redemptive light, talk of *fighting for peace* looks radically and life-affirmingly different from that myth of redemptive violence that is commonly read into *SW*. The saga possesses something of the quality of the peace affirmed by Augustine as the "respect for and development of human life . . . [through] the assiduous practice of fraternity . . . [and] 'the tranquility of order.'" This "peace is the work of justice and the effect of charity."[46] That indeed is the Jedi way, the way that the aged Jedi Master Yoda discloses in the Dagobah swamp during his first encounter with Luke (*ESB*): "Wars not make one great." Wars may not, but the just life of self-giving service or charity does.

This is where *SW* at its best possesses radical potential to witness to a set of nonviolent values that understand personhood or personal identity to be properly relational and persons to be truly interdependent. One inspired by such a vision will attempt to contribute to the flourishing of a freedom that is not individualistic, that is primarily creative and not reactive, and that does not discriminate against others on the basis of race, class, gender, nationality, and so on. Only that kind of society and the people who form it will find it easier to relate to others in ways that do not need to resort to violence and thus provide a challenge to the very dynamics and conditions that make wars possible. This would make better sense of appeals to peace, justice, and reconciliation by Christians who claim to follow a crucified Savior than those who entertain the sentiment advertised on some Midwestern billboards in 1975: "God, guns, and guts: that's what made America great!"[47]

Chapter Seven

Feeling the Force

The Ethics of the Good Life

*W*hen Christians talk of "salvation," all too often they slip into ways of thinking that are both world-denying and sentimental. Particularly with regard to the second of these, the rhetoric of salvation has more to do with assuaging beleaguered souls than with encouraging the virtue of living well. In this form the Gospel is understood to be God's gift for the purpose of bestowing eternal life (here understood as life after death) to the individual believer. There are several theological problems with this kind of perspective, most notably that it is otherwordly and heavenly minded. But because chapter 8 will deal with that more fully, this chapter will instead point to a couple of other problems.

First, this perspective tends to suggest that salvation is a *saving from* much more than it is a *saving to*. In this way salvation is troublingly preoccupied "with sin, to the detriment of . . . the all-encompassing presence of the Spirit within the world[,] . . . of creation and embodied existence as God's gift . . . [and] the divine purpose of the restoration of all things."[1] Of course, the very fact that its mind is focused on heaven (imagined to be *a place* that is *not here*) means that these Christian minds are not focused on this world or on its healing. But it is one thing for God radically to overwhelm and transform sin and quite another simply to announce that God avoids the sinful conditions that dehumanize, distort, and despoil the good that God has created. Jesus' own way of living and dying does not take his followers *out of the world* and simply save them *from* sin, evil, suffering, and so on but instead saves them *for* good (meaning faithful) living *in* this world, God's world (John 1:3; Col. 1:15). We should remember that Christ's raised body remains a *body*, even if it is a transformed body (1 Cor. 15), and this has to do theologically with the divine judgment that *vindicates God's creating.* This gospel does not allow for any "escape pod" approach that resists the world qua world but instead resists the *sinful values and*

117

structures, the manifold injustices, and the dynamics that generate them in this world, in order to refer all things to the Good that God, Creator and Redeemer, is. After all, the Latin term for salvation, *salus*, has to do with being well or in good health.

Second, perhaps even more crucially, the otherworldly account encourages, and in turn is popularly sustained by, a morally ambiguous sense of self-concern. As a youth, Lucas responded keenly to the rituals of a local Lutheran church, the congregation of his parents' housekeeper. He later admitted to Dale Pollock that it had been "interesting and different" from his own Methodist upbringing. Nonetheless, he was disturbed by the Christianities he was familiar with, troubled particularly by what he saw as the unacknowledged selfishness of their message: Christian "self-centered religion."[2] In contrast to both this kind of Christianity and the moral cynicism of post-Vietnam America, Lucas deigned to "introduce a kind of basic morality," initially doing so through *ANH*'s confident moral consciousness.[3] Pollock comments that "Lucas was imposing his values on the rest of the world, but he felt they were the *right* values." The language of imposition here is misleading, since it has connotations of coercion; Lucas only *attempts* to *persuade* others without denying them the *space* and *ability* to make their *own* responses. Yet how can Lucas assume that his values are the *right* values? Our discussion concerning his pluralist approach in chapter 2 suggests that these are assumed and untested humanistic values, values that themselves have a Christian background. While we will not critique this any further, we should at least recognize that these assumptions need to be critically tested. If nothing else, we can recognize again that "Lucas offers more than just escapist entertainment; he gives us a vision of what should be."[4] This vision is particularly interesting since it challenges the kinds of ethics that promote and are concerned with the self while at the same time it imagines ways to resist those self-understandings and attitudes that ultimately order and sustain oppressive social relations.

Responsibility and Service:
"Judge Me by My Size, Do You?"

The Lies of Truthful Jedi and the Truth of the Lying Sith

What separates the Sith (formerly "dark Jedi") from the Jedi is neither their ability to use the power of the Force nor their origins. Rather, their difference has to do with their motivations and moral character. Put starkly, they are different because they have strikingly diverging approaches to how they should live, work, and be responsible agents in and through the Force. When it comes to the matter of the lying Jedi, this fundamental difference must be remembered. Augustine explains that "it seems certain that every lie is a sin, though it makes a great difference with what intention and on what subject one lies. . . . But in the case of men who have reached this standard [of goodness], it is not the deceit, but their good intention, that is justly praised, and sometimes even rewarded."[5] In other words, the difference lies in the goal of the lying, as Shanti Fader argues:

> Truth-telling for the Sith has nothing to do with increasing wisdom and understanding; it's just another tool to help them gain power or hurt their opponents. Ironically, in speaking more literal, factual truths, they lose the higher spirit of truth—that integrity that comes when honesty is practised for the sake of illuminating the human soul. . . . The lesson of the lying Jedi is that truth depends on perspective, on intention, on intuitive understanding, and finally on a compassion that's willing to see the whole picture and not just a single "point of view."[6]

Obi-Wan's lie to Luke is designed to shelter the young man from a harsh reality that the Jedi Master feels he is as yet ill-equipped to handle. With experience and understanding Luke becomes better able to face the truth later and is therefore better able to resist the threat that it may pose to his well-being. The lie, then, is deliberately construed *for another's benefit*. An example of Jedi mind control for the good of another occurs in the Outlander gambling club in Coruscant's underlevels (*AOTC*). Obi-Wan is offered some lethal narcotics ("death-sticks") by a slythmonger, but through mental manipulation the Jedi forces the dealer actively to admit, "I want to go home and rethink my life." In stark contrast, Palpatine's tricks serve only to vault *himself* into power. In other words, in his deception of others, Palpatine differs from the Jedi who also deceive not in degree but qualitatively *in kind*.

The Sith use others to do their bidding and in this way come to adopt an irreversible and almost godlike position. Consequently, as *ANH*'s novelization makes clear, the kind of rule Palpatine engages in as Emperor separates him from being one of the people, and hence "the cries of the people for justice did not reach his ears."[7] In stark contrast, the Jedi values imply that authentic existence is relational at its core. Their training in virtue always has as its end promoting peace and justice for others (*all* others), and they do this in a loyal service that is free from conceit, fear, and personal ambition.

GARY PUBLIC LIBRARY

Living Symbiotically

This theme of good relations pervades the *SW* movies. Lucas is being guided no doubt by Campbell, who, despite his tendencies toward individualism especially in his later work, claims in *Hero* that "the totality—the fullness of man—is not in the separate member, but in the body of the society as a whole. . . . From his group he has derived his techniques of life, in the language in which he thinks, the ideas on which he thrives; through the past of that society descended the genes that built his body."[8]

Hanson and Kay's comment that "the fate of the Star Wars galaxy will hinge upon the individual, the microcosm, not the group" is distinctly misleading.[9] The relational sense of the saga vitally exposes and deconstructs the kinds of individualisms that exalt *the* hero in the myths of the modern Western world. It is the Emperor who plays the role of the individualist; he even implies that Luke's faith in his friends is actually his weakness (*ROTJ*). While he is subsequently shown to be drastically mistaken, his Sith instincts are the antithesis of symbiotic living. The Sith are unable and unwilling to love, to have compassion, or to engage in the project of peacefully creating unity between those who are different. They simply understand life in terms not of the Good of good relations ("relations of difference") but only of what is good for them, and they use others to achieve that (homogenization or "relations of the same"). Therefore, while the classic trilogy draws readily on hero mythology, it does not succumb to the myth of the great individual unleashed and unencumbered—a John Rambo of *Rambo II* and *III* dispensing good old American justice to the evil "Commies" in defiance of complicitous bureaucratic American political forces.

One of the things going awry in the cultural celebration of the hero is that heroism is exalted for its own sake: the hero is adored simply for being a hero. Consequently the means (the heroic action), rather than the end or the goal of the hero's action (the people or cause for whom the hero acts), becomes what is celebrated. We have seen that to a significant extent Luke's imagination seems to have been shaped by just this sort of hero myth. But Yoda exposes his frivolous and greedy yearning for excitement and adventure—not entirely dissimilar from Anakin's love of battle and susceptibility to the flattery of popular adulation—for lacking virtue: "A Jedi craves not these things." Luke, as Yoda admits in *ESB*, still has much to learn.

There is another problem in this type of hero myth. It tends to depend on a prior conflict and is thus a reactive notion. In other words, situations arise that enable someone *subsequently* to act heroically. In this form the "hero" cannot be a concept that is morally creative or proactive in and of itself.

GARY PUBLIC LIBRARY

In contrast, *SW*'s vision is a creatively socialistic one, celebrating the making of a people together. This is why there are many identifiable forms of dependence involved in the development of the so-called hero of the classic trilogy. For instance, in *ANH* Luke learns through the *guidance of another*, Obi-Wan Kenobi (and through Yoda in *ESB*); he is *dependent upon* the roguish Han Solo in order to escape from the Death Star and finally to save him from Darth Vader; he feels a strong *attraction to* Princess Leia; and he is also *dependent upon* the contributions of Rebel squadrons in the Battle of Yavin, as well as on both the mechanics who have serviced his X-Wing fighter and the astromech droid R2D2. As Nathan says, "While much of '70s Hollywood—the type that *Star Wars* is supposed to have extinguished—brilliantly exposed the fragility of relationships, *Star Wars* reminded us that those relationships are the most important thing in the universe."[10]

This is given a theological shape by talk of the interconnection of all things, the symbiotic chains of all life-forms in the Force, which is why knowing the ways of the Force is necessary to setting life in an authentic relation to all things. To exploit any aspect of that arrangement for personal—or national, we could add—gain is to risk disturbing the complex and delicate balance of the web of mutual relations. Whatever affects one affects all indirectly. This idea makes particular sense in our own situation, shaped as it is by a global market economy and global communication technologies. For instance, before I even leave for work in the morning, I am beholden to a great many others around the world (for my Taiwanese manufactured alarm clock; Colombian coffee; cereal packaged in Poland; French and Brazilian shower products; Indonesian produced clothes, and so on).

But there is even more to it than this. Some particularly sinister possibilities are created by the very matrix of my relations: perhaps without knowing it, I could invest in banks and companies involved in arms sales to third-world countries; eat ice cream from corporations that abuse poor women and their babies in Asia or that lend vast sums of money to poor African countries at unrepayable interest levels; holiday in areas that for the sake of the tourist trade evict tenants and destroy villages; use heating energy and car fuel that contribute to environmental damage; choose goods from manufacturers that exploit laborers in order to keep my purchase price low; and so on. Everything I do has some kind of effect on someone else, and much of it is detrimental to his or her well-being. The ethics of consumerism either blinds us to that fact or subdues the potential for pangs of conscience since, as Richard Foster observes, our grasping at possessing things has "a way of crowding out much interest in civil rights or inner-city poverty or the starved masses of

India. Greed has a way of severing the cords of compassion."[11] Consumerism tends to become a "weapon of mass distraction," and ironically the consumerism of the movies' fans for all things *SW* may well distract them from the moral sensibility of the saga.

Cloning and Character: The Virtue of Responsible Persons

The use of the cloning biotechnology discussed earlier (chapter 3) is interesting in this regard (*AOTC, ROTS*). The Republic's senators are unwittingly manipulated by Palpatine in the Clone Army Creation Act (Jar Jar himself proposes granting the Chancellor emergency powers, the very powers that are first utilized to create the Grand Army of the Republic). And yet we cannot let these senators off too lightly, since their support tragically contributes to the Republic's downfall. But they are ignorant, because they are manipulated by the dark shroud Sidious casts over events. So should we not return a plea of "diminished responsibility" here? But questions of responsibility do not begin and end there. We need to trace back their networks of responsibility and insight and ask some difficult questions: What kind of society falls prey to self-flattery, to the need to instrumentalize life, to supporting the security provided by totalitarian regimes, and to turning a blind eye to abuses? Martin Luther King announced that we have a moral responsibility to be intelligent:[12] "Nothing in all the world is more dangerous than sincere ignorance and conscientious stupidity."[13] People too readily and lazily appeal to ignorance in order to let themselves, their society, culture, nation, and so on, off the hook. Perhaps they do so because they have not developed the type of moral character required to think carefully and proactively about the interrelation of things. In *SW* Padmé alone seems to be well equipped suspiciously to interrogate the swift drive to war. Ignorance is not an excuse for the mess the world is in—whether we are ignorant or not, the hungry still need to be fed, the exploited still cry out for justice, the lonely still weep for company, and so on. Our ignorance will not help them. But does that make us any less responsible for them and their plight?

Luke comes to learn the truth of the authentic relationships of all things, and his relational sensibility encourages him to forgo the completion of his training in order to rush nobly—but rather rashly, it would seem from both Yoda and Obi-Wan's warnings and from subsequent events—to attempt to save his friends at his own expense (*ESB*). This act of self-giving echoes his later self-offering for his enemy Vader (*ROTJ*). Luke, on the one hand, may be driven here by affection rather than practical wisdom—after all, he is evidently not yet ready to face Vader—but, on the other hand, he is morally not constrained by pragmatic considerations of possible success or the desire to protect himself. Instead he merely wants to do what is right, and in this he has come a long way, from his petulant teen years, in the development of a virtuous Jedi life. Lucas intriguingly does not read the scene in terms of Luke facing a tragic dilemma. He believes that Luke is taking "the easy route": "It's pivotal [that] Luke doesn't have patience, he doesn't want to finish his training, and he's being succumbed by his emotional feelings for his friends rather than the practical feelings of 'I've got to get this job done before I can actually save them.'"[14]

Significantly Han Solo also undergoes something of a transformation of outlook through the course of the classic trilogy, and accordingly he is a much more interesting and important character than Harrison Ford, his actor, perceived: "Han Solo flies a spaceship, and shouts his mouth off, and that's about it."[15] The Han of *ANH* is cynical and full of himself. In the first place, he is self-reliant: "Look, your worshipfulness," he asserts to Leia, "I take orders from just one person, me!" Accordingly, he has difficulty recognizing that he is dependent on others in Leia's rescue from the Death Star. After all, crucial in this event are Obi-Wan, who disables the tractor beam and sacrifices himself in battle with Vader; Luke, Chewbacca, and Leia, who take part in the shootouts; C3PO and R2D2, who shut down the trash compactor; and Luke, who helps destroy the *Falcon*'s four pursuing TIE fighters. Yet Han thinks of the rescue as if it is his own achievement: "Not a bad bit of rescuing, huh? You know, sometimes I amaze even myself." Of course, his work for, and recent debt to, Jabba the Hutt reveals that he cannot be utterly free from commitment to, and dependency on, others.

In the second place, he is essentially self-concerned. He initially refuses to help liberate the soon-to-be-executed Leia and at the outset also evades aiding the soon-to-be-destroyed Rebellion at the Battle of Yavin. On this second occasion Han even tempts Luke to forgo his own chosen responsibilities and instead join the lucrative smuggling enterprise. A disappointed Luke scathingly enjoins, "Well, take care of yourself, Han. I guess it's what you're best at, isn't it?" The older man seems to reject the possibility of being responsible to anyone or anything but himself and his own greed, as is clearly evident in his rhetorical question: "What good's a reward if you ain't around to use it?" Precisely because "money is all that" he loves (Leia to Han), he is able to be enlisted in the cause of rescuing the damsel in distress. It is noteworthy that by this stage Han does not need the money to "save my neck" (Han to Chewie); the negotiated payment for delivery of Obi-Wan, Luke, and the droids safely to Alderaan had already seen to that. Han's greed later prompts Leia damningly to observe to Luke, "Your friend is quite a mercenary. I wonder if he really cares about anything, or anybody."

Nonetheless, unlike Palpatine's rapacious desire for power and Jabba's particularly disgusting and loathsome consumptiveness, Han's loyalty to Chewbacca and his burgeoning fraternal affection for Luke suggest some deeply hidden capacity to care for others. So while the smuggler's process of transformation is as slow as Luke's own (in the midst of a continued display of egoistic self-interest), he returns in the *Falcon* to aid Luke at the crucial moment in the assault on the Death Star; demonstrates self-sacrifice in risking his life on Hoth to rescue his younger companion (*ESB*); falls in love with Leia; dignifiedly allows himself to be carbon frozen on Bespin in the hope that his friends may be freed; and eventually becomes a general in the Rebel Alliance responsible for destroying the shield generator on the moon of Endor (*ROTJ*). It is particularly through his relationships with Luke and Leia that Han comes to see the importance of causes greater than himself and to participate in the goals to which they have devoted themselves. "Han has been transformed from an arrogant and self-centered smuggler into a moral leader."[16]

But, as we saw with Anakin, with the relations between sentient creatures comes the possibility of moral difficulty and tragic dilemma. Richard Dees believes that the Lando Calrissian of *ESB* provides a tragic illustration of conflicting duties to his responsible relations. A kind of Han Solo character initially, this gambling scoundrel and rogue has become the responsible administrative leader of the Bespin mining colony. Yet he *betrays* Han and Leia. Dees argues that Lando has been given no choice but to become the betrayer: he is responsible to the Bespin mining colony and accordingly acts against his friend in order to resist tyrannical Imperial control over the business and its people. Lando's choice is seemingly the utilitarian one of the greatest good for the greatest number. "To his credit," Dees observes, "when he realizes that his goals are hopeless, he does what he can both to evacuate as much of the colony as possible and to save Leia, Chewie, and Threepio from Vader. After losing his colony he doesn't think of himself at all."[17] He compassionately gives himself for others and later actively attempts to right the wrong of his earlier Faustian pact with Vader (for which he could hardly be accused of being morally culpable, according to Dees). "Far from being a narrow egoist, Lando is in fact one of the most morally courageous figures in the *Star Wars* saga."[18]

This, however, is not the stamp Lucas puts on the situation. Lando is "a foil for Han," a type of Han from *ANH*.[19] The important issue is whether

Lando truly feels himself to have no moral choice or—and this is more likely—is merely willing to give up the life of his old friend Solo (and the lives of his friends) for simple quantifiable economic considerations. In this second possibility he is not too far removed from those who speak of human casualties in military calculations as collateral damage, evaluating people's worth in dehumanized terms. Lando's actions suggest that his so-called friend's well-being is less valuable than his business enterprise; Han's life consequently becomes a commodifiable product, part of a tragic business transaction. The Luke who rushes to save his friends, even if he dies trying, and the Han who is carbon frozen are the important foils here.

The theology of *SW* is difficult to pin down—as it should be, given that it is not an explicitly theologically constructed vision (chapter 2). But the interconnectedness of all life does seem to be the *fruit of the Force* in some way and is therefore exalted as the movies' Good. In this there is a distinct echo of the theme of God's creative blessing on the delicate balance of interconnected created life. But the image of the Force lacks a theology of creation that can proclaim all life is good and valuable, precisely because the life-giving Force, by the evaluating hands of which all life comes, is good in itself. The Force lacks sufficient content to enable us to say something of the practical significance of the way God values all God's creatures. Nevertheless, the sense provided by the idea of the symbiosis in the Force does have this kind of role—life, *all* life, participates in and is participated in by the Force and is therefore valuable and to be served. The implication is that authentic value cannot be measured on the basis of contingent factors such as race (or species in *SW*), creed, intelligence, wealth, physical prowess, and so on. Nor do our responsibilities to others' lives become annulled when these others live in ways contrary to "the will of the Force"—which is one of the reasons Luke continues to hope for Vader/Anakin (chapter 8). Consequently, given the rich and dynamic notion of the delicate interrelation of all living things in and through the Force, it is little wonder that authentic Jedi virtue resists "the oppression of the Sith" (Mace, *ROTS*).

The relation that Luke is wholly unprepared for is the stunningly disclosed kinship with his still-living father (*ESB*). The value Luke places in family is now put in jeopardy, and his whole outlook on life is dramatically challenged. He struggles psychologically with whether to follow the path of his biological father, Vader (the Sith way), or that of his recently acquired surrogate father, Obi-Wan (the Jedi way). Just how far has he himself begun his own journey toward the broad road (see Matt. 7:13–14) of the dark side?

The Tempting Broad Road

Preachers on Jesus' testing in the desert (Matt. 4:1–11) often make the rather banal and supposedly comforting comment that he was tempted as we are (cf. Heb. 2:18). But the character of those temptations is hereby insufficiently studied. In these enticements Jesus refuses a certain kind of power and the means of acquiring it. In the temptation on the mountain (the third temptation) he is lured by the prospect that through his bowing down and worshiping the devil, all the nations could be his. His refusal to travel that path is not itself a denial of politics or power, as if the life he lives is not full of significance for the way public relations are conducted. Rather, it is a denial of a politics of self-interest that suppresses or manipulates the full personhood of others. Many of Jesus' Jewish contemporaries believed God's coming Messiah would employ an aggressive approach in forcefully liberating Judea from Roman occupation. Whatever Jesus' own conception of messiahship, it certainly was not this, which is perhaps why the Synoptic Gospel traditions (Matthew, Mark, and Luke) portray him as identifying himself more with the Suffering Servant of Isaiah than with the Messiah as such. In other words, he rejects a way of relating to others that would, in fact, be a denial of who he is. The way he rejects is the easier one, the one that could produce results and do so much more obviously and swiftly, but that would run roughshod over the people who would get in the way. Jesus is no utilitarian, reflecting morally on the greatest good for the greatest number. Nor does he entertain a realpolitik that in the name of being practical would make compromises over people's lives. He painfully engages in the hard work of building free relations with others. Jesus lives and dies wholly for others, opposing injustice through peacemaking justice, utilizing patient persuasion through the labor of argument and witness, rather than through dominating coercion. (That is also the import of the second temptation, the overwhelming appeal of the spectacular.)

Likewise Luke has to resist that "easier and more seductive" (Yoda, *ESB*) path to the dark side. And this learning to choose well, as his temperamental and frequently petulant behavior on Dagobah reveals, is long and arduous. His impatience continually brings temptations to quick and easy shortcuts. Crucially the virtue of patience is mentioned four times concerning Luke in the space of a few minutes in the movie. After all, prior to discovering his host's true Jedi identity, Luke cannot enjoy the hospitality offered out of desperation to quickly fulfill his task, while Yoda has been waiting for twenty-two or so years on the swamp planet of Dagobah for the young man's arrival. According to the aged Jedi Master's counsel, "A Jedi must have the deepest commitment, the most serious mind." In contrast, he observes concerning Luke: "All his life has he looked away to the future, to the horizon, never his mind on where he was, what he was doing. Adventure, excitement. A Jedi craves not these things. You are reckless." (The virtues of patience and self-giving do not seem to permeate many *SW* fans' values—Brooker tells of one who paid $1,500 to see *TPM* three days early.)[20] These are the traits of the dark side, the path that the impatient Anakin took (although, interestingly, the Lords of the Sith themselves, including Sidious, had displayed an inexhaustible self-restraining patience when waiting for a millennium before unmasking themselves). Luke demonstrates in the swamps of Dagobah that he has insufficiently given himself over to his training, improperly holding on to what he should be, according to Yoda, "unlearning." Just how close he comes to embracing the dark side in the path of his father is revealed through an important set of images.

First, there is what Yoda afterward calls "the failure of the cave"—the test of Luke's spirit. The Jedi Master advises the apprentice not to take in his weapons, since what is in the cave is "only what you take with you." But Luke, still caught in the thrall of the hero myth and the violent solution to the threat of the other, comes face-to-face with himself in a highly disturbing form—in the guise of Darth Vader himself. Even the hero can tread perilously close to the dark side. In fact, the evil enemy lies as much within as without.

Second, he dons dark robes in *ROTJ* and Force-chokes two Gamorrean guards in Jabba's palace, in a move that reflects Vader. Third, by the close of *ESB* Luke is forced by the loss of his right hand (the hand Anakin first lost in defeat by Dooku) to have a mechanical prosthesis surgically grafted on. The symbolic value of this is most evident when he stares in dismay at his prosthesis and at his opponent's own severed one after enragedly defeating Vader before the delighted Emperor in the second Death Star's throne room.

Fear Leads to the Dark Side

Hanson and Kay reveal just how little they understand the vice of anger, as well as that of pride, when they puzzle that "though these emotions sound evil, they are part of the human spirit."[21] However, pride, for instance, unless it is a pleasure taken in the well-being of others, has fundamentally to do with exalting oneself. This disposition can be contrasted with that of Obi-Wan, who displays the utmost humility when he refrains from listing his highly notable achievements, Jedi powers, and Force-prowess in *ANH*. It is precisely the Jedi Order's arrogant sense of superiority, self-righteousness, and indispensability to the Republic that makes it both blind to the Sith's reemergence and complicit finally in its own downfall. Their very pride weakens their ability critically to discern the signs of the times. "In some ways the Jedi had led a life of royalty. The order had been wealthy, privileged, entitled. *And that was why . . . [the Jedi] didn't see it coming*[,] . . .why so many of the Jedi had turned a blind eye to the trap Palpatine had been setting. Because they had refused to accept that such entitlement could ever come to an end."[22] Perhaps Palpatine's comment to Anakin that the Jedi are seeking to hold "onto power" is not too far from the truth, then. The question, *who watches the watchers?* is as relevant for the Jedi as for government itself.

To these vices we should add fear. But can fear not also be a virtue? For instance, had Anakin been more fearful of Count Dooku, he would not have foolishly rushed into a self-destructive charge, irresponsibly leaving Obi-Wan exposed to Dooku's power (*AOTC*). Similarly, can fear for others not be a morally energizing emotion? The context of Yoda's warning suggests that he has a certain sort of fear in mind. Partly he is discouraging Luke from being the type of person who is determined primarily by self-concern—the Empire exists through institutionalizing others' fear of it. But, more than this, fear is a quality that leads to the dark side itself. As discussed in chapter 3, the burden of fear extends not merely to the Emperor's citizens and the military officials who offend him, but importantly moves him too. Augustine observes that "many are miserable because they are in love with things that should not be loved."[23] So while the absolute object of his inappropriate love is himself, and accordingly his ability to have power and to wield that power over all others, he nonetheless fears not having enough power, and once he possesses absolute power, he ends up like Plagueis shackled to dreading its loss. To adapt the words of Boethius, while striking "fear into his subjects, [Palpatine] yet fears them more himself."[24] The connection between fear and love is important, as McCabe explains:

> Take as a picture of this condition children who in an obvious sort of way are deprived of love. They are insecure and defensive. They need to justify themselves all the time. They can't admit to being wrong. They constantly have to preserve their self-esteem by making excuses for themselves, by building up a self-flattering image of themselves. But all the time they live in fear.[25]

Quite simply, Palpatine does not experience love, either as something truly given to him or as something he is able to give to others. And this lovelessness creates the basic insecurity manifested in his self-securing "reign of [galactic] terror."[26] The Jedi are trained not to fear in this sense because the object or goal of their love is not themselves, and thus they can enjoy the Good for its own sake, not for the securing or promoting of their own position and status.

McCabe's point works particularly well in relation to Anakin. Noticeably one of the main ingredients in his tragedy is fear, his pathological fear of losing Padmé, and this reveals what he *really loves*. In the conversation between them on the transport ship taking them to Naboo (*AOTC*), Anakin recognizes that "attachment is forbidden" by the Jedi, presumably since with attachment comes the need to possess and the fear of loss of that possession. This is the spin that Yoda puts on it when he warns Anakin, "The shadow of greed, attachment is" (*ROTS*). The Padawan continues, "Compassion, which I would define as unconditional love, is central to a Jedi's life. So you might say we are encouraged to love." So far so good, for at least in word Anakin acknowledges the Jedi commitment to serving others in compassion. However, his later revelations of passionate love suggest that he conflates the passion for compassion and the passion of infatuation. His anxiety is less about what will happen to Padmé than about what the loss of his possession will do to him, his loss of being loved and giving love. His underlying worry is over what love will be returned to him, and in this way it is never truly a giving away of love at all. This looks more like the securing of contractual relations and impatience with contingency than the risk-laden and messy spontaneity of free persons whose only desire is the flourishing of the beloved herself.

Bortolin's observation reveals the heart of Anakin's problem: "Romantic love is infatuation for a particular person and is often wrapped up with selfish desires and needs that have nothing really to do with the person we believe we love."[27] Sounding just as much like Yoda, Teresa of Avila (1515–82) argues, "When we desire anyone's affection, we always seek it because of some interest, profit or pleasure of our own."[28] Anakin's love looks more like greedy and possessive self-gratification than self-renouncing self-giving. So even when he does give himself to his beloved Padmé, his gift has the egoistic quality Martin Luther King Jr. observed in much human behavior: "It is possible for one to be self-centered in his self-sacrifice."[29]

Anakin's love never matures from this, although he has not been helped by a Jedi code that forbiddingly identifies every form of romantic love with improper attachment. Is this asceticism itself not an improper expression of a Jedi fear: a fear "of the loss of self-control that comes to the 'I' of passionate love which is at the same time a 'We'"?[30] (It is not insignificant that according to the Expanded Universe literature concerning the New Jedi Order, post-*ROTJ* the restored Order permits Luke to marry former dark

Jedi or "Emperor's Hand" Mara Jade.) It may well be that Yoda has not fully understood the meaning of detachment. After all, when reflecting on the Christian process of purifying desire by speaking of detachment from all things, St. John of the Cross emphasizes that he is "not treating here of the lack of things" that would really imply "no detachment on the part of the soul" at all.[31] He is concerned with the possessive ego, which *desires things* rather than desires a proper relation to them in service to the common Good (God). Crucially, "perfection consists in voiding and stripping and purifying the soul of every desire" of this possessive kind.[32]

In fact, numerous commentators seem largely to misunderstand the self-disinterested principle of detachment, erroneously accusing it of a lack of love for others. Rather, having no *need* of others' love entails that one does not use others to fulfill one's needs, but puts one in a better position to be endlessly available for creative acts of charity. "When we become quiet enough to let go of people, we learn compassion for them," claims Foster.[33]

A Jedi should be aware of these pressures and temptations, so as not to repress his or her instincts but face and purge them instead, channeling his or her emotions through the transformation of desire (the goal sought and lived for). The training of the Jedi is a cultivation of the right kind of desire, or intuitive and knowledgeable education in controlling his or her instincts, habituated in the character-making practice of virtue. One implication of this schooling in wisdom is that a Jedi is defined not by legalistic adherence to a known and formulaic code or inflexible set of written rules but rather by embodying "the will of the Force" and instinctively living a life that is formed at its core by the excessive richness of creative virtue. (Dexter rightly distinguishes precisely between [pure] knowledge and wisdom [*AOTC*], opening the possibility of sounding something like Augustine, who claims that "knowledge is valuable when charity informs it. Without charity, knowledge inflates.")[34] That development of virtuous character or wisdom is why the intensively Force-conscious Qui-Gon tells Anakin to "concentrate on the moment," act on instinct, and "feel," not think. Similarly Obi-Wan requests that Luke let go of his perceptions and act on instinct (*ANH*).

Contrary to some criticisms, this is not an appeal to irrationality in favor of blind and untamed intuition.[35] Individualistic Western consumer culture finds thinking about anything that matters too difficult to do; the last thing it *needs* to hear would be such an appeal to irrationality. Instead the Jedi sound here more like the prophet Jeremiah, who speaks of the divine law written on our hearts (e.g., Jer. 31:33). The problem is that while Qui-Gon has a sense of the guiding of the Force, the Jedi Council finds ways of keeping it at a distance and has both become somewhat complacent and lost its way.

It has "become more intent on following ancient rulings of the council than listening to the living Force speaking to them, and this is a grave mistake. For it is the laws created by mortals that will be inherently flawed, as there is no perfect individual to create a perfect law. And the Jedi fail to see this wisdom. Only laws decreed by God himself possess the divine perfection that one must adhere to."[36] Significantly Yoda comes to admit that he had wrongly underestimated Qui-Gon's Force-instincts, when it is too late for the old Republic and the Jedi Order (*ROTS*).

Anakin is unable (unwilling?) to struggle sufficiently to develop this kind of self-control and to learn mechanisms for coping with his most intense emotions. Hence when he understandably attacks the Tusken Raiders responsible for his mother's death, he does so less to administer justice than to gain revenge (*AOTC*). "Revenge" is, of course, precisely the concept Darth Maul desires (*TPM*). The results are catastrophic, not merely for the Sand People the Padawan indiscriminately slaughters, but for Anakin too, for it is in this act of wanton carnage that he steps ever closer to the path to the dark side.

Embodied Life

An important implication of Jedi wisdom is that life—*this* life and the *whole* of it—needs to be transformed. There is no separation of public and private here, as has been common in much of the modern Western imagination. The public is not something *additional* to the personal or the inner person, as if under certain conditions it can be given up without any loss to that inner person. Yet Jerome Donnelly nevertheless detects in *SW* a lingering dualistic "disdain for creaturely flesh and blood . . . by . . . [*SW*'s] predilection for technology," a demeaning of the human that "ultimately results in *dehumanization*."[37] Lucas's world is seemingly one of interchangeable parts, much as Vader's (*ROTS*) and Luke's (*ESB*) severed biological limbs are mechanically replaceable. Donnelly forgets, however, that Vader is less than human as a result. The backstory to *ROTS* includes a reference to several members of the Jedi Council who believe that when Anakin loses his right arm, he loses something of his humanity. Donnelly then argues that the droids not only have distinctly human characteristics but can interchangeably assume human roles, thereby operating as minds severed from organic bodies. Intriguingly, Mark Hamill once famously commented, "I have a sneaking suspicion that if there were a way to make movies without actors, George would do it."[38]

Nevertheless, in relation to the narrative itself Pollock rightly observes that "Lucas thinks *Star Wars* is about *people*, not spaceships, . . . The special effects help only to create a new universe in which the story takes place and in which the characters interact."[39] The technologies never *replace* but *serve* the Good, the embodied being-for-others. Concerning *THX 1138* Lucas reveals that "I was fascinated by the futuristic society, the idea of rocket ships and lasers up against somebody with a stick. The little guys were winning and technology was losing—I liked that."[40] His creation of the Wookiee, Ewok, and Gungan species accordingly celebrates those peoples who are more ecologically conscious than the technocratic Empire. But they are not without their technologies, and neither is the Rebel Alliance, and so the difference is not between a simple technophobia and technophilia as such. Lyden's comment about the films' "technophobic message" is mistaken.[41]

Instead, the main differences lie in the *way technology is used* and the *purpose it is used for*. The Imperial and Trade Federation environments express a coldly utilitarian technophilia. The latter needlessly destroy natural habitats by crushing everything that stands in the way of their droid war machine (*TPM*). In contrast, the more lush and organic environments (Naboo, Endor, Kashyyk, and the fourth moon of Yavin) are populated by the more identifiably good characters. In fact Geonosis, the planet central to the construction of the Separatist war machine (*AOTC*), is visually associated with hell in its coloring, steam vents, subterranean demonlike insect inhabitants, and cauldrons of molten metal. Its underground/underworld assembly conveyor belts produce only technologies of death. The movies therefore imply that while science can break the light barrier, create interstellar travel, generate artificial intelligence, provide nerve-sensitive prostheses, and manufacture planet-destroying weapons, human intentionality and character change little. Lucas's worry, then—in contrast to *2001: A Space Odyssey* and *The Terminator* movies—is more about the users of the machines than the machines outgrowing their users.

Donnelly claims, thirdly, that Yoda endorses a gnostic contempt for physicality when he teaches, "Luminous beings are we, not this crude matter" (*ESB*).[42] The Jedi Master apparently also articulates an ethic of detachment that goes beyond Christian freedom from excessive attachment into an emotionless (Buddhist?) impassiveness, implying that our acceptance of death should be so complete that we do not even mourn the dead (*ROTS*). But we need to be careful here. While three return in the form of Jedi spirits, this is not a simple freedom from the constraints of physicality. (It is noteworthy that Obi-Wan's disembodied Force-existence was the product of a request of Marcia Lucas at the time not to have him killed off.)[43] True, they are not embodied in any ordinary sense, but they are not wholly disembodied either. In fact, they have a continuously identifiable, circumscribed, and personal form of presence that possesses its own kind of bodily logic, a different kind of matter and existence that is nonetheless continuous with their predeath physical identities. So even if Yoda does dismiss the body—and it is not necessarily clear that he does—the saga embraces both personal immortality in the form of an *identifiable* life beyond death, rather than some kind of mere impersonal and abstract oneness with the Force, and the necessary relation of personhood to embodiedness, even if personhood is more than material (which is why Yoda informs Luke, "Luminous beings are we, not this crude matter"). It is interesting that some of the Expanded Universe material, in contrast—in particular Timothy Zahn's *Heir to the Empire* trilogy—speaks of the transmigration of the Emperor's spirit from his body destroyed by Vader to clones of himself he has made.[44] However, this is not only contrary to the spirit of embodiment in *SW* but, as we will see in chapter 8, diverges from the feeling of resolution in *ROTJ*. The official *SW* databank simply records that Vader "hurled the Emperor into the Death Star's reactor core, killing him."[45]

Wickedness comes not from embodiment as such but from the desires of *distorted* persons and their lack of a rightly ordered and practiced life of self-denial. In this way Jedi wisdom can encourage a right regard for bodiliness that is in stark contrast with the inordinate voraciousness of the gluttonously self-indulgent Jabba the Hutt (*ROTJ*).

Conclusion: Bringing "Balance to the Force"

The classic trilogy never explores in detail just what the Rebellion is fighting for. Words such as "freedom," "justice," and "peace" are used without their concrete meaning being revealed, perhaps suggesting that this is little more than empty reactionary rhetoric. Yet *SW* does perceptibly play with the imagery of two broad ways of living, two ways of valuing and desiring. As Lucas explains, "The film is ultimately about the dark side and the light side, and those sides are designed around compassion and greed."[46] But does the notion of "balancing" the Force not contradict this? Only if balance is between two aspects of the Force (see chapter 2) that thereby requires something less than the complete eradication of evil (see chapter 3). Instead, the Jedi and, significantly, Lucas understand the term "balance" to refer to the complete *eradication of the Sith*.[47] So Obi-Wan cries to the defeated young Vader, "You were to bring balance to the Force, not leave it in darkness" (*ROTS*). Whatever is meant by balance, then, it certainly does not mean a harmonizing of good and evil (as in the TV series *Charmed*, for instance).

Caputo, then, is right to make the "distinctly anti-Manichaean" observation, "The war in *Star Wars* does not transpire between two equal but opposed Forces but turns on a disturbance or lack of balance within the one and only Force."[48] It perhaps has more to do with the Greek philosopher Aristotle's (384–322 BC) sense of tempering the good moral life in prudential reasoning rather than a metaphysical balance between two eternal principles or forces.

Here Lucas's *SW* may actually provide a better sense of what reconciliation might mean than does a tremendous amount of Christian practice, past and present. In contrast to the escape-pod theology and spirituality of much Christianity, *ANH* launches the droids into space from Tantive IV (now captured by the Imperial Star Destroyer *Devastator*) not so they could escape the troubles and turmoils of being related to others but rather so that R2D2 could venture forth as a messenger/witness (C3PO is largely oblivious to the demands of the "mission").

All in all, while opposition to the tyranny of collectivism is a common American theme, what sets *SW* apart from much other pop culture, and even from much of the mainstream American (and possibly British) cultural consciousness, is its critique of individualism and a freedom that actually fragments the responsible freedom of being appropriately together. Personhood has an essentially social nature; this means that relations of aggressive and competitive egotism are distortions of what it means to be a person.

Chapter Eight

A New Hope

Redemption in *Star Wars*

*T*here has been a tendency in many modern Christian theologies to put questions of eschatology (Greek *eschata*, "last things") at the end of their systems of doctrine. Among other things this divorces eschatology from the doctrines of the Trinity, creation, and incarnation. When this happens, otherworldly tendencies develop in a way that forgets God's blessing on the created (material) world. This is why observations like those of Karl Marx (1818–83) are morally important when they detect that Christianity is this-life-denying. Christian belief helps us diagnose real ills, he suggests, but it offers an illusory placebo—a hope for another life in another, compensating world—that not only fails to deal appropriately with those problems but even distracts us from searching for suitable therapies. While there may be a consoling hope for an afterlife among those suffering, there is no hope for change, justice, and happiness in this life.

The popular dualistic reading of *SW* suggests that it too has a muted sense of hope, and that is only for the "good characters." "There is no point in attempting to 'save' any of the Imperial troops"—they are, quite simply, beyond hope, argues Henderson.[1] Of course, *AOTC* and *ROTS* explain why these troops are irredeemable, although literature during the midst of the classic trilogy likewise suggested this—given the deliberate restriction of their cloned individuality they are more like biomachinery than human beings. But we have consistently argued that a dualist reading of *SW* is just inappropriate. There is indeed a pronounced sense of hope, which climaxes in a feeling that redemption has been achieved. "Without explicitly saying so, *Return of the Jedi* leaves the viewer with the distinct impression that 'everyone lived happily ever after.'"[2] Amid all the postbattle jubilation in *ANH*, the audience is aware that Darth Vader has survived and the Empire remains largely intact. But *ROTJ*, in contrast, closes with the annihilation of the Sith Order; the destruction of most of the Imperial Fleet and the Second Death Star; Anakin

135

Skywalker having been raised to redeemed life; justice having been done; and the ground having been cleared for the restoration of the great fallen Republic. There is a sense of closure, finality, the *eschaton* (Greek, "end") come. And so, while the Expanded Universe literature continues the civil war, with the Imperial fleet marshaling its resources under a cloned Palpatine and Grand Admiral Thrawn, this seriously detracts from the symbolism of *ROTJ*. It is possibly the eschatological spirit of *ROTJ* that prevented Lucas from filming his originally planned *Episodes VII–IX*, although there are suggestions that he had been planning to visit on-screen the post-*ROTJ* universe at some point. Nonetheless, this eschatological-like mood is one of the reasons why *TFA* sits uneasily within the saga's frame.

But what does hope mean? One of Lucas's comments on *ANH* suggests that it has to do with a feel-good factor: "The whole emotion I am trying to get at the end of this film is for you to be emotionally and spiritually uplifted and to feel absolutely good about life."[3] Wilkinson suggests something else as well: "It encourages the imagination to believe that there is real hope and that good *will win*. The dominant pessimism is violated in a story of *optimism*."[4] However, it is important to test and properly sever the association of hope and feel-good optimism if hope is really to be *hope*. And that is what the saga itself has the potential to do, thereby providing resources for developing a hope that is much less illusory.

"Always in Motion the Future Is" (Yoda)

Optimism *knows* the future and knows that it will be good (incidentally, pessimism too *knows* the future, but knows that it is bad). While some types of hope also attempt to *know* the future, so that those who hope can exercise some kind of *control* over it, they recognize that they can never fully know or decisively control that future. But the hope of a Force-conscious individual in *SW* is somewhat different from even this understanding of hope. His or her hope is *not determined by knowledge or even expectation of success* (like the hope for victory in battle being determined by the expectation of successful tactics and military personnel), which becomes a mistaken hope if it is unsuccessful (the battle is lost). Hope in this sense, as we will see later, is properly a way of taking moral responsibility for what is Good and actively desiring that the "will of the Force" be done.

Yoda occasionally speaks as if he does indeed have the ability to foresee (and therefore control) events. In a broadly similar fashion, Qui-Gon insightfully surmises that young Anakin "can see things before they happen" (*TPM*). These examples suggest less hope for the future than an optimistic knowledge of what will happen, and these echo certain types of Christian apocalypticism that imagine eschatology has to do with a God-enabled foreseeing of future events. This idea of prescient Jedi invokes images of an *overwhelming destiny* underlying history. This would suggest that some can see the future because that is the way the future *will be*. Is this why Qui-Gon, for instance, declares to young Anakin that "our meeting was not a coincidence. Nothing happens by accident" (*TPM*)? Perhaps the similarity between the characterizations of the tragic figures of Anakin and Oedipus could support this idea of irrevocable fate. For Anakin, as for Oedipus, it is precisely the attempt to avoid the foreseen disaster (Padmé's death) that generates the conditions of his own fall. Is his mistake, though, the attempt to evade destiny, or the manner of his attempted escape? Christian apocalyptic generally denies that we can control our futures, precisely because they are controlled by Another. So Christians at best are consequently rendered little more than spectators, though they may be comforted and secured by the knowledge they have been given. In this way the apocalypticists *know* the outcome of future events, which will be bad for the world (it will be destroyed) but will be good for the Christian seer (who will be saved). *SW* does not reveal how the Jedi Masters achieve foresight, but it is the *Jedi* seemingly most in tune with the Force who possess this ability.

But we need to be careful here, since *SW* tends *not* to present destiny in terms of such inescapability. Instead, Luke, for instance, is advised *actively* to follow his destiny, thereby suggesting it is a path that can be followed *or* rejected and requires an act of will and effort in the face of temptation and other difficulties. His destiny could take a different route, depending on his actions: "If once you start down the dark path, forever will it dominate your destiny, consume you it will, as it did Obi-Wan's apprentice" (Yoda to Luke, *ESB*). Perversely Vader even appeals to Luke's "destiny" in destroying the Emperor in order to "together . . . rule the galaxy as father and son." And while Yoda asserts that Vader has gone this dark route, we learn through Anakin's redemption that even the great Jedi Master has inappropriately lost hope at this point (*ROTJ*). Destiny talk, then, primarily concerns *the proper purpose of one's existence*. It is what Christians should mean when they speak broadly of God's creative call before the foundation of the world, although this too has been presented in causally deterministic ways. So Lucas claims that "the greater Force has to do with destiny. In working with the Force, you can find your destiny and you can choose to either follow it, or not."[5]

Crucially, in the second place, the ability of the future-sighted unambiguously to guide their steps "into the future" is considerably curtailed. Yoda admits deficient knowledge of young Anakin's future: "Clouded this boy's future is" (*TPM*). After all, "Always in motion the future is." This sounds less like apocalyptic foresight than sober nescience or ignorance, the kind that takes more seriously Jesus' precautionary words concerning the inability to "know on what day your Lord is coming" (Matt. 24:42). But it is also significant that this potential for prescience is shrouded by the disruptive operation of the dark side. The presence of the Sith subverts and distorts any natural teleology or course of events. This echoes several Christian accounts of God's providential governance that admit we cannot know just where God's unambiguous rule in Christ can be seen in contemporary events and experiences.

The way *SW* clearly sets "the ways of the Force" against the way of the Sith, however, ultimately diverges from much Christian apocalyptic in at least four critical ways. Firstly, while apocalypticism foresees events *in*—or, rather, toward the end of—history, it is not at all clear that this is true of Luke's hope. In this way, Jedi hope differs in kind from even the more cautious approaches to future knowing that nevertheless attempt to *know* what is to come. As will become clear later, Luke's hope for Vader's transformation is not invalidated by its seeming failure. Secondly, much Christian apocalyptic is fundamentally individualistic, worrying essentially about *individuals'* eternal destiny, whereas *SW*'s vision is communitarian and involves personal responsibility for the *common* flourishing of *all*. Thirdly, Christian apocalyptic is frequently self-centered, fretting over individuals' eternal *destiny*, whereas *SW* depicts the Jedi wisdom of complete and utter self-giving. The Jedi spurn *possessive* attachments fundamentally because they renounce self-aggrandizing self-interest in favor of primarily serving others' true interests, the flourishing of all beings in the Force. Finally, Christian apocalyptic is plagued by a sense of world denial or world destruction that worries about individuals' *heavenly* destiny (usually in terms of their *souls*), whereas *SW* recreates the good life in the experienceable universe. While Christian apocalyptic, then, is able rightly to hold all social projects and supposed utopian achievements in critical suspicion, unlike the more positively creative suspicion of Jedi hope, it has little transformative power and thus can dangerously degenerate into utter despair over this world. Admittedly, Yoda's warning to Anakin not to mourn those "who transform into the Force" (*ROTS*) might unwittingly underestimate the injustice of enforced death. Yet *SW* is indeed concerned with hope for all things and persons—even for Darth Vader!

The Redemption of Darth Vader

"He's More Machine Now than Man"

Wink observes, "Cartoon and comic heroes cast no shadows. . . . Repentance and confession are as alien to them as the love of enemies and non-violence." This is particularly a problem given that such pop materials both express certain cultural trends and also reinforce and disseminate them.[6] Henderson's comment concerning the lack of hope for the stormtroopers suggests that *SW* suffers from this too. But while this perspective may make some sense of *ANH*, it is less appropriate to the succeeding movies, which begin to explore evil in more nuanced ways. One important way this happens is through the theme of redemption, particularly the redemption of Darth Vader.

Vader is portrayed in the blackest of colors in *ANH*, garbed in an SS-inspired costume that signifies his inhumanity. In *ESB* that wickedness is mitigated a little, so that even though he knows he is Luke's father, he nevertheless warns his progeny, "Don't make me destroy you"; earlier he had promised the Emperor, "He will join us or die, Master." Even if Vader had no intention of killing Luke, the symbolic value of severing his son's hand is itself immensely brutal. Vader is still corrupted by wickedness even in *ROTJ*, so that he commends the dark side to Luke: "You don't know the power of the dark side. . . . The Emperor will show you the true nature of the Force." He later demands that Luke, and if not him then his sister, "will turn to the dark side." Even if he was the hero of Obi-Wan's earlier eulogy to Luke, there is no doubt just how far he has fallen. According to Obi-Wan, Vader has become "more machine than man" (*ESB*). To all intents and purposes Anakin Skywalker is truly dead, killed by the damnable Vader, and only the "irredeemably dark" subhuman (not even inhuman) Sith Lord lives in his place, "kept alive only by machinery and his own black will."[7]

Hoping There Is Still Some Good Left in Him

In the midst of what seems to be overwhelming evidence to the contrary, Luke nonetheless refuses to believe Obi-Wan's rhetoric and instead actively takes responsibility for Vader. Luke's move here resonates with Augustine's instruction to hate the fault and *not* the person whose fault it is.[8] In what might be called his hoping against hope, the Jedi even refuses to believe that Anakin has been utterly destroyed; he certainly refuses to celebrate possibly having to kill this evil other, even if his father is finally irredeemable. Does Luke hope because of some sentimental understanding of the inherent goodness of people? He does announce on the Endor moon that he feels "the good" still in his archnemesis (as Padmé too declares on her deathbed, *ROTS*). Yet he is sensing here Vader's *real* moral struggles at this time and is therefore not pleading from some optimistic anthropology. Besides, a sentimentalized anthropology of this sort would make little sense of the facts that numerous characters (Palpatine, Maul, Dooku, Jango and Boba Fett, and Jabba) remain conspicuously unredeemed and that *Episodes IV–VI* do not otherwise suggest any remnant of the Good in Vader himself. After all, the Dark Lord of the Sith's offer to Luke to join him against the Emperor (*ESB*) has arguably less to do with family loyalty than with the desire to preserve the Emperor's political power.

It is precisely this dark shroud hanging over him that makes Vader's redemption so shockingly surprising, and it particularly reveals the simplistic nature of Anglo-American audiences' readings of good and evil and their dominating sense of justice as retribution. As Anker observes, "The very surprise it occasions effectively uncovers the bad manners of contemporary cynicism and hopelessness. . . . The effect of . . . the unlikely return itself pivots on the audience's usual gullibility about the way the world usually works, which is badly."[9]

Luke obviously has some sense that his hope for Vader can be fulfilled, which is why he acknowledges, "I sense the good in you, Father." Yet in the light of the Jedi commitment to the Good of all life-forms in the life-giving Force, we may argue that Luke takes responsibility for Vader because *it is wrong to do wrong to another* or, better, *it is right to do good to another,* whether or not there is any prospect of being successful. This is precisely why he is prevented from giving up on Vader in despair, even at the point when his father claims his own damnation: "It is too late for me, Son." After all, Jesus suffers and dies because, in peacemaking love for even his enemies, he resisted evil irrespective of whether his divinely redeeming life and message were understood and finally transformative of any others. Luke's hope *desires* fulfillment, of course, but is *not wholly dependent upon it*, which is why he offers himself as a sacrificial victim when he thinks he has finally failed. Utilitarian calculative reasoning is not the driving force of his moral responsibility, which is why he does not slip into valuing the person of Vader himself on the basis of what he has done, achieved, or become. Vader's true evaluation is in what the symbiosis of life in the Force declares him to be. Luke's hope, then, echoes Barth's claim that the Christian community "need neither ask nor worry what the result will be, what success it will enjoy or not enjoy, so long as it is obedient."[10] The young Jedi will not dehumanizingly betray his most bitter of foes by killing him when he is battered and beaten—in marked contrast with the young Anakin, who was unable to resist

Palpatine's tempting him into the state-sanctioned murder of the defeated Dooku years earlier (*ROTS*).

When Luke casts his lightsaber away, he retrieves control over his moral judgment. He can now act neither out of a craving for revenge nor out of a lust for dominating power. In taking this route, Luke refuses to acknowledge that power and enmity are ultimate. For this reason, in a moment of utter self-dispossession, he acts for the good of his heretofore most fearsome enemy by surprisingly *not* repaying violence with further violence in a self-perpetuating conflict. By inviting upon himself the full force of the Emperor's Force-Lightning, Luke finally gives himself, not merely for his friends (*ESB*) or an alternate set of abstract moral principles, but for his enemy too. "He has at last comprehended the heart of Yoda's teachings: that the universe runs by love and that love should pervade all thought and action."[11] There is a striking overlap between the Luke of this climactic duel scene and the God of the cross who gives God's own self (cf. Phil. 2) in order not to give up on humanity, thereby expressing the divine desire to break the power of human enmity without violence. Luke, in a profoundly Christlike move, refuses to leave even the fallen human being of Vader (the Adamic archetype) unhoped for but offers himself up in order to break the long-standing enmity between them in the offer of an embrace beyond violence. This enables him creatively to become a channel of redemptive significance.

Here the hope of the Jedi youth could remind numerous apocalyptically minded Christians about the creative and recreative grace of God. In spite of everything, as Volf argues, "the economy of undeserved grace has primacy over the economy of moral deserts. . . . Human beings are *always already in the covenant* as those who have *always already broken the covenant*."[12] Volf's use of general language with the term "human beings" is important. All creatures belong to the God who creates in and through the divine creative Word (John 1:3; cf. Col. 1:16), and it is to these that God moves in redemptive form. There is actually a profound blasphemy against the creation-blessing *Creator* lurking in apocalyptic dualisms that leave all of God's fallen people unhoped for or merely partially hoped for (hope for their *souls* or the souls of *some* only). The image of hell all too easily expresses victims' self-assertive anger and is thereby frequently driven by a sense of hopelessness for the victimizers, who require redemption as much as the victims.

Luke's hope is rewarded in one of Lucas's masterstrokes, the stunning surprise that retroactively illuminates and enriches the whole texture of the classic trilogy: Vader's repentance, the resurrection (new "return") of *the* Jedi Anakin Skywalker, and the casting down of the satanic Palpatine (cf. Rev. 20:10). His son's incalculable hope, compassion, and resistance to Palpatine's temptations of power remind Vader of the moral integrity he once had as an idealistic young Jedi and force him to face the consequences of his own failure to resist many years before. Luke's is a completely gratuitous judgment of mercy on Vader's life and worth. The dark figure's ultimate value as a person cannot be extinguished by the shroud of the Sith and his dark deeds herein. Vader's response is to remember who he once was, discover his filial relation to Luke, and react in a responding compassion for his son. And in the ultimate moment of reconciliation they literally see one another face-to-face when Anakin's mask is removed (cf. 1 Cor. 13:12).

Hope and the Tragic Quality of Redemption

ROTJ's closing mood has the feel of a redemption achieved. There is, for example, an important consummating return to the theme of the symbiosis of the multiplicity of life-forms. The Endor moon stages the harmonious gathering into a fellowship of praise of diverse races, and similar forms of communal celebration are seen on Bespin, Coruscant, and Tatooine, thus representing universal and comprehensive harmony or the community redeemed in the Force. So Anker suggestively concludes that "the ragtag assembly of characters ends up forming a new family of mutuality that looks a lot like what the New Testament envisions as the constituency of the family of God."[13]

Lucas himself has spoken in a biblical allusion of light's overcoming darkness, and despite the terrible gravitas and unsettling pathos in *ROTS*, there is vital symbolic value both in the way the deathly resurrection of Vader is intercut with the new life of the twins and in its *ending* with the sounding of the musical motif of *ANH* as Luke is held by his new guardians on Tatooine. Yet we must be wary of overemphasizing these themes in a way that depicts redemption too easily and thus lazily trivializes all that has happened. Hanson and Kay, for instance, strangely and glibly deny Anakin his tragic quality by proclaiming that his "strange and incomprehensible journey" is "one of success."[14] At what cost does the eventual "success" come? Yoda's cautioning of Obi-Wan serves as something of a warning: "Victory! Victory you say . . . , not victory. The shroud of the dark side has fallen. Begun the Clone War has" (*AOTC*). This most accomplished of Jedi Masters is attentive to the significance of war as a failure in human relations and to its ruinous destruction, which means that it should be better spoken of in terms of catastrophe, calamity, and disaster. The mood in *ROTJ* may accord too little weight to this sensibility, but it most certainly is compensated for in the prequels.

Unless we feel the sense of bittersweetness of the numerous joyous and reconciliatory moments in tragedies, we have entirely missed their point. For instance, tragic dramas often display an *anagoresis* ("recognition") or a kind of repentance on the part of the tragic protagonist. Vader's own personal transformation echoes something of William Shakespeare's King Lear, who in his final moments of life is reconciled with his most beloved daughter, Cordelia, whom through his own sufferings, he painfully comes to realize, he has wronged terribly and tragically. Yet despite the presence of such redemptive themes, real tragedy is the torment of the irreparable sense of too little too late and the uncomfortable feeling that there can be no adequate "compensation" or healing of wounds.[15]

So it is for Anakin. While he finally sees Luke face-to-face as his true self, their reconciling gaze, like that of Lear and Cordelia, is all too brief. Anakin dies, as do Lear and his beloved daughter. His becoming one with the Force, despite what Yoda argues with respect to not grieving but rather celebrating this event (*ROTS*), cannot compensate for that brevity and for the fact that he never is able to embrace his daughter. This has the character of too little too late, even if *ROTJ* prevents the audience from gazing on it for too long. Certainly the galaxy can now be stronger because of Vader's redemptive intervention, but this is by no means a simple restoration of providential justice. Whatever readers want to argue with regard to Vader's redemptive end or the sense of eternal justice in the galactic Force, there remains in his salvation a disturbing tragic quality that cannot be undone: the consequences of Vader's evil, in spite of personal repentance, remain and stain his legacy— Padmé remains dead; Luke and Leia are raised apart for nineteen years; the Jedi Order is almost wholly obliterated, and all but two of its greatest Jedi are massacred; the stores of recorded Jedi wisdom stay irretrievably destroyed or utterly corrupted; and Anakin's own great potential in the Force is never realized. The symbolic value of Qui-Gon's death is similarly important: "This is a horrific, post-modern notion that Lucas has conjured. The hero *cannot* overcome all circumstances, prevail against all odds, good does not always win over evil . . . the hero is as mortal as the villain."[16]

The six-volume saga certainly cannot be read as *pure* tragedy—whatever that may be—but it poignantly possesses a profoundly tragic sense that subverts easy talk of new life, salvation, and redemption. Anakin's tragedy leaves it irreducibly bearing his scars forevermore. "There are scars, it seems," Nicholas Lash declares from Revelation 5:6, "in heaven."[17]

Conclusion

In our contemporary climate, Western hopes in particular have been touched by pessimism, despair, and cynicism. Even in 1965 William Lynch could write of a contemporary fascination with hopelessness—no doubt reflecting the anxieties felt after the Cuban missile crisis of 1962—and that was before Vietnam, the AIDS crisis, and the consciousness of ecological disaster.[18] Today the fragile and partial hopes that still exist have been largely reduced to the individualist "me-first attitude" that is shaped by market relations. It is little wonder, then, that the desire for some form of escape continues to be attractive; this partly accounts for the growing popularity of hedonistic diets of narcotics and consumer therapy, momentary consolations that slide toward the insatiable demand for "more and more." Many nostalgically regularly search for some kind of securely grounded, unambiguous, and ultimate hope. In this context, when heaven becomes the belief of an alienated humanity (Ludwig Feuerbach, 1804–72) or a comforting escapist response to the pain of an alienated existence (Marx), then its cardinal function is to get one through life. But it does this in a way that unwittingly intensifies "the love of self, disguised beyond recognition, at least to those who perpetrate this pious fraud." This finally reduces "God to a means to the believer's own ends."[19]

Read in the light of their tragic quality, the redemptive therapy provided by the *SW* saga is not *comforting* as such and accordingly does not support any desire that strengthens self-centeredness. Hope cannot, as in numerous problematic Christian accounts, provide a self-securing consolation; offer a "compensating heaven"; soothe the wounded soul with knowledge of a resolution to the so-called problem of evil; or provide an escape route into a different world that disposes us to be indifferent to this one. Instead, while it intensifies the sense of the fragility and tragic nature of moral endeavor in a messy world, it vitally helps us identify and resist evil and prompts us to charity. We are therein forced to "unlearn" our ways of dominating others (as displayed by the tribal racism of the Imperial peace) that destructively subvert the original and final symbiosis of all life-forms.

Jedi wisdom imagines a way of living that necessarily supports considerations of flourishing together. Any hope generated on these grounds does protect hopers from despair, but only because it does not allow the hopers to focus on their own emotional state. The Jedi are called to a never ending self-dispossessiveness that subverts their need for possessive guarantees, instead enabling them simply to live faithfully into their futures for the sake of the flourishing of all things. As Qui-Gon asserts, "I will do what I must." A hope aware of a tragic quality of existence, then, "is very different from a blank depression. It combines a recognition of the chanciness of life, the ultimate and uncompensatable waste of value and a resolution to live the best life available within these limits."[20]

In a scene in Peter Jackson's cinematic version of *The Fellowship of the Ring*, Frodo the Hobbit balks at the size of his task, for on him rests the very future of the human race: "I wish the ring had never come to me. I wish none of this had happened." Gandalf the Wizard wisely responds: "So do all who live to see such times; but that is not for them to decide. All you have to decide is what to do with the time that is given to you." In this way, the *SW* saga too may be more theo-ethically interesting than viewers who experience it as simple entertainment may imagine.

Chapter Nine

Whose Force Awakens?

J. J. Abrams's *Star Wars*'s Return to Violence

> *There has been an awakening. Have you felt it?*
> —Supreme Leader Snoke

*T*his lengthy final chapter reflects on the newest cinematic addition to the *SW* saga, addressing two sets of issues. The first is the substantial narrative, thematic, and character overlaps between *TFA* and the classic trilogy, particularly *ANH*. The blogosphere is full of observations that J. J. Abrams's *SW* movie is nostalgic for George Lucas's *ANH*. A number of these take the form of complaints that it in fact verges on being a rehash of the first movie in the saga. The second issue demands that closer attention be paid to the differences between these two versions of the *SW* franchise. These differences are actually not trivial, or at least not morally trivial. In this regard, the new movie is in many ways not "the story of history repeating itself," as the director tries to suggest in an interview for *The Hollywood Reporter*.[1] The changes are not limited to some attempts at repairing the pacing of the *SW* prequel movies, or removing characters who particularly irritated the fans (like Jar Jar Binks), or returning to more set-driven and model-making conditions in reaction to the CGI-laden special editions of the classic trilogy and the three prequel movies. The differences lie in the quite particular interpretation of *SW* that Abrams offers and is nostalgic for. What this amounts to is a sense that while it reverberates with much of Lucas's early form, it offers some crucial modifications of the very moral spirit of the *SW* movies made by Lucas. What is suggestive is not merely those things chosen to be nostalgically reproduced but equally those things that have been omitted, for whatever reason.

Of course it needs to be said that when assessing the newest movie in the *SW* series to appear at the time of this writing, one must exercise some caution. *TFA* is, after all, the first movie in a new trilogy, and, as this book has argued on numerous occasions, the *SW* movies that succeeded the one that became known as *ANH* shone new light on the 1977 cinematic masterpiece. In other words, *Episodes V* and *VI*, not to mention *I–III*, demand that *IV* be reinterpreted.

"Chewie, We're Home" (Han)

As the trailers and advertisements end, the audience of the first movie in the *Lord of the Rings* trilogy settles back and the lights switch off while the curtain recedes. The production and distribution logos briefly move and twinkle on the screen and are followed by a momentary darkness. Peter Jackson's epic cinematic study of Middle Earth begins with the voice of a soft-spoken woman, accompanied by a musical theme with a tone of lament: "the world is changed." And so begins Peter Jackson's epic cinematic interest in Middle Earth. On another evening, this time in December 2015, the darkness momentarily preceding the theatrical picture is visually lit with the now-familiar glowing line: "A long time ago, in a galaxy far, far away." The world may have changed, as have the hands responsible for the saga, with Lucas's lucrative sale of the franchise to the Disney Corporation, but this opening line suggests that *SW* remains the same yesterday and today (and forever?). It is little wonder that one of the prerelease trailers included the line uttered by Han as he enters the *Millennium Falcon*, "Chewie, we're home." The conflict in the space fairy tale continues. . . .

The *SW* saga has a narrative echo throughout; the referencing of past cultural materials and products in *ANH* means it is engaged in its own *pastiche* of adventure serials: Kurosawa's *Hidden Fortress*, John Ford's westerns, and other influences; the Han/Lando parallel; the attack on the Death Stars in *ANH/ROTJ*; the Luke/Anakin correspondences; the Leia/Padmé overlaps, and so on. The director and cowriter of *TFA*, J. J. Abrams, recognizes this and makes no claims to be doing anything radically different with his particular contribution to the series. In fact, his own defense of the direction he has taken appeals to his contribution being a "derivative of all these things George loves so much." So he states, "It was obviously a wildly intentional thing that we go backwards, in some ways, to go forwards in the important ways. . . . Ultimately," he claims, "the structure of *Star Wars* itself is as classic and tried-and-true as you can get."[2] This second comment is distinctly misleading since, as chapter 4 explains, there are at the very least two main macronarrative arcs that cover the two sets of Lucas's trilogies. The telling implication, though, is that the self-confessed *SW* fan Abrams discounts the prequels, and the overwhelming echoes that abound in *TFA* are predominantly of *ANH*. There is, then, only one *SW* "structure" and not two "structures." The reverberations and repetitions are themselves either the result of a fanboy's *homage* to the original material he has loved or the outcome of a director and pair of writers seriously devoid of novel ideas. If the latter, perhaps a lazy script can be somewhat excused by the fact that the writers had to rush the writing in order to begin churning out Disney's mass-produced *SW* movies.[3]

First, there are grand dramatic similarities between the newest movie and its predecessors: for instance, the heroic journey by a main protagonist from a desert planet, a journey that involves what Obi-Wan calls stepping into the "larger world" of the Force (an echo of the stories of both Luke and Anakin).[4] The dramatic conflictual arc features not only a grand lightsaber battle but a SOMF (Small One-(Wo)Man Fighter) attack, particularly with X-Wings (the T-70s are upgraded from the classic trilogy's T-65), on a spherical world-annihilating superweapon. Even the name "Starkiller Base" is an echo of the name "Death Star." More specifically, it is taken from the surname Lucas had for some time considered giving to his young protagonist Luke, but he decided against it because of the problematic values that the name "Starkiller" would suggest and because the cult murderer Charles Manson had sometimes been referred to as "the Star killer."[5]

Second, there are countless other visual and narrative echoes. To name only a few: The opening shot of the movie focuses on a Star Destroyer. A marketably cutesy astromech droid, BB-8, carries vital information and is to be delivered into the hands of the movies' heroes. The *Millennium Falcon* is in a dilapidated state (the *Falcon* being on Jakku at Niima Outpost, unlocked and even in flyable condition, an all-too-convenient plot device), and the heroes hide in the smuggling compartments under its floors. Han and Chewbacca are smugglers running from criminal money lenders who are collecting the debts owed to their gangs. There are visual references to Han and Luke's laser canon battle with the TIE Fighters. There is a cantina-like scene with a motley crew of customers, only now it is on Takodana rather than Tatooine. The hero receives a lightsaber (this time it is Rey rather than Luke). A ship containing important information in a droid is tracked back to its hidden base. A garbage chute and trash compactor are referenced. An important elderly character dies by lightsaber. The onscreen presence of Jedi is limited (in contrast to *Episodes I–III*). The examples are numerous. It is worth mentioning that Rey in *TFA* is the same age as Luke in *ANH*: nineteen. References to *Episodes IV–VI* abound with the character of Kylo Ren. Aboard the Star Destroyer the *Finalizer*, the black cowled and imposingly masked Master of the Knights of Ren cryptically addresses a battered and distorted helmet that had belonged to his grandfather, telling it that he will continue Darth Vader's work. Moreover, Ren is described as having been a young Jedi who had betrayed and murdered the emerging New Jedi Order's students, a clear echo of Obi-Wan's description of Vader's history in *ANH*. Also, Ren's position in the First Order's command structure mimics Vader's in that of the Empire's—he reports directly to Supreme Leader Snoke just as Vader did to Emperor Palpatine, and "his agenda always trumps military objectives."[6] This brings him into conflict with Hux, a General with "little understanding of or patience for the mystical side" who echoes Grand Moff Tarkin's disdain for Vader's ancient religion. Lucas's cowriter on *ESB* and *ROTJ*, Lawrence Kasdan, was one of the cowriters of *TFA*, and Alan Dean Foster composed the novel, just as he had done for *ANH*.

In fact, the echoes and reprises of themes, images, and plot from *ANH* in particular are so numerous that in an interview with Charlie Rose, *SW*'s creator George Lucas chose to criticize this element of mimicry in the new movie as being less *homage* than conservative repetition. "They wanted to do a retro movie. I don't like that. Every movie I work very hard to make them completely different, with different planets, different spaceships, make it new."[7] Of course, here he is being a little disingenuous; in particular, much of the narrative flow of the climax of *ROTJ* recapitulates that of *ANH*. Nevertheless, his point is a very fair artistic one, and it is certainly spot-on with regard to *TFA* and its overdependence on imitation. He even laments that it did not take risks with the franchise but was too keen on making a movie to please the fans.[8] (There is a debate in *SW* fandom as to whether the line by Lor San Tekka "This will begin to make things right" is a reassuring gesture to fans that with Abrams's *TFA* the franchise will return to the form that many felt had been lost with the prequels. The following mentioning of the prophecy of bringing "balance to the Force" certainly seems to be a deliberate reference to Mace Windu's question in *TPM*.)[9] Speaking more generally of the formulaic productions of the contemporary Hollywood industry, Lucas quips, "Of course, the only way you could really do that [viz., make money] is not take chances. Only do something that's proven. You gotta remember *Star Wars* came from nowhere. *American Graffiti* came from nowhere. There was nothing like it. Now, if you do anything that's not a sequel or not a TV series or doesn't look like one, they won't do it!"

However, questions still have to be asked about the form of the echo taken in J. J. Abrams's *TFA*. Is *Episode VII* really a referential return to Lucas's *SW*, or does it reflect a substantial and significant transmutation?

The Adventures of Rey:
Matters of Gender in the Force

One quite obvious difference suggests that *TFA* has learned from the criticisms often leveled at the characterizations of Leia and Padmé. Certainly it is the case that a good deal of the journalistic and scholarly criticism has been overdrawn, and I have argued more extensively elsewhere that many of the ideological critical readings of the female characters are actually poorly done, given, among other things, the narrative context of the material.[10] But nonetheless, it is difficult to quell nagging concerns about the mythical characterization of the "mother" and "daughter" figures in the two sets of trilogies. As characters, Leia and Padmé bear the heavy burden of being the sole females in significant speaking roles among the central protagonists. In the second draft of *ANH* in a telling comment, Lucas writes that at the end Leia is "revealed as her true goddess-like self."[11] Of course there is plenty of potential for developing Leia as a Jedi Knight given the familial revelations in *ROTJ*, and such a move might have alleviated critics' concerns over her position of being in largely a supportive role to the more dramatically important males in *Episodes IV–VI*.[12] Lucas had considered this when he decided that Luke would have a twin sister. In his planning of *ESB* in late 1977 he announces,

> I also want to develop Luke's sister. The idea is that Luke's father had two children who were twins. He took one of them to an uncle on one side of the universe and one to the other side of the universe, so that they would be safe. If one got killed, the other wouldn't even know that the other one was there. She also becomes a Jedi—she's doing the same thing simultaneously that Luke is doing. Eventually in some episode, not this one [viz., *Episode V*], we could cope with Luke and his sister, and how she is the female Jedi and he is the male Jedi.[13]

TFA, for its part, reintroduces the audience to Leia, now acting as a general in the Resistance, but it also introduces Rey as the central protagonist. Moreover, four other women are given speaking roles, even if only briefly: the good-humored Resistance medical officer, Doctor Kolonia; the Resistance pilot involved in the bombing run against Starkiller base, Jess Pava; the former smuggler-turned-tavern owner, Maz Kanata (who is apparently Force-conscious); and the distinctively chrome-armored stormtrooper commander, Captain Phasma. A brief comment about the shift of titles for Leia is in order at this point, since it may well have a bearing on the way *TFA* offers a kind of critical repair of elements of the classic trilogy. As has been mentioned earlier, the characterization of the female protagonist as a princess had as much to do with Lucas's love for Kurosawa's *Hidden Fortress* as it had with his regard for fairy tales and chivalric stories (such as the Merlin-Arthur-Guinevere romance cycles). Moreover, *ANH* actually attempted to deconstruct and reconceive the notion of the princess-in-the-tower who needs to be rescued. Yet the very concept still remains bound in popular culture to prefeminist sensibilities, despite not only Leia's performance but that of the likes of Fiona from *Shrek*. Is this why it is the *elderly* Lor San Tekka who is portrayed as still referring to her as royalty, and the typically socially *insensitive* C3PO who does so as well? Leia's role in *TFA* is as a military commander, and a certain gravitas comes with that position in popular cinema. Of course, there is also a reason for her refusal to continue using the political title. According to the *Visual Dictionary*, "Many thought Leia Organa was unreasonably suspicious of the peace process that defanged the Galactic Empire . . . and she was estranged from the Senate for her refusal to let the ghosts of the last war stay dead."[14]

One notable reparative reference to *ANH* occurs when Rey first encounters Finn. When a pair of stormtroopers runs toward them, the young man patronizingly grabs Rey's hand to help her flee only to be greeted with a shocked, "What are you doing?," followed by an even more annoyed, "Let go of me!" and a rough shake of the hand as she frees herself from his grip. Soon she is in front of Finn, *leading him away* from their pursuers, imploring him to "come on." Moments later, when Finn grabs Rey's hand again, the irritated scavenger barks, "Stop taking my hand." Finally, after surviving a TIE Fighter blast, Rey offers her hand to Finn in a role reversal. The scene is as comic as it is dramatic, but its reparative references back to *ANH* are unmistakable and noteworthy. For all Leia's leadership qualities, and the clever deflation of the image of the passive princess awaiting her white knight with Leia's puncturing comments to Luke and Han ("This is some rescue," for instance), she still does become precisely a damsel in distress at certain points, clutching Luke's guiding hand and a little later grabbing onto him as they swing over the shaft in the Death Star. Of course, one cannot overlook the fact that toward the end of *ESB*, it is Leia who turns the *Falcon* back into the dangerous path of the pursuing TIE Fighters in order to rescue a wounded and traumatized Luke. Importantly the roles of savior are reversed. In *TFA* Rey's years on the wastelands of Jakku have forced her to become self-reliant in order simply to survive. The scene in which she is first introduced to Finn at Niima Outpost sets further tone to what this survival entails. The young man catches sight of her being attacked by two of the Crolute Unkar Plutt's thugs, only to see her successfully defend herself before he can even reach her to offer heroic assistance. Later in the movie, Finn, along with Han and Chewbacca, seeks to rescue Rey from the clutches of the First Order in Starkiller Base. However, as the defected stormtrooper outlines his rescue plan, Han draws attention to the fact that Rey is impressively *effecting her own escape*.

That she is something of an echo of Luke Skywalker is rather obvious. As mentioned earlier, both are the same age when they first appear in the saga. They have been raised on harsh desert worlds, Rey on Jakku and Luke (and Anakin before him) on Tatooine. Both have to scratch out a living, and it is a meager one at that—Luke through his work on his uncle's moisture farm, Rey through scavenging and trading her salvaged materials to the junkyard owner, Unkar Plutt. Luke and Rey's respective journey's into heroic adventure begin soon after they come into possession of an astromech droid that conceals important plans. Unlike Luke, however, the audience is not entreated to displays of petulance and frustration by Rey at her lot in life, and that makes her in many ways an even more watchable character, although in other ways it can also make her difficult to relate to. The closest *TFA* comes to this is with her attempt to escape the call into the "larger world," fleeing into the forest on Takodana. The reason she appears more emotionally resilient than Luke is largely the result of the fact that she is awaiting her family's return to the desolate planet. She, in other words, lives each day in hope, in contrast to Luke, who endures every moment on Tatooine as mundanely dispiriting. Luke is bound to his home world by his responsibility to his uncle and aunt, whereas Rey is bound to hers by her anticipation of her family's reappearance (as the young Anakin, for his part, is bound to Tatooine by virtue of both being a slave and being responsible to his mother, Shmi). By fulfilling his responsibilities to help his uncle on the farm in *ANH* rather than satisfying his own desires for adventure, Luke demonstrates some moral depth. In a slight twist, Rey's moral depth is shown in the opposite direction—while her personal desire is to stay on Jakku (and she later expresses her need to return there), her care for the well-being of others, for BB-8 and his mission initially and then for finding Luke, demands that she venture off-world. The young woman, like her predecessor in *ANH*, is a dreamer—but she dreams of other, lushly vegetated worlds and of her family, while Luke dreams of escapist adventure and heroic excitement. Both Luke and Rey (like Anakin) share the gifts of mechanical expertise. "Rey is a gifted mechanic, seemingly having an innate sense of how machinery fits together and functions."[15] The highly capable, resourceful, and spirited young woman, like Luke (as well as Anakin before him) has become a particularly skilled pilot (although given that neither of them had left their planets, their advanced skills as space pilots is somewhat puzzling). In another scene in which she sits in front of one of the feet of the toppled AT-AT that serves as her home, she wears a salvaged Rebel Alliance flight helmet. Immediately one thinks of the Luke of *ESB* garbed in flight uniform and dropping from the AT-AT on Hoth, which he destroys with a well-placed explosive. There are even a couple of understated mini-temptation scenes. One of these occurs in Maz's castle, when Finn unsuccessfully tries to persuade Rey to flee with him to get away from the reach of the First Order. The offer comes during a tender moment in which the former stormtrooper displays his affection for his companion, and that adds a certain poignancy not only to his self-revelation but also to the pain of the parting of these friends. Moreover, there is an echo of what in Campbellian conceptuality would be referred to as the "refusal of the call" here. Where Luke refuses to join Obi-Wan initially until circumstances on his home planet leave him with little choice, Rey refuses to answer the call of the lightsaber (Maz uses precisely this language of "calling") and flees into the forest until her capture by Kylo Ren leaves her with no other option. This is arguably an important, but largely the only, humanizing sign of her fragility in the movie. It is the one moment that disrupts the sense of Rey being as a 'Mary Sue' or idealized character.

In one draft of the script of *ANH*, Lucas had replaced his young hero with a young woman—Luke replaced by Leia. Abrams and Kasdan have followed up on this, and the various parallels between these characters reinforce the notion that in the early planning of *SW*, Luke and Leia were interchangeable. What this entails for Rey's characterization remains to be seen, especially when her origins and identity remain shrouded in mystery. The various connections with the Luke story may well prove to be significant, just as her name might (*rey* comes from the Spanish *rex* meaning king, but also may have to do with the light of the sun). Clues to her origin include her accented speech, which suggests a connection with either Coruscant or with aristocracy of some kind, her Force-consciousness, and the fact that neither of her parents are seen in the movie nor is her surname provided. Wherever the succeeding episodes go with her character, *TFA* offers the audience a likeable and robustly heroic female lead, although given her talents and evident lack of weakness, it is difficult to imagine what kind of character-development remains open to the writers of the forthcoming pair of episodes. More importantly, though, the introduction of Rey both displays real selfless heroism that properly engages in responsible action rather than the selfabsorbed longing for excitement and also acknowledges that a *SW* narrative can focus on a young woman.

Nonetheless, there is a telling difference between the Luke and Rey story arcs, and one that is not ethically insignificant. The general issue has to do with the ease with which Rey comes to Force-consciousness, taking the form not merely of a kind of immediate and intuitive sense of the Force but also of a set of Force-wielding talents that have circumvented the way in which other characters in the *SW* universe have needed training. It is important to spend some time unpacking what has changed with this element of the *SW* movies.

It has often been noted that in *ANH* the Force is largely a plot device, a kind of consciousness enhancement. Without it, for instance, Luke's torpedo would likely have impacted on the surface as had happened with the bombing run of Red Leader in the attack on the Death Star. This reductive reading of the Force within the movie as a mere plot device is contradicted by the way Obi Wan describes the Force. One thing that is clear from the film is the need for training. Luke, who we learn is the "new hope" (even if in *ESB* Yoda reveals that there is "another"), is slowly inducted into awareness of it under the tutelage of Obi Wan, and later Yoda. In August 1977, three months after the theatrical release of *ANH*, Lucas explained that "the Force really doesn't have anything to do with the lightsaber. Anybody can have a lightsaber."[16] True to form, of course, General Grievous in *ROTS* has several that he has taken from the bodies of the Jedi he has slain, and he does so out of technical skill and training alone rather than from and through an ability to marshal the Force in combat. Instead, *SW*'s visionary continues, "The Force is really a way of feeling; it's a way of being with life. It really has nothing to do with weapons." In *ESB*, of course, we see the great Jedi Master Yoda brandish nothing but his gimer stick. The "power to have extrasensory perception and to be able to see things and hear things, read minds and levitate things" is then mentioned. But what is crucial is that this "power" is not the first or primary thing that Lucas conceives of as being Force-conscious. He then speaks of the higher Force awareness of those who "have more midi-chlorians in their cells," something not mentioned in his films until *TPM* in 1999 and a topic that continues to cause consternation among a substantial section of *SW*'s fans. His next statement about the Force is just as significant:

> The Force is a perception of the reality that exists around us. You have to come to learn it. It's not something you just get. It takes many, many years. Luke is on the road to knowing the Force, but it will be another twenty years before he actually begins to cope with it on a real level. He's still an amateur. . . . The Force is always there, however. Anyone who studied and worked hard could learn it.[17]

Of course Lucas had to telescope Luke's apprenticeship in the Force for dramatic effect, so that by *ROTJ* Luke declares to the Emperor, "I am a Jedi Knight like my father before me." The prequels, however, properly suggest that although the apprenticeship as a Jedi Padawan is of limited duration, contemplating and being an *apprentice in* the Force is a lifetime's activity.

Because of the end of the Jedi Masters, guiding their Padawans in feeling and knowledge of the Force, Lucas admits that while "anyone who studied and worked hard could learn it . . . you would have to do it on your own."[18] While that comment is understandable in the context of the dissolution and destruction of the Jedi Order, it does sit perilously close to the culturally influential spirit of self-reliance that the trajectory of the movie's depiction of teamwork and friendship subverts. *SW*'s director does himself tend toward this spirit of the self-made person in occasional interviews.[19] Even so, his practice is better than his theory here—in *ANH* we see Luke being inducted into a tradition of learning, guided or educated by the sagacious Obi-Wan; in *ESB* we watch him "unlearn" what he has learned through the highly experienced Yoda; in the prequels we come to understand the importance of the practice of discipling, of pairing up an apprentice with a Master. After all, the Force needs to be interpreted, and no interpretation is free from social influence. The Force can even be *misinterpreted* when used for nefariously self-aggrandizing purposes. Moreover, the very social reconditioning of many of the characters is vital to their learning. So Han (and possibly Lando as well) is transformed by his relations, particularly those with Leia and Luke, as well as enduring a symbolic rebirth when defrosted in Jabba's palace.

In this context *TFA* offers a number of troubling moments centered on Rey.[20] On the one hand, Rey's "first steps" into the Force are interpreted by Maz Kanata, who admits, "I am no Jedi, but I know the Force." That in itself is a suggestive claim. What does knowledge of the Force mean when it does not take place within the tradition of Force-study, Force-interpretation, and Force-meditation? It may simply mean that Maz was never trained to be a Knight, but the reference is not to a particular level of Jedi but simply to "Jedi." She continues by making a claim that echoes Yoda's teaching in *ESB*: "It moves through and surrounds every living thing." Those fans who railed against *TPM* will have appreciated the absence of any reference to midi-chlorians while keeping the spirit of both the universality of the Force and the implications for symbiotic harmony of life in and through that Force. "Close your eyes. Feel it," Maz tells Rey, who is clearly upset, distressed by the visions that followed her touching of the lightsaber and awakened to the fact that those whom she awaited on Jakku would probably never return. (How is the lightsaber "calling" to Rey in the first place?)[21]

Again the reference is to Yoda's pedagogy in Force-consciousness: "Feel the Force around you." Feeling the Force, when it is combined with an education in the Force, is one thing. It provides a more holistic sense to what is meant by 'knowledge' of the Force. The difficulty with what ensues in *TFA*, however, suggests something different—an immediacy of knowing the Force that does not require a teacher other than the Force itself, which "will guide you" when one closes one's eyes and concentrates on the Force. The fact that the one character who offers her training is Kylo Ren does not help, since it functions as an ominous (but underdeveloped) mini-temptation moment.

In *ANH* Luke is surprised by Obi-Wan's Force mind-manipulation of a sandtrooper on entering Mos Eisley. The Jedi mentor explains that "the Force can have a strong influence on the weak-minded." Rey, in contrast, suddenly discovers that she, without any education in the capabilities of Force-conscious, can manipulate her guard to undo her restraints and to leave his blaster for her as he leaves. While in the wampa's cave on Hoth in *ESB*, the Jedi apprentice Force-summons the lightsaber into his hand for the first time on screen. He has already received some direction from Obi-Wan and presumably has received further guidance from his tutor via his ghostly presence as well. Again, in contrast, on the same day (or at least very soon after) Rey discovers her connection with the Force, she is able to summon the lightsaber into her hand even while Kylo Ren attempts to do the same. What makes this an even more astonishing act is that the fallen Jedi formerly known as Ben Solo has already demonstrated the immensity of his control of the dark side of the Force by halting a laser blast in mid-air for quite some time.

The further telescoping of the way the power of the Force is cultivated by the main protagonist is significant. There is an issue of the exaggerated speed of rash narrative plotting in order to get Rey, now very much a "Mary Sue" type of character, into a position where she can defeat Ren in a lightsaber battle. But what is more telling is the fact that apart from a brief comment from Maz about the Force, the writers have chosen to dispense at this point with any sense of mentoring, discipling in the Force. And this is a move that otherwise appears in the context of material that has copied and resituated much of *ANH*. This is, of course, a new development that is well-equipped to pander to the optimistic message of North American and North West European hyper-individualism that appeals to *self-reliance*, and to various New Age *self-help* spiritualities. Force-consciousness is now being reduced in Disney *SW*'s to a "do-it-yourself" or "just do it" approach.

Before leaving this section focused on female characters, it is worth mentioning Captain Phasma. Hers is a quite different case altogether from those of Rey and Leia. Although one must be careful not to speculate on the direction her characterization will take in the future movies, in *TFA* she fits uncomfortably into the *SW* movies. The stormtrooper commander is the first female character in the *SW* movies who is placed on the side of the military machine that fights the movies' heroes. *AOTC*'s Zam Wesell functioned in a different way, since the Clawdite character was construed as a bounty hunter rather than as part of the Confederacy of Independent Systems (the "Separatists"). Shu Mai, the Gossam character from Castell who is the President of the Commerce Guild, makes only a very brief appearance around the Separatists' war table. While Asajj Ventress has been an interesting character in her own right in the two sets of Clone War animations, Lucas chose not to use her, and that choice has served an important conceptual function—Palpatine's Empire is depicted as a force of domination, not just of political and military authority, but also of patriarchal ascendancy and racial/species supremacism.[22] (The fact that General Grievous was Kaleesh and Darth Maul was Zabrak does not undermine this point, since they were both deliberately *used* and therefore expendable. No tears were seen to be shed by Sidious when they were killed, in contrast to the tender moment with the mutilated Anakin on Mustafar.)

What is the significance of *TFA*'s thus-far rather thinly developed character Phasma? At this stage it is difficult to say. Certainly something has potentially been lost—the critical weight provided by the representation of patriarchy in the very structure of Lucas's construal of the Empire, a system of relations that the classic trilogy seems to try to undo. On the other hand, arguably the presence of a female First Order infantry officer, combined with the strong female presence in the Resistance, may suggest that patriarchy is a spent force not worth even critical representation on-screen. The *Star Wars, The Force Awakens: The Visual Dictionary* states that Phasma "pays little heed to outdated notions of inequality between genders, an idea common on undeveloped worlds."[23] Yet, as an object of the Resistance's violent action, any female First Order character, and likewise with the female Resistance fighters who are the target of the First Order's violent deeds, her introduction may well contribute to the growing screen violence against women. Even so, the movie has simply made too little of Phasma to know what to do with her just yet, and therefore any critical reading of her significance both to the unfolding saga and as a moment of cultural representation should be offered with considerable hesitation. The underdevelopment of her character means that, unlike *ANH*, this newest addition to the franchise does not function well as a stand-alone movie. The writers and director of the forthcoming *Episode VIII* have considerable work to do to fill in some vast gaps in the new story.

"You Looked at Me Like No One Ever Had" (Finn to Rey)

Matters of Race

A further area in which *TFA* shifts the vision of the emerging (*Episodes I–III*) and then emergent (*Episodes IV–VI*) Empire is with the character of Finn. The first time we see him he is unnoticeable, because the shot is of the battle-prepared stormtroopers descending to Tuanul in Jakku's Kelvin Ravine in their Atmospheric Assault Landers. Given the helmets and the uniforms, we are unaware that there is anything distinctive about him. The camera singles him out only when he rushes over to a dying comrade, FN-2003, who touchingly places a bloody hand on his helmet. (How a trooper shot with Poe Dameron's blaster rifle has a bloody hand anyway is another plot hole made for dramatic effect. It certainly makes the *SW* combat more realistic than the bloodless, computerized, cartoonish violence of the prequels, but it is an odd wound given the laser weaponry involved, unless the fatally wounded trooper's fall to the ground resulted in a cut hand.) That mark of blood now sets him apart, and the experience of watching a comrade die has a traumatic effect on him. However, he seems to have no qualms about blasting his way out of the Star Destroyer, killing his comrades in the process. (This is an example of a number of glaring gaps in the storytelling.) Immediately after his combat-initiation scene, he moves in a startled fashion, quickly jerking his head to look left and right in panic. He comes closer to absconding from the ranks of the First Order when he refuses to kill a villager, a scene cut from the movie, most likely for pacing purposes. (It was a little too long and was also made unnecessary by virtue of the fact that when the prisoners were being executed, the trooper we later learn is number FN-2187 fails to fire and even lowers his weapon as his conformist colleagues engage in a ruthless acquiescence to orders).

There is nonetheless an issue of how and why twenty-three years of First Order propaganda and the pressure of his acquiescent peers do not take control of his psyche. Later on Takodana, he admits to Rey, "I wasn't gonna kill for them." What is interesting is the use of the "them" when describing the First Order. By this point in the story he is fleeing from his past, but the move to regarding the Order as "other" is too neat. In the flow of the movie, his defection is far too swift when it is left unaccompanied by a significant backstory. This is a not an insignificant moral matter with regard to the transformation of character. The sense is that some people are inherently good, and for them no amount of training in wickedness will disfigure or morally impair them. So *The Visual Dictionary* claims, "It would seem that Finn's good nature—a gentleness, humor and unerring moral compass—could not be wiped from his mind as it is from others who undergo stormtrooper training."[24] The sense of this not only involves a naiveté over the way that virtue is *learned*, but it points toward a lurking Manichaean tendency in the movie—the "pure us" (those who innately know and do the good) versus the "evil them" (those bent on dominating others and those who conform to their authority). This is what underpins not only FN-2187's inability to kill the Tuanul villagers but the ease of his dispatching First Order personnel when fleeing the *Finalizer* with Poe. To return to the difficulty with his "conversion," it would seem that no amount of training or habituation in wickedness will make one vicious, and the good will always win out. The sense of moral development and its relation to the good and to wickedness here is more like that of children's movies and comic books, of a portrayal of humanity being good at heart (or at least those who are not essentially other and therefore irredeemable, those whom Abrams explicitly refers to as the "baddies"). On this sensibility I will have more to say later in the chapter, and much has already been written about it in my earlier chapters. Suffice to say for now, it is a morally disturbing sensibility that lurks throughout this movie, especially so given the care that Lucas took, at least from *ESB* onward, to undo any residual Manichaean-like dualism and a naiveté over the way virtue and vice are formed with the education of character.[25]

There is, however, another feature of Finn's desertion that is actually morally helpful. Military personnel are hired, trained, and conditioned to obey authority (*Full Metal Jacket* presents a version of that conditioning during a time of war), even when the orders they receive might trouble them. FN-2187 hesitates to carry out the villager-extermination order and exhibits signs of compassion and trauma, which show not only his strength of character but also his *moral integrity*. It is little wonder that after the battle he is listed for mental reconditioning and renewal therapy. Simple and unreflective conformity is a recipe for moral blindness and tragedy.

It is only later that FN-2187 removes his helmet and the trooper is unmasked as a young black man. There are several thought-provoking things worth reflecting on here. The casting of a black man as a major character early in the movie suggests that *TFA* has learned something from the criticisms of racial tokenism related to the incorporation of Lando Calrissian. Also worth considering are the racial criticisms of the depiction of the Tusken Raiders or Sand People, Jar Jar, the Neimoidians, and Watto. (There are arguably racial stereotypes in *TFA* as well, with the distinctive Glaswegian brogue of Bala-Tik of the Guavian Death Gang and the Triad-like Kanjiklub).[26] Lucas had been concerned about hiring James Earl Jones for Vader's voice since, as the only black actor in *ANH*, he would also be playing the villain. However, Fred Roos convinced the director to cast Jones because of the commanding presence that his baritone voice would add to David Prowse's physicality in the suit.[27] Lando was designed in order to ensure that there would indeed be a durable and heroic black character in the *SW* saga, although as with the sole female presence of Leia, it smacked of tokenism. (One might still legitimately ask whether there is sufficient racial representation in *TFA* or whether it relies too much on the nonhuman characters to provide a more substantive sense of racial difference. Poe Dameron, at least, is played by a Guatemalan actor; Admiral Statura by an Asian-American actor; and Maz by a Kenyan-Mexican actress, although she is animated over in order to play a diminutive nonhuman character.) Moreover, the classic trilogy's Vietnam references would have been enhanced if the Empire, despite (or possibly precisely because of) its white supremacism, had generated or recruited a majority of its disposable troops from young nonwhite males. As Henry Giroux argues, "a disproportionate number of soldiers who fought in Vietnam were poor, were high school dropouts, and were African American or Latino."[28]

Yet, according to Gregory E. Rutledge, "a black stormtrooper is as much out of place as, nostalgically, blacks and Native Americans are to the American Revolution cultural logic."[29] An interesting possibility is that this could precisely be a reference to nonwhite troops who are used and led by middle-class white officers, the most expendable of the various military personnel. When Finn later reveals that his time had been employed in "sanitation," the point may have been scripted simply for comedic effect. He is no trooper well-versed in killing or in being of any particular use as an informant to the Resistance. It might also partially offer an explanation of why he was unduly scarred by his experiences in his first combat mission. Equally, the reference might simply humanize the character so that the audience does not lump him in with all those who have been trained to be killers. But why would one of the sanitation services personnel be sent into combat unless this is a reference to the First Order's military stock running low? The speech scene with General Hux before the gathered military masses certainly does not support this theory. *The Visual Dictionary*'s explanation is that "[a]s part of his training rotation, FN-2187 also logged many hours on sanitation detail, dirty work that nevertheless needed doing."[30] Even so, why this sanitation work was being done by highly, and presumably expensively, trained and combat-skilled personnel rather than droids appears more than a little peculiar. Of course, the very exercise of exterminating the inhabitants of a "sacred village" is itself a form of cleansing, a political act to cleanse the galaxy of the religious groups that were outlawed during the Imperial regime.[31] With that in mind, talk of "sanitation" becomes a considerably more sinister matter.

Crucially, at least, after Finn's highly symbolic removal of each armored plate of his stormtrooper uniform, this young man's clothing against the backdrop of the desert is reduced to simple black undergarments (begging the question of how he survived the crash). The image is one of his losing his identity. His sense of self has to be constructed subsequently when his journey becomes informed by each of his encounters, especially those with Rey. When he dons Poe's jacket, this lack of self is reinforced because, for a moment, he takes on another's identity as a Resistance fighter. Initially his desires take the form of simple self-preservation and self-interest. When he liberates Poe from his restraints on the *Finalizer*, he responds to the Resistance pilot's question "Why are you helping me?" with a moral assertion, "Because it's the right thing to do." The more experienced warrior sees through this rhetoric and recognizes that the earlier question of "Can you fly a TIE Fighter?" reveals a different motivation: "You need a pilot." In this there may well be a reference back to Lando, minus the gambler backstory of course, at the moment when the latter opted not to side with Han, Leia, and Chewbacca once the threat of Darth Vader loomed menacingly large over his (and Cloud City's) future. However, a further attack of conscience, coupled with his burgeoning friendship with Rey, pushes him in a different and more ethically responsible direction. That his rapidly growing rapport with others is properly humanizing is suggested by a comment he makes to Rey: "you looked at me like no one ever had. I was ashamed of what I was." The young woman, in other words, has had a redemptive effect on Finn, looking at him like an equal, a human being worthy of respect and amity rather than a numbered object programmed to conform to brutal orders for the purposes of enslaving and destroying the lives of the nonconformists and their government, or what General Hux calls "a regime that acquiesces to disorder."

The character of Finn cannot but raise the issue of the clones, a matter that was even mentioned by Ren when he criticized General Hux for the defection of FN-2187 (Finn).[32] From a very young age, Finn was trained to obey (he was "programmed" according to Hux) and was cultivated in the mythology of the First Order, as well as trained in the skills required for the role. This indoctrination does have a similar effect to the earlier system of cloning. This is reinforced by the naming of the troopers by numbers and the masking of their faces, a process of deindividualization as well as an instrumentalization of their lives. Nonetheless, what the movie does not do in any shape or form is rehumanize any of its "sinister First Order" characters other than Finn, and thereby it does not critique the deadly instrumentalization of the lives of others in the way that becomes so important in *AOTC* and *ROTS* (nor does it offer a critique of the values of unfettered capitalism such as that which run through Lucas's saga). This perpetuates the dehumanization of others and hints at the issue from which real ethical concerns with the new material emerge.

"We Must Face Them, Fight Them!" (Maz): The Return to Political Conflictuality

In one of three episodes of the television show *Robot Chicken* specifically dedicated to *SW*, there is a sketch involving two Imperial officers on board one of the Star Destroyers. The context is the engagement of hostilities against the fleet of the Rebel Alliance at the end of *ROTJ*. One particularly animated officer excitedly commands: "Convene all ships on Endor. I want the moon obliterated and the Rebels [eradicated] from the face of the galaxy." To this the more junior of the pair responds, "Sorry sir, but actually we can't. The Rebels won." "What do you mean 'they won'?" asks the first, puzzled. "We have tens of thousands of ships; we control countless worlds; we have millions of troops at our disposal." At this point the second officer interrupts: "But they just blew up the Second Death Star and killed the Emperor." More perturbed than ever, the senior officer quips, "So?" to which the response comes, "So, that means that they won." Not to be put off by this odd situation, the higher-ranking official asks again "How does that mean 'they won'? They blew up the First Death Star years ago and the fighting continued." The difference, his subordinate admits, is that in the first of these victories "they didn't kill the Emperor. They have to do both."

The sketch has a Monty Pythonesque quality, with the comedy lying in the observational value of a "not suffering fools gladly" scenario, identifying a significant plot hole in the ending of the story. But it raises an important matter that many fans and post-*ROTJ* Expanded Universe materials have attempted to address in different ways. Of course, the finality of the celebratory scenes at the close of the movie make sense within the archetypal design of Lucas's plot and the characters integral to that plot. It was for this reason that chapter 8 addressed the conclusion of the movie as having an *eschatological quality* about it. On a political level, the Imperial collapse relates somewhat to the overlaps between the Nazi regime and Lucas's Empire. There is one telling difference here, though, and that is that when Hitler and his staff committed suicide in their bunker, the German forces were at that stage beleaguered and hemmed in by the Allied troops advancing into the German heartlands from the west and the Soviets from the east. In *ROTJ* the Imperial forces were confronted and beaten by a considerably inferior force after the former had the upper hand until the death of Palpatine. Again, while the connection between the Empire and Nixon's forces in Vietnam are also in Lucas's view, *ROTJ*'s overlaps with real events is minimal. It is certainly not an allegory. After all, the retreat from Vietnam did not cause the collapse of the United States and her allies, and it was not the consequence of the assassination of the president, and there has been no straightforward happy-ever-after scenario for the peoples of Southeast Asia.

SW is without question a set of violent movies. The reference to military conflict in its very title is, of course, a giveaway. Psychologists Elizabeth A. Kus and Janina Scarlet draw attention to various studies of the issue of copycatting screened violence. In one study, "men who watched films in which women were sexually abused became more likely to display harassing or violent behaviors toward women."[33] However, the important ethical question is not whether there is violence or not but what the violence is for and how it is portrayed. After all, a good many antiwar movies are replete with violent acts and images.

At the very least, violence as a form of *entertainment* can slip an audience exposed to it into a moral slumber so that the complex causes of violence evade us even in the moments of our more critical alertness. *TFA* contains three scenes in which the consequences of the violent action are made more appropriately audience-involving than simply audience-entertaining. Entertaining violence renders violent behavior as fun, to be celebrated and enjoyed. In contrast, the realism of the troop drop into Tuanul and the subsequent gunning down of mainly unarmed villagers adds a timely poignancy to the drama. At this moment the violence is not to be enjoyed. Rather it is deadly, unjust, and brutal. In a later scene, the audience is forced to see the faces of senators on Hosnian Prime as the Starkiller laser bolt approaches. The solemn John Williams musical theme echoes the emotionally powerful Order 66 in *ROTS*, with its heartbreaking scene when the elegant Jedi Masters are cut down by the troops on Palpatine's orders. This is a marked step up from the destruction of Alderaan in *ANH*, in which the emotion is carried quite lightly through a momentary dropping of Leia's emotional reserve with a quivering no and Obi-Wan's claim about the crying out and subsequent silencing of a million voices.[34] Likewise the lengthy scene in which Han is killed by his son, the Master of the Knights of Ren, is reasonably well done. After Han appeals emotionally to Ren (or, rather, Ben) to give up the dark and destructive cult he has been manipulated by, the young man begins to cry, evidently suffering emotional turmoil. The fact that the camera lingers on the figures in the execution and prolongs the death scene intensifies its importance. The screaming reactions of Rey, Finn, and Chewbacca effectively intensify the significance of the death for the *SW* universe. They act as something of a chorus to guide the audience's reaction. Lucas, for his part, had resisted actor Harrison Ford's appeal to him to kill Han in *ROTJ*, since his character was largely dramatically unnecessary throughout that episode once he was removed from Jabba's clutches. The writer resisted and announced to his creative team that he did not like movies killing off the main characters, particularly because of the trauma that would ensue for a young audience. The point is a good one, but the fact that Abrams and Kasdan have done what Lucas had earlier refused to do at least emphasizes the waste of life that can and does come with war.

While this is all well and good, and generates potential for some ethically interesting material, *TFA* slips too easily into the "good violence" motif that troubles particularly *ANH*. But *TFA* does so in such a way as to mitigate one or two of the elements that in the first *SW* movie could potentially offset the sacralisation of a violent order. What is involved here can be unpacked in several ways, although I will focus only on two elements in Abrams's and Kasdan's *SW* movie: the necessity of the violence (this section of the chapter) and the dualistic interpretation of the Force (the following and final section of the chapter).

Peter Jackson's Lady Galadriel, the Lady of the forest elves of Lothlorien, announces that the world has changed, and her lament comes in the context of assuming that this has involved a *fall* from a certain kind of global peace-fulness into the impending destruction of the kingdoms, in fact Middle Earth itself, through war. So she says, "Much that once was is *lost* for none now live who remember it." Of course, peace does not sell movie tickets. Disney's choice to return to the ongoing violent conflict in *SW* reinforces the idea that the conflict is never-ending, irresolvable by any means other than violent resistance. According to cultural commentator Leonidas Donskis, "Violence shown every day ceases to provoke amazement, or disgust. It, as it were, grows on you."[35] In other words, it is *naturalized*, made part of our every-day horizons. In this regard the selection of items worth reporting on in the print and television news is telling and reinforces the idea that violence and conflict are not only inescapable but also pervasive in our world, countries, cities, streets, and so on. There is no reference in *TFA*, as there is in *ANH*, to a time of prior peace or even to a hope for a future peaceful reconciliation. Abrams's and Kasdan's sensibility for *SW* is that it involves a never-ending conflict precisely because it is grounded in an *eternal* conflict. This fram-ing of the drama is sustained by a less careful prevention of the theological sensibility often referred to as "Manichaean dualism" than has been the case with Lucas's *SW*. Certainly the mood of something akin to an eschatological realization of galactic or cosmic peace in *ROTJ* is both dramatically unrealistic and premature (given, theologically, the drama of life lived before the consummating *eschaton* or End). Nonetheless, it does at least symbolically offer a vital form of resistance to the dominance of a Manichaean sensibility. This resistant note is enhanced when one bears in mind the language of the fall of Vader in *ANH*, the narrative of the near-fall of Luke (*ROTJ*), the redemption of Vader (*ROTJ*), and the tragic parallels of the demise of the Republic, Anakin, and Padmé (*AOTC*, *ROTS*).

But worse, this not wanting to think about violence is reinforced by the multiplication of certain cultural and political appeals to values and myths that are increasingly embedded in common talk about violence and its perpetrators. This means that there is a further form of naturalization involved in certain depictions of violence and conflict rather than any simple resignation to unending conflict: that of the naturalization of conflictual values such as those of self-assertion, self-interest, reactive anger, binary divisions between "us" and "them," and so on. Paul Verhoeven, the director of *Robocop* and *Starship Troopers*, once revealingly admitted that "the US is desperate for a new enemy. . . . The Communists were the enemy, and the Nazis before them, but now that wonderful enemy everyone can fight has been lost. Alien sci-fi gives us a terrifying enemy that's politically correct. They're bad. They're evil. And they're not even human."[36] Verhoeven's lack of irony in using the phrase "politically correct" while also using terms for the aliens such as "enemy" and "evil" is revealing of a powerful strand in American political culture.

It is this sensibility that commentators are so concerned about when they look at the forms of ideological representation in movies, television, music, and literature. The literary critic Terry Eagleton laments, "In the so-called war against terror, 'evil' is used to foreclose the possibility of historical explanation."[37] Speaking of a politics "perpetuating its own self-blindness," Eagleton observes how moral reflexivity is deferred by the morally simplistic character of a variety of euphemisms, slogans, and images.[38] Among other things, these not only legitimate any national conflict but also reinforce the notion of "sacrifice" for those brutalized in the process, those whose lives are wasted by a system that disposes of them to embracing a scapegoat mechanism. Their lives become disposable when the governing system demands it, and critical interrogation of that system is simplistically denied by reason-evading appeals to, for instance, patriotism and duty, freedom and honor, and even my/our "way of life." The system, in other words, generates a set of categories and language that serves as something of a pathology of denial.

It is too early to say whether there will be an anti-Manichaean form of redemption in Disney's *SW*, a shocking turn in Lucas's *ROTJ* that upsets the Manichaean exclusion of the enemy as pure and irredeemable "other." According to Chris Taylor, "The redemption of Darth Vader would rub some fans the wrong way."[39] Even the ghostwriter of *ANH*'s novelization, Alan Dean Foster, dismissed it: "It's like Hitler's on his deathbed and he repents and everything's okay. 'I've murdered eight million people, but I'm sorry.' I just couldn't go with that."[40] Foster is right to suggest that the moment of repentance cannot undo the terrible damage Vader has inflicted on the galaxy, and he is also correct to suggest that there should not be any glib presentation of it. On the other hand, his comments indicate just how difficult it is to conceive of *forgiveness* and *reconciliation*, especially in the most difficult of conditions. According to Taylor, *ROTJ*'s producer Lawrence Kazanjian, a devout Christian, was likewise perturbed by the event "until Lucas pointed out that his religion emphasized forgiveness. Thereafter Kazanjian was a convert and came up with the suggestion that Anakin Skywalker's ghost should make an appearance at the end alongside Obi-Wan and Yoda."

TFA's depiction of Kylo Ren's backstory at least offers similar potential. Ben Solo, son of Leia and Han, was seduced to the dark side when he fell under the influence of Snoke, with the result that he joined the Supreme Leader's cause and annihilated the Jedi Academy. Lor San Tekka and Han both remind him of his heritage in an effort to convince him to reject the Supreme Leader's dark hold on him. In particular, the references to following Vader's work are useful markers of his motivations and ambitions and of the deliberate parallels between the two characters. Even the turmoil and the petulant behavior he demonstrates are reminiscent of the Anakin of *AOTC* and *ROTS*, and it is seemingly only with the execution of his father that he begins to resolve his identity crisis.[41] The awakening, it would appear, is not only of Rey becoming Force-conscious but of Ren coming into his own in the dark side. Even if the narrative arc of Kylo Ren takes a similar direction, he has been responsible for, among other things, the annihilation of the new Jedi Academy, an entire Jakku village, and his own father, Han Solo. In that regard, any character transformation would need to be handled sensitively and without anything that would undermine the tragic significance of his actions. However, without a moment of repentance and forgiveness, he may contribute to the sense of an irretrievable fall from grace that dominates the mind-set of those who believe in retributive and not restorationist justice.

In the meantime, however, the depiction of the opposition between the

Resistance and the First Order is clean-cut. The visual references to Nazism not only remain striking (after all, the First Order emerges from the ashes of the Empire) but are even enhanced by virtue of the loss of Lucas's references to the empires of Rome and the United States. True, the English-accented naval officers continue to offer a nod to the British Empire, but without Lucas's implicit critique of America during the Vietnam War, the implication is that the Resistance in *TFA* is more akin to the American forces fighting against British imperialism.[42] This observation would make sense of an *Apocalypse Now*-like image. The TIE Fighter attack on Takodana occurs with the screen-filling sun as a backdrop, only now it has John Williams's score rather than Richard Wagner's *Flight of the Valkyries*. If that textual reference is indeed intended, then the point of Francis Ford Coppola's movie has been entirely missed, since for him it is the American helicopter gunships that are the airborne attack force, while *TFA* certainly makes no other equation of the First Order with the United States and its allies in Vietnam.

What is more, the various political contexts of the different sets of movies are significant. Lucas has often mentioned that the real-world context of the classic trilogy was the rising tide of reactionary politics in the United States, from the escalation of the Vietnam conflict through to the ascension to the Oval Office of Ronald Reagan. The plucky band of Rebel fighter terrorists in this milieu play a significant role against the regime of the superpower. So in an early draft of *SW* in 1973 Lucas envisaged a "large technological empire going after a small group of freedom fighters."[43] During this time he was also working on *Apocalypse Now*, a movie he would have directed had it not been for its producer's (Francis Ford Coppola) inability to secure a studio that would finance it. Lucas jokes that if he had directed, he would have been run out of the country by the government.

The tragic direction taken by the narratives of the prequel trilogy, especially *AOTC* and *ROTS*, occur during a period when the government of one of the world's superpowers attempted to reshape large sections of the world in its own image *with military force* and with distinct connections to powerful business interests. In 2012 Lucas said that "I'm a very ardent patriot, but I'm also a very ardent believer in democracy, not capitalist democracy" or a government "bought" by the rich.[44] He continued by announcing that the prequels had been designed to "subliminally" convey the message of "what happens to you if you've got a dysfunctional government that's corrupt and doesn't work." Of course, the directions of the trilogy's drama had been broadly planned for some years before the turn of events under the Bush administration, yet "it was hard to see a movie that featured a Republic sliding into a dictatorship via the granting of emergency war powers, and not think you were watching a specific commentary on George W. Bush's administration post-9/11."[45] Commenting on the political implications of *ROTS*, Lucas publicly likened Bush to Nixon and Iraq to Vietnam, adding "I didn't think I'd get this close."[46]

In contrast, in *TFA* the superpower or dominant political system is the New Republic, and it is the First Order that is thereafter cast in the mold of the lesser political power. The Resistance is certainly militarily smaller again, but it is something of a strike team operating to protect the sovereign New Republic. That means that the First Order takes the role of a terrorist organization that possesses a weapon of mass destruction. The resonance of this in the current geopolitical context is markedly different from that of Lucas's *SW* movies, especially the first trilogy that had the political fallout over the Vietnam conflict and therefore more consciously depicted issues of colonialism in its background. In this regard, it is telling that General Hux's impassioned speech to his amassed forces, with sizable red and black banners in the background, is a visual reference to Hitler's delivery of powerful rhetoric in venues such as Nuremburg. But his language does not refer to the ethnicity of those internal to the regime that have betrayed it or to the need for living space for the German people. Rather, it centers on moral matters, and in the contemporary world-scene this has another resonance for identifying those to be fought as evil others: the New Republic "lies to the galaxy while secretly supporting the treachery of the loathsome Resistance. . . . All remaining systems will bow to the First Order." This is a fundamentalism requiring complete political and ideological takeover, a fundamentalism enthusing the gathered ranks against those portrayed as politically decadent. Alan Dean Foster's novelization even uses this language of "decadence" more generally to describe the New Republic.[47] This characterization is picked up later when Kylo Ren sneers at Rey and confronts her about "the murderers, traitors, and thieves you call friends." Here the New Republic and the Resistance are as irredeemably "other" to the First Order as it is to them. With such regimes there can be no compromise, no conversation, no cooperation, no negotiation, only conflict and annihilation, only opposition from what is described as "a brave Resistance." In a childish way Abrams even refers to them in an interview as the "baddies." They are binary opposites, but yet in some ways they are mirror images of each other. The resistant conflict is not eschatological as much as apocalyptic, involving not reconciliation and peacefulness as much as all-out conflict to the bitter end.

Perhaps this is the reason why the deadly violence against the heroic characters and the New Republic is often depicted with a lot of emotional engagement, while the violence against the First Order is portrayed with qualities more associated with entertaining violence—such as a jubilant score when the X-Wings appear to save the day at Takodana; the swiftness of the dispatch of the stormtroopers by Han, Chewbacca, and Finn; and the euphoria of the fighter attack on the superweapon. Displayed is the *need* for violent action against the enemy without regret, reluctance, or a lamenting sense of tragedy. If anything, the *necessary* disposability of the First Order in the various battles is offered in sharper relief since the deaths of the Resistance and New Republic characters are depicted with a sensitivity that is lacking in the depiction of the deaths of First Order personnel. Of course, this motif is made even more significant now by virtue of the revelation that the stormtroopers are not the distinctly limited biomechanical life-forms of mass-produced clones or the mechanical enemy manufactured on Genosian production lines. The First Order offers nothing other than the rule of death, pure death and a destructive order. As the screen crawl states, it is "sinister" and "will not rest until Skywalker, the last of the Jedi, has been destroyed." This is a highly significant message from an entertainment company that, according to Henry Giroux, "is more than a corporate giant; it is also a cultural institution that fiercely protects its legendary status as a purveyor of innocence and moral virtue."[48]

To that end, it is unsurprising that despite the peace treaty and severe galactic disarming that was imposed on the remnants of the Empire after the war, Leia Organa is depicted in the backstories as warning that the measures were insufficiently stringent, and the newest trilogy in the saga proves her words "tragically prophetic."[49] This seems to be a reference to the growing fascist threat in the early 1930s, impelled by a feeling of betrayal over the humiliating and disarming Treaty of Versailles of 1919. "Leia Organa's warning about the suspicious activities of the First Order" follows the warnings that were given over the policy of Allied appeasement of the Nazis until the conflict was unavoidable. On the other hand, the message in the contemporary global context is one of more stark measures being required, a situation that would escalate the level of fear in an already-insecure environment. Either way, there is no sense of the complicity of the Allies/New Republic in contributing to the conditions that led to the rise of these fascist orders or absolutist political regimes. Instead, in the movie's novel Leia says the Resistance is engaged in a "war that won't end until either it or the Resistance is destroyed."[50] This arch-hawkishness enables deflection away from the "us" to "them," and the "them/others" are to be fought and defeated for "our" security. Moreover, it indicates that military disarmament is politically premature and complacently naive and leaves a political order particularly vulnerable to its enemies. Leia organizes the Resistance while never questioning what it is that constitutes an enemy in the first place nor suggesting that there is any virtue in a policy of staggered disarmament.[51]

Whose Force Is It Anyway?

I argued in chapter 6 and even more fully elsewhere that despite the number of criticisms that Lucas's *SW* promotes values that would unproblematically render violence natural, necessary, and even to be desired, these reproaches are in fact overstated.[52] What they miss is the sets of values that his movies promote that have considerable potential for contesting the very desires and beliefs that make war a seeming inevitability. Most of this book has reasoned that it is simply a mistake to claim that evil is "*not* a privation but an aspect of the Force."[53] Yet while Peter Lee's just-cited claim is quite mistaken about Lucas's Force, it is an uncomfortable one when applied to *TFA*: "*Star Wars*'s binary forces of 'light' and 'dark' sides . . . paralleled notions of American righteousness against an 'Other.'"[54] This means that at a highly significant point, *TFA* simply evacuates its narrative material of Lucas's morally enlightening and peaceable moments in the symbiotic Force. As a result, it offers no sense of the good life beyond a thin account of comradery in combat and the annihilation of one's enemies. (Accordingly, Lucas's critique of savage forms of corporate self-interest disappear.)

One of the inspirations behind Lucas's term 'the Force' was a short movie made by Arthur Lipsett in 1963 titled *21-87*. The movie was an abstract motion-collage that offered a reflection on the mechanization of society and a sense of what Taylor calls "transcendence."[55] The impact of this piece can be seen in Lucas's 1967 award-winning short student movie *Electronic Labyrinth: THX 1138 4EB*, which was expanded into his 1971 dystopian tone poem more simply titled "THX 1138." In a deleted scene in the latter movie, the titular character announces that "there must be something independent; a force, reality." And in *ANH* in a scene set in a detention block, Han announces to Luke, "We gotta find out which cell of this Princess of yours is in. Here it is—21-87." Moreover the mechanizing society that reduces people to numbers is something Lucas continues with through the reference to the Imperial stormtroopers by their number (*TFA* keeps this, at least). This is life reduced to its barest, to its purely instrumental or use value. However, after about three minutes of Lipsett's impressionistic piece comes a statement that made a profound impression and provided aid to Lucas's shaping of the spirituality of his first *SW*. "Many people feel that in sort of the contemplation of nature and in communication with other living things, they become aware of *some kind of force*, or *something*, behind this apparent mask, which we see in front of us, and they call it God." "The Force" and "God." It is not appropriate in the context of the *SW* movies to describe this "God" in dualistic terms. Certainly the Force is used for different ends, according to whether one is Sith or Jedi. But the Force itself is not neutral, since it is pervading all things and giving them life, according to Yoda in *ESB*. This is what Lucas admits to Pollock in a rather theologically simplistic fashion: "I was trying to say that there is a God and that there is both a good side and a bad side. You have a choice between them, but the world works better if you're on the good side."[56]

Early in *TFA* Lor San Tekka informs Poe that "without the Jedi there can be no balance in the Force." What this means is not further explained. The context is his giving the map of the location of Luke Skywalker, in which case presumably the "balance" would have to do with Luke's being more involved in the affairs of the galaxy, such as training a new generation of Jedi. At this stage there is no sense that the Sith are in operation, and so the reference does not have to be taken as a dualistic claim that there has to be light and dark, Jedi and Sith necessarily. On the other hand, the elderly man's previous admission ("This will begin to make things right. I've travelled too far and seen too much to ignore the despair in the galaxy") may well suggest that the "balance" has to do with the Jedi's elimination of the wickedness that brings despair to the galaxy. If this is the case, then the reference dovetails with Lucas's portrayal of the "balance" involving the very destruction of the Sith themselves. Support for this reading comes from Poe, the Resistance pilot, when he immediately responds, "Well, because of you, now we have a chance."

The difficulty, however, comes when the Force is referred to as having a "light" side: Maz claims that "the light, it's always been there," and a hopeful Leia later says to Han that "there is still light in him [viz., Ren], I know it." In Lucas's *SW* there is "the Force," and the reference to "the dark side of the Force" offers a perspective for the audience on the fact that the Sith and the Empire are wicked, distorting the Force for their own ends. This is what makes the exchanges between Palpatine and Anakin and then between Anakin and Obi-Wan on the nature of the Force so interesting and powerful in *ROTS*. However, once the language of the "light side" enters the saga, the image becomes not one of the light that enters the darkness and extinguishes it but rather the flip side of the Force's dark side. Tellingly the director himself comments:

I don't know if it was so explicit, but I always felt like it was implicit: The idea that the Force was this one thing, but there was a dark "side" of the Force. And that was always the temptation of power and greed, and yet—it didn't feel like it was a separate thing, but it was all inclusive. You know, it's almost like the flipside of the coin.[57]

Judging by much of the Expanded Universe literature and fan sites such as the wiki titled *Wookieepedia*, which speak about *sides* or *aspects* of the Force, this is a common interpretation of Lucas's material even if it does not fit well with numerous elements of Lucas's movies (see chapters 3–8) and generates significant moral difficulties with its dualistic sensibility. *The Complete Star Wars Encyclopedia* likewise claims that "there are two sides to the Force: The light side bestows great knowledge, peace, and an inner serenity; the dark side is filled with fear, anger, and the vilest aggression."[58] Here is a spirituality of conflict, *necessary* conflict, and therefore of a *normalization and sacralization of the violent order* against the enemy. It is this that takes the movie's conformity to hawkish sentiment beyond a mere ethos of personal survivalism. There seems to be a spiritual imperative to belligerently "balance" the Force.

Conclusion

In his study of the development of George Lucas's *SW*, Chris Taylor explains that Lucas envisioned the saga taking a franchise path like the James Bond series, with a variety of directors and interpretations.

Now people will start building on it. I've put up the concrete slab of the walls and now everybody can have fun drawing the pictures and putting on the little gargoyles and doing all the really fun stuff. And it's a competition. I'm hoping if I get friends of mine they will want to do a much better film, like, "I'll show George that I can do a film twice that good," and I think they can, but then I want to do the last one, so I can do one twice as good as everybody else.[59]

However, other comments suggest that "fun" is a term that should be used carefully with regard to Lucas's creation. For instance, when reflecting on the qualities sought in a director for *ROTJ*, he admits that he looked for:

somebody who doesn't just think it's kids' junk. Somebody who understands what's going on. A lot of people don't understand; they think it's some quick and easy kind of thing you throw out, with not much behind it.

But the truth of it is, there's a lot going on behind it, and the director has to have that sensibility.[60]

While Lucas wrote and oversaw *ESB* and *ROTJ* subsequent to this interview with *Rolling Stone*'s Paul Scanlon, himself to return to the director's chair for the trilogy of prequels, this dream of multiple directors became reality in 2012 when the franchise's rights were sold to Disney. The result seems not to have been to his liking, as the criticisms mentioned earlier regarding this "retro" movie make clear. When he launched an attack on Disney as "white-slavers," Lucas's reflections on the new *SW Episode*, however, became more cryptic, not least since after a nervous laugh he moved off the topic.[61] One reading might suggest that it is the product of painfully responding to someone else raising the child he has nurtured for so long. So he not only refers to the movies as his "kids" but even speaks of the sale in the language of a "break-up" and a "divorce." Perhaps he is now instead in the position of being the grumpy grandfather who does not appreciate the way the grandchildren are being reared, especially since he claims his input was explicitly rejected.[62] A *Guardian* newspaper article even titled its story covering this "Attack of the Moans."[63] However, if the reflections above are sound, then perhaps his concerns are actually ethical ones, and if they are not, then at least they should be. *TFA* simply assumes and displays a different set of moral values from those pervading Lucas's writing of *Episodes I–VI*, or at least those he established once he had repaired the rather misleading (because verging on a Manichaean-like dualism) direction *ANH* had taken. As he reflects,

> I feel very strongly about the role myths and fairy tales play in setting up young people for the way they're supposed to conduct themselves in society. It's the kind of thing Bruno Bettelheim talks about, the importance of childhood. I realized before I did *Star Wars* that there was no contemporary fairy tale and that the number of parents who sit down and tell their children fairy tales is dwindling. As families begin to break up, kids are left more to the television, and they don't hear bedtime stories. As a result, people are learning their mythology from TV, which makes them very confused because it has no point of view, no sense of morality. Fairy tales, religion, all were designed to teach the right way to live and give a moral anchor.[64]

If this is indeed the case, it may strike many as being odd. After all, as Giroux notices, "Popular audiences tend to reject any link between ideology and the prolific entertainment world of Disney."[65] The problem is that there are no innocent pieces of cultural work. A whole host of assumptions about what is valuable, worth expressing, and so on pervade cultural products, even those that appear to be the most child-friendly. In that regard, Lucas is being a little disingenuous by claiming that, for instance, "TV . . . has no point of view, no sense of morality." It does, but multiple points of view are expressed in a variety of shows that take diffuse forms. For many, even "Disney's pretense of innocence appears . . . as little more than a promotional mask that covers its aggressive marketing techniques and its influence in educating children to become active consumers."[66] Of course, this critical observation should, in turn, raise questions about the commercial direction that *SW* itself took—its successful merchandising that, in fact, generated the profits that enabled Lucas to make *ESB* and *ROTJ*, not to mention the prequels. Just as crucially, claims of innocence are powerful forms of rhetoric that mask the ways in which the media operates. So, continues Giroux, "Disney's 'innocence' renders it unaccountable for the way it shapes children's sense of reality: its sanitized notions of identity, difference, and history in the seemingly apolitical cultural universe of the 'magic kingdom.'" Learning to pay critical attention to media, even to Disney's productions, is vital for a healthy dose of democratic intelligence. According to Walter Lippmann in 1920, "There can be no liberty for a community which lacks the means by which to detect lies."[67] Consequently,

> rather than being viewed as a commercial venture innocently distributing pleasure to young people, the Disney empire must be seen as a pedagogical and policy-making enterprise actively engaged in the cultural landscaping of national identity and the "schooling" of the minds of young children. This is not to suggest that there is something sinister behind what Disney does. It points only to the need to address the role of fantasy, desire, and innocence in securing particular ideological interests, legitimating specific social relations, and making a claim on the meaning of public memory. Disney needs to be held accountable, which will require that parents, educators, and others challenge and disrupt both the institutional power and the images, representations, and values offered by Disney's teaching machine.[68]

Brad Evans and Henry Giroux argue that current conditions in fact require "a critique of violence that . . . encourages us to think beyond its necessity, so as to make clear that in a world in which violence is normalized, it once again becomes possible to imagine the unimaginable."[69] Numerous critics have claimed that Lucas's *SW* saga is distinctly unhelpful here, reinforcing what Walter Wink has called the "myth of redemptive violence." My analysis has suggested that this is actually to do Lucas's material a considerable disservice and to simply miss too much that occurs in his movies. *TFA* is a quite different case, however. The issue is not only with what the movie does but also with what it chooses to leave out, and it is those gaps especially, with the lack of any reference to the good life of peace, that are particularly revealing of what it values. We live in a time of the intensification of a "politics of fear" in the geopolitical sphere. We do not need the gospel of redemptive violence and wars of simple retributive justice; we need a form of robust peacemaking that changes the very myths of "self" and "other" we live by and that can cause violent competition. As Walter Brueggemann argues, "The great crisis among us is the crisis of 'the common good,' the sense of community solidarity that binds all in a common destiny—haves and have-nots, the rich and the poor. We face a crisis about the common good because there are powerful forces at work among us to resist the common good, to violate community solidarity, and to deny a common destiny."[70] What *TFA* provides is less a vision of the "common good" than of a good available to some that must be violently protected from the evil "others," the conformist myth of "us-versus-them," the combination of the politics of fear and the politics of purity. The theopolitical implications of this ethical infantilization of the *SW* saga are pronounced, and the popularity of the type of nostalgic path of dualistic *SW* interpretation that *Episode VII* takes may well force one to claim with Padmé, "So this is how liberty dies, with thunderous applause!"

Afterword

*I*n his study of film and religion, S. Brent Plate claims that "[f]ilms create worlds."[1] Of course, given the space operatic nature of the movies of the *SW* saga, the notion of world creation would seem rather obvious. But the imaginative creativity of science-*fiction* is not what Plate refers to. Movies, he argues, "do not passively mimic or directly display what is 'out there,' but actively reshape elements of the lived world and twist them in new ways that are projected onscreen and given over to an audience." What Plate is trying to get at here is the idea that movies are themselves *interpretations* of what he has called "the lived world." Not only are they selective in what they present, but they tie the material together in such a way as to assume and present a certain set of value judgments. In this way the screen offers audiences a lens. In its framing of "the real" it helps to shape and interpret that reality and provide a means through which to view the real. It is for this reason that George Lucas speaks of the moral responsibility of movie makers. In an interview with John Seabrook published in 1997, for instance, he claims that "everyone teaches in every work of art. In almost everything you do, you teach, whether you are aware of it or not. Everybody teaches all the time. Some people aren't aware of what they are teaching. They should be wiser. Everyone teaches all the time."[2] Likewise, fantasy writer Ursula K. Le Guin declares that artists have not only a duty to teach but equally a duty to be very careful about what it is that is being taught through their work. She claims that "there is . . . [a] responsibility to ensure that one's work does not, even if inadvertently, employ and continue derogatory stereotypes, appropriate for selfish purposes elements of other's cultures, and present women and minorities as Other."[3] In this regard, a classic example of inadvertent problematic teaching is D. W. Griffith's masterpiece *The Birth of a Nation*. The director was bemused by criticisms that his epic American Civil War movie could be accused of racism. That form of race representation was certainly not what

176

he intended for his picture. And yet it is difficult to watch the depiction of black men abusing white women, with the Ku Klux Klan riding in to save the day accompanied by the powerful Wagnerian theme of *The Flight of the Valkyries*, without recognizing that the criticisms of this work do indeed hit their target, and do so rather too easily.

Given the way the theatrical screen's lens functions to depict values particular to the movie creators, it is important for viewers to develop a critical awareness or "media literacy." The cultural commentator and educationalist Neil Postman has argued that the problem posed to the health of a culture resides not "in *what* people watch. The problem is in *that* we watch. The solution must be found in *how* we watch."[4] This entails that "no medium is excessively dangerous if its users understand what its dangers are."[5] Appealing to Aldous Huxley's novel *Brave New World*, Postman argues that the problem is not that people are "laughing instead of thinking" but rather that they do not know what they are laughing about and why they have stopped thinking.[6]

But what is it that the *SW* saga teaches? George Lucas's version of *SW* eclectically draws on numerous different types of sources for its ideas, plots, characterizations, and images. For example, *ANH* has much in common with Campbell's *Hero*; its style fuses science-fiction, Westerns, and even fairy tales; it draws nostalgically on a 1950s morality; and so on. According to many, the nostalgic effect has to do with its return to clear-cut values by which good and evil are clearly set over against each other in a way that exhibits the power of the writer/directors to stamp their vision of what is valuable, what form the good life takes, and what it is that disrupts the good. However, this book has argued something quite different, even if it has to be admitted that *SW* can offer only a very broadly and cartoonishly drawn prescription for the flourishing of life and well-ordered relations between persons and things.

For Irvin Kershner, Lucas's director for *ESB*, *SW* is a morality play. In many ways what this involves has been summed up by Lucas in a simple statement: everyone has "obligations to your fellow Man, to other people that are around you."[7] It is important to notice the profound difference between this sensibility and Joseph Campbell's injunction to "pursue your bliss," a message more suited to a consumer culture than Lucas's. Commenting on Campbell's self-centered ethic here, Gregory Rutledge sensibly observes its dangerous ambiguity: "The blissful pursuit of the power of myth, in the U.S. and globally, has given us a galaxy of (epic) heroes, and brutal slavery, colonialism, and massive cultural indoctrination."[8] Lucas himself offers a number of critical comments on just such an ethic in his more ethically responsible and socially expansive understanding of selfhood: "Pleasure's fun, but just accept the fact that it's here and gone. Joy lasts forever. Pleasure's purely self-centered. It's all about your pleasure. It's about you. A selfish, self-centered emotion created by a selfish moment for you. Joy is compassion. Joy is giving yourself to something else, or somebody else. It is much more powerful than pleasure. If you get hung up on pleasure, you're doomed. If you pursue joy you'll find everlasting happiness."[9] It is that approach to self-hood and its socially engaged responsibility to try to relate to others that Luke has to learn. In his explanations of the concepts around which the script of the then-forthcoming *ESB* would be written, Lucas reflects late in 1977:

> Like in the desert sequence [in Tatooine in *ANH*] was really a horror film sequence, like the *Exorcist* [1973], dealing with the devil. This can be developed into a good conflict—basically Jesus's temptation in the desert scene. It would be interesting, a good idea, if in this one Vader tries to tempt Luke.[10]

Here Luke's eventual resistance to the temptations forms a marked contrast to the trajectory of the Anakin story in the prequels. For this falling Jedi, the self-dispossessing learning education never fully takes place. Lucas does a masterful job of dramatizing, through the tragic drama of Anakin's story, what he means by dooming oneself by self-centeredness. The ethical pattern in Lucas's *SW*, then, is radically different at this point from that of Campbell, and it markedly diverges from the way that *SW* is often read as celebrating the *individual* or promoting without critical repair "the hero myth" and valorizing self-reliance and even self-improvement.

For Lucas, the issue largely centers on the greedy self, a way of being in the world that needs to be unlearned. The avaricious Jabba the Hutt is merely an extreme expression of the temperament that the primary imagination behind *SW* depicts through the likes of Han Solo, possibly Lando Calrissian (although this character's exact motivations are not entirely clear), the bounty hunters, Anakin Skywalker, the commercial and mercantile powers (the Trade Federation, the InterGalactic Banking Clan, the Techno Union, and the Commerce Guild),[11] and most notably the Sith. Accordingly, Lucas observes that the "issue of greed, of getting things and owning things and having things and not being able to let go of things . . . is the opposite of compassion—of not thinking of yourself all the time."[12] The problem with greed, then, is that it operates from an inappropriate view of the self and of the self's relations to others and to everything that self encounters.

Many will ask the question about the values/nostalgia in a more specific form. Is *SW*'s nostalgia recognizable as *Christian* morality? Because it displays a notable eclecticism at the mythological level, its theological significance does not specifically lie here. In fact, its morality is much more interesting than the question would allow and messes up all the neatly framed dualisms that often occur in Christian rhetoric: for instance, "us/them," "church/world," and "Christian/non-Christian." The boundaries are much more slippery than those suggest (although perhaps sharper than so-called "liberal Christianity" has tended to assume).

SW can make for uncomfortable viewing, and here I do not refer to the common complaints over acting or dialogue quality, special effects over-kill, or irritating characters (in particular, Jar Jar Binks, ten-year-old Anakin Skywalker, the Ewoks, and the Anakin-like temper tantrums of Kylo Ren). Rather, I mean that Lucas's version of the saga can challenge modern Western liberal societies with their deep sense of individualism that is indifferent to the other, their avoidance of responsible consideration of a common good, their exaltation of competition into all areas of life to the neglect even of social compassion and the justice of protective welfare for the most vulnerable people, and their consequent making of self-promotion or self-interest into a virtue. Telotte recognizes that Lucas's first feature, *THX 1138*, "lays bare some of the more disturbing elements of American cultural ideology—particularly an inherent racism, a deadening disjunction between the individual and his or her work, and a capitalist reduction of everything and everyone to bottom-line budgetary numbers."[13] In its own way Lucas's grand six-episode epic continues to investigate some of these themes and explores the kinds of self-understandings that generate and sustain them. In Telotte's language about *THX*, it "challenges us to be less naive in the face of a mediated world, to be more wary about the sorts of images [and ideologies] we consume."

Consequently, by offering a countermyth, when it is in Lucas's hands the saga offers some possibilities for hope: in particular asking us to think about the redemptive relationship between moral agency, moral character, and personal desire, especially with regard to the social nature and responsibilities of human life. Because of the way the virtues are portrayed as forms of socially relating, Lucas's *SW* movies deconstruct the Manichaean sensibility that pervades much of the popular culture of the modern West, which features so prominently in political rhetoric and which has even appeared problematically in Disney's first foray into the universe of *SW* films. "No one who is evil thinks they are evil; they always think they are doing good even though they're not. . . . [*Episode III*] is a matter of how a person who is good turns to becoming [*sic*] evil."[14] Likewise, when planning *ESB* the creator of *SW* suggests:

I'd like the end to be a moral conflict, in addition to a physical one. It should have Vader using a moral law that we learned earlier, but Vader turns it around. It has to be a mystical thing. Something you can look at from two sides. In the end, Vader is trying to undo everything Luke just learned. The real drama is whether Luke will become Darth Vader or not. We have tested him and he is weak. He really had to struggle to stay good. He has the same potentiality that Darth Vader had.[15]

Of course, it took Lucas some time to emerge from the dualism that *ANH* veered toward. In a conversation with Alan Dean Foster (the novel's 'ghost-writer—the publishing company insisted Lucas's name appear as author) in late 1975, the director claims that the Force is "a force field that has a good side and a bad side, and every person has this force field around them; and when you die your aura doesn't die with you, it joins the rest of the life force."[16]

This is where the sequels are particularly important. The redemption of Vader, among other things, not only subverts this Manichaean tendency but crucially disturbs the deeply culturally ingrained sense that justice is retributive before it is restorative. In this regard, the well-known renaming of *Episode VI* as the *return* rather than the *revenge* of the Jedi is important. Lawrence Kazanjian informed Lucas that *return* makes for a "weak title," but in a story planning meeting in July 1981, the writer informed his movie's producer that "Jedi don't take revenge; it's not in their nature; it's just not the way that they are."[17]

That said, however, even Lucas's *SW* remains morally ambiguous in places—his movies offer no compellingly concrete vision of hope beyond a reasonably vague fairy-tale-like happy-ever-after; they leave the nomadic Tusken Raiders or Sand People who resonate with Westerns' portrayals of the indigenous North American peoples as "vicious, mindless monsters"; the eschatological mood of the close of *ROTJ* may still be too glibly utopian given that, despite the transformations that have taken place, the galaxy and its leadership will still be populated by diverse peoples with their conflicting interests and desires; and ultimately they fail to sufficiently clarify the relationship of the redemption and violence (albeit more in the classic trilogy and Abrams's *TFA*). Nevertheless, despite the vague interplay between violence and nonviolence, these films can perhaps alert us to the uneasy relationship of the cultural imagination, human responsibility, and the violent gods in our world. By *AOTC* and *ROTS* Lucas certainly appears to explore deep anxieties about the alliance of religion and violence—the Jedi attempt to remain politically impartial at first is portrayed both as a form of resistance to government (government cannot claim Jedi support) and as a compromise caused by a blindness to the underlying truth of things that is so devastatingly exploited by the power-hungry Palpatine/Sidious. There is a yearning in our own world for a spirituality that can resolve the tensions between religion and power with integrity, and if *SW* is unable to identify what that might look like, at least it has the courage to try to imagine its possibility and reveal our need for it. (I am yet to be convinced that *TFA* is as ethically constructive.) This is vital to the health of our existence together, whether that be in the relational microdynamics of person-to-person interactions or the macrodynamics of international affairs. It would also be a mistake to imagine that Christianity itself can *resolve* such pressures of power: not merely because it is unconsciously too caught up in the swirl of power itself to be able to see straight but also because it consciously recognizes that sin pervades all forms of life in a fallen world. What Christians cannot afford to do, at least if they are being faithful to the God who makes peace through a cross, is either unwittingly or directly support relations of greed, envy, hate, division, malice, manipulation, and distrust. The way of the God of Jesus Christ is not itself one of possession or grasping for self-fulfillment but a way of gracious and divine Self-giving. In a secular world that less and less requires what it calls "metaphysical stop-gaps," the challenge for people of faith is to dynamically communicate the vital relevance of their religious loyalties in meaningfully creative ways that seek a just and lasting peace, a peace that resists and replaces the self-aggrandizement that invariably underlies violence.

In many ways, of course, Lucas's *SW* is a problematic set of "theological texts," but its theological interests will be missed by those of us who find it difficult to discern divine wisdom diffused throughout God's world. So when someone like Card complains that "the philosophy behind Star Wars is every bit as sophisticated as the science—in other words, mostly wrong and always silly," he clearly demonstrates just how little certain critics have simply not been listening sufficiently carefully.[18] Assertions such as Card's are dishonest, problematically ungenerous, and always silly.

This, though, means reading *SW* well or healthily. Sir Alec Guinness tells the story of a twelve- or thirteen-year-old boy whom he met at a science-fiction convention in San Francisco. The experienced actor expressed his worry over the boy's unashamed admission that he had seen *SW* (meaning here *ANH*) one hundred and ten times. Guinness advised, "I beg you never to see it again because this is going to be an ill effect on your life," and he commented later that "people were seeking something which didn't exist for them," a fantasy that prevented them from dealing with their own lives.[19] *SW* can and has been read and used as an escapist fantasy in this way—the viewers lose themselves in another world. And yet it can also be read as a way of returning us to ourselves by providing a framework for beginning to think about who we are and where we are going. It is that which should challenge Christians whose hope looks distinctly escapist in an other-worldly sense and therein encourage world-affirming hopes of moral responsibility for the good of all God's creatures. The saga's morality is not to be found on the surface of some clearly defined doctrinal teaching but in the "fetching, luminous, and finally exultant" exhibition of character, the heroism of friendship, the courage of virtue, the disposing of self-interest in servanthood, the disciplining of desire especially in the purification of our addiction to desires that are shaped by fear and anger, and in the reconciling practices of forgiveness and repentance.[20] Consequently, as Bowman recognizes, SW's "message . . . is invariably not about learning to master occult powers or attaining a mystical experience. The Force is really . . . about two different ways of living, two different motivations in life." In this way Lucas's SW may become a parabolic resource that reveals something of the shape of a Christian discipleship lived under the shadow of the cross. "To be a servant," Wood argues, "is to be liberated from self-concern. It is to be so fully devoted to the common good that one hardly thinks of one's own wants and needs at all."[21] This, as St. John of the Cross makes clear, is a cross-shaped life Christians have found particularly difficult to live:

> for they prefer feeding and clothing their natural selves with spiritual feelings and consolations, to stripping themselves of all things, and denying themselves all things, for God's sake. For they think that it suffices to deny themselves worldly things without annihilating and purifying themselves of spiritual attachment. . . . This is not self-denial and detachment of spirit, but spiritual gluttony. Herein, spiritually, they become enemies of the Cross of Christ. . . . [Therefore,] I see that Christ is known very little by those who consider themselves His friends: we see them seeking in Him their own pleasures and consolations because of their great love for themselves, but not loving His bitter trials and His death because of their great love for Him.[22]

St. John's observation is one that those with a prophetic sense make in every generation. As Kathryn Tanner laments, Christian history demonstrates how easily "Christian beliefs about God and the world" function to "support . . . a status quo of injustice" rather than provide the "resource for commitment to progressive social change."[23] In the light of that, being a Christian, then, may indeed require a good dose of the Jedi's disciplined life of learning virtue together in its disciplining of disordered desire after all. In this way, "this seemingly straightforward tale of good *and* evil . . . remains such a resounding modern parable."[24] Although the early signs are not promising, whether the forthcoming Disney-owned additions to the SW series can be spoken of in a similar way remains to be seen.

Notes

Introduction

1. Adam Roberts, *Science Fiction* (London and New York: Routledge, 2000), 84.

2. Peter Krämer, *The New Hollywood: From Bonnie and Clyde to Star Wars* (London and New York: Wallflower, 2005), 102.

3. Citation in Garry Jenkins, *Empire Building: The Remarkable Real Life Story of Star Wars* (London: Simon & Schuster, 1997), 284.

4. Ibid., 287.

5. Martin Scorsese, cited in John Baxter, *George Lucas: A Biography* (London: Harper Collins, 1999), 246.

6. Robin Wood, *Hollywood from Vietnam to Reagan* (New York: Columbia University Press, 1986), 162f.

7. Citations from "Great Galloping Galaxies!" *Time* (May 23, 1983), 74–80 (75); Brian Aldiss, cited in Patricia Monk, "Not Just 'Cosmic Skullduggery': A Partial Reconsideration of Space Opera" *Extrapolation* 334 (1992), 294–316 (296).

8. Citation from Andrew Gordon, "Star Wars: A Myth for Our Time," *Literature/Film Quarterly* 6.4 (1978), 314–26 (315).

9. See J. W. Rinzler, *The Making of Star Wars: The Definitive Story behind the Original Film* (London: Ebury Press, 2008), 26. Dan Rubey notes, "Aristocratic characters like Princess Leia and Ben (Obi-Wan) Kenobi speak in the high-flown ornamental rhetoric of romance and epic fantasy" ("Not So Long Ago Nor Far Away: New Variations on Old Themes and Questioning Star Wars' Revival of Heroic Archetypes," in Douglas Brode and Leah Deyneka, eds., *Myth, Media, and Culture in Star Wars* [Lanham, Toronto, Plymouth: The Scarecrow Press, 2012], 47–64 [56]).

10. Samuel L. Jackson, "Story," *Star Wars Episode II: Attack of the Clones*, DVD Disc 2 (Lucasfilm Ltd., 2002).

11. Gary Kurtz, cited in Baxter, *George Lucas*, 166.

12. Warren Buckland, "Close Encounters with *Raiders of the Lost Ark*: Notes on Narrative Aspects of the New Hollywood Blockbuster," in Steve Neale and Murray Smith, eds., *Contemporary Hollywood Cinema* (London and New York: Routledge, 1998), 166–77 (166, 175).

13. Stanley Kauffmann, cited in Baxter, *George Lucas*, 244.

14. Rowan Williams, *The Truce of God* (London: Collins, 1983), 16.

15. Bryan P. Stone, *Faith and the Film: Theological Themes at the Cinema* (St. Louis: Chalice Press, 2000), 5f.

183

16. Lucas, cited in John Seabrook, *Nobrow: The Culture of Marketing—The Marketing of Culture* (New York: Knopf, 2000), 146.

17. The tendency among intellectuals to equate "culture" with "high culture" remains strong, but it is problematic. These tend to be cultural works of only a small part of any society's cultural production and consumption, and arguably they have considerably less impact (at least direct impact) than movies and television.

18. This material is taken from *The Politics of Big Fantasy: Studies in Cultural Suspicion* (Jefferson, NC: McFarland Press, 2014), 5–6.

19. George Lucas, in Sally Kline, ed., *George Lucas: Interviews* (Jackson: University of Mississippi, 1999), 143.

20. George Lucas, interviewed by Bill Moyers, in *The Mythology of Star Wars*. This was transcripted as "Of Myth and Men," *Time* 153, no. 16 (April 26, 1999): 90–94.

21. Lucas, cited in Stephen Zito, "George Lucas Goes Far Out," in Kline, 45–54 (53).

22. Lucas, cited in Dale Pollock, *Skywalking: The Life and Films of George Lucas, the Creator of Star Wars* (Hollywood, New York, London, Toronto: Samuel French, 1990), 144.

23. Lucas, in Tim Rayment, "Master of the Universe," *Sunday Times Magazine* (May 16, 1999): 14–24 (20).

24. Pollock, *Skywalking*, 271.

25. Rohan Gowland, "The Phantom Menace of Idealism: Film Review," *The Guardian* (June 16, 1999), www.zipworld.com.au/~cpa/garchive/958star.htm, consulted 30-05-05.

26. http://www.crossroad.to/text/responses/StarWars.html, consulted 29-05-05. A different example comes from one blog review of the first edition of my book. It might be summed up by the question that calls into theological question the exploration of the movies' politics: "What has Washington to do with Jerusalem?"

27. Ian Maher, *Faith and Film: Close Encounters of an Evangelistic Kind* (Cambridge: Grove Books, 2002), 5.

28. Matt Bielby, *Total Film* (April 1997), cited in David Wilkinson, *The Power of the Force: The Spirituality of the Star Wars* (Oxford: Lion, 2000), 14.

29. Ian Nathan, "Star Wars, 1977–1997: The Legend," *Empire* (April 1997), cited in Wilkinson, 14.

30. *SW* has inspired what some commentators have called "hyper-real" religiosity. See Adam Possamai, "Popular Religion," in Peter B. Clarke and Pewter Bayer, eds., *The World's Religions: Continuities and Transformations* (London and New York: Routledge, 2009), 479–92.

31. Krämer, *The New Hollywood*, 101.

32. Citation from Dale Pollock, *Skywalking: The Life and Films of George Lucas, the Creator of Star Wars* (Hollywood, New York, London, Toronto: Samuel French, 1990), 272.

33. Wilkinson, *The Power of the Force*, 139.

34. George Lucas, cited in J. W. Rinzler, *The Making of The Empire Strikes Back: The Definitive Story* (New York: Ballantine, 2010), 38.

35. Dick Staub, interview with Stan Guthrie, "On the *Star Wars* Myth," *Christianity Today* (May 16, 2005), http://www.christianitytoday.com/ct/2005/120/22.0.html, consulted 26-05-05; cf. Dick Staub, *Christian Wisdom of the Jedi Masters* (San Francisco: Jossey-Bass, 2005).

36. Douglas John Hall, "Bound and Free: On Being a Christian Theologian," *Theology Today* 59 (2002): 421–27 (427).

37. Timothy J. Gorringe, *Furthering Humanity: A Theology of Culture* (Aldershot and Burlington: Ashgate, 2004), 3.

38. An incident in Connie Neal's *The Gospel according to Harry Potter* illustrates how many Christians can approach "culture" badly by refusing to listen with appropriate attention (*The Gospel according to Harry Potter: Spirituality in the Stories of the World's Most Famous Seeker* [Louisville, KY: Westminster John Knox Press, 2002]). In order to dismiss the "truthfulness" of the Harry Potter books, her Christian radio interviewer contemptuously quoted: "There is no good or evil, only power and those too weak to seek it." Neal recalls that this statement was made by one of the books' *villains* and that this very perspective was opposed by the books' underlying philosophy. Quite simply the interviewer's approach was abusive of the texts (which she had not even been bothered to read and understand), of Mrs. Neal (whose book she likewise had not read), and of a Christian faith that supposedly follows One who refused to be self-assertive and coercive of others (see Phil. 2:6–11). The interviewer, in other words, had not developed a properly *Christian mode* of cultural discernment.

39. R. Albert Mohler, "Faith vs. the Force," *World Magazine* 21, no. 1 (December 31, 2005), http://www.worldmag.com/mohler/mohler.cfm?id=5923, consulted 26-05-05.

40. Martin Luther King, *Strength to Love* (London: Collins Fontana, 1969), 44.

41. J. R. R. Tolkien, *"The Monsters and the Critics" and Other Essays*, Christopher Tolkien (Boston: Houghton Mifflin, 1984), 155.

42. Kevin S. Decker and Jason T. Ebrel, "The Force Is with You . . . but You're Not a Jedi Yet," in Kevin S. Decker and Jason T. Ebrel, eds., *Star Wars and Philosophy: More Powerful Than You Can Possibly Imagine* (Chicago and La Salle, IL: Open Court, 2005), xiii–xvi (xiv).

43. Lucas, in Rinzler, *The Making of The Empire Strikes Back*, 44.

44. See Matthew Bortolin, *The Dharma of Star Wars* (Boston: Wisdom Publications, 2005); John Porter, *The Tao of Star Wars* (Atlanta: Humanics, 2003).

45. Cited in Charlotte Higgins, "Final Star Wars Bears Message for America," *The Guardian* (May 16, 2005), http://film.guardian.co.uk/cannes2005/story/0,15927,1484795,00.html#article_continue, consulted 26-05-05.

Chapter 1: A New Myth

1. Orson Scott Card, "'*Star Wars*' Our Public Religion," *USA Today* (March 17, 1997), 13A.

2. James L. Ford, "Buddhism, Christianity, and *The Matrix*: The Dialectic of Myth-Making in Contemporary Cinema," *Journal of Religion and Film* 4, no.2 (October 2000), http://digitalcommons.unomaha.edu/cgi/viewcontent.cgi?article=1807&context=jrf, 24, consulted 12-02-16.

3. Conrad Kottak and Kathryn Kozaitis, *On Being Different*, 2nd ed. (New York: McGraw-Hill Higher Education, 2002), 2.

4. Baxter, *George Lucas*, 245.

5. Lucas, interviewed by Bill Moyers, in *The Mythology of Star Wars* (May 1999). This was transcripted as "Of Myth and Men," *Time* 153, no. 16 (April 26, 1999), 90. Cf. Lucas, cited in Dale Pollock, *Skywalking: The Life and Films of George Lucas, the Creator of Star Wars* (Hollywood, New York, London, Toronto: Samuel French, 1990), 144.

6. Lucas, cited in Tim Rayment, "Master of the Universe," in *The Sunday Times Magazine* (May 16, 1999), 14–24 (20).

7. Steven Spielberg, cited in J. W. Rinzler, *The Making of Star Wars: The Definitive Story behind the Original Film* (London: Ebury Press, 2008), 328.

8. These were published as Joseph Campbell and Bill Moyers, *The Power of Myth* (New York: Doubleday, 1988).

9. Carl Silvio and Tony M. Vinci, "Introduction. Moving Away from Myth: *Star Wars* as Cultural Artifact," in Carl Silvio and Tony M. Vinci, eds., *Culture, Identities and Technology in the* Star Wars *Films: Essays on the Two Trilogies* (Jefferson, NC: McFarland and Company Inc., 2007), 1–8 (2).

10. Liam Neeson, in *Star Wars Episode I: The Phantom Menace* (2001), DVD Disc2.

11. The popular account of the relationship of *SW* and Campbell's myth-studies has, however, been contested. In this richly detailed and illuminating work, Michael Kaminski certainly recognizes the prevalence of claims about Campbellian influence on Lucas, at least for the creation of 1977's *SW*; however, he contests this for several reasons (*The Secret History of Star Wars: The Art of Storytelling and the Making of a Modern Epic* [Kingston, ON: Legacy Books Press, 2008]). One of his theses is that the connection was unintentional, unconscious, and thus somewhat accidental.

First, Kaminski notes that there are occasions when Lucas distanced his script writing from Campbell. For instance, in a BBC interview of 1999, Lucas claimed, "I was going along on my own story, I was trying to write whatever I felt. And then I would go back once I'd written a script, I would go back and check it against the classic model of the hero's journey and that sort of thing to see if I had gone off the deep end, and simply by following my own inspiration, the thing that intrigued me most is that it was very close to the model" (cited in Kaminski, 215). As Peter Biskind notes, "Lucas wanted to be taken seriously as an artist, be paid the kind of attention the critics lavished on Coppola and Scorsese" (*Easy Riders, Raging Bulls: Sex-Drugs-and-Rock 'n' Roll Generation Saved Hollywood* [New York: Touchstone, 1998], 319). Nevertheless, there are several things that Kaminski should be more careful about here. Notably, this is not a claim about "unconscious" mimicking at all but an admission that Lucas had read about the "hero myth" and wanted to follow it, at least broadly; that his own script was deliberately checked against this form of myth. (Lucas does not say here whether he would have changed the script had he found significant deviation, but the implication is that the myth form is something of a narrative touchstone.) Also, this interview dates from 1999, and, as we will see below, Kaminski has been making the point that Lucas's later reflections are unreliable guides. "[B]y following my own inspiration" is a way of sounding more original and creative than a mimicker. Finally, while Lucas does not tend to name his mythic sources in earlier interviews, there is no reason to assume that Campbell's work is not among them, unnamed perhaps, again, in order to emphasize Lucas's own creativity in writing *SW*. Kaminski's argument is a speculative one built on silence—there is simply no direct evidence to contest Lucas's appeal to Campbell, among others.

Second, Kaminski argues that initially *SW* "was viewed as a fun and exciting adventure film, with a positive and spiritual message—but not anything particularly deep and history-making beyond being a current hit" (213). *SW* was initially conceived from pulp science-fiction materials. Yet such an argument seems to have succumbed to the common, but deeply problematic and unsustainable, separation of pulp and fantasy adventure genres from the mythological. There is a disturbingly real logical problem with the use of *only* in Kaminski's naive argument that Lucas "intended [*Star Wars*] only as a thrilling adventure to stimulate the imagination of young people" (217). So Kaminski, naively missing the way no cultural product is ideologically neutral, speaks of *SW* as "nothing more than an exciting action picture" (219).

Third, Kaminski reasons that Lucas picked up motifs from the likes of Campbell largely unconsciously. When related to the previous argument this means that Kaminski's Lucas intended to construct a pulp narrative but had unconsciously assumed many elements from older mythic traditions. Lucas's eclecticism involves the absorption of "myths and fairy tales, especially in later drafts" (66). Does this unwitting absorption also include the more scholarly reflections on myths?

It is far from inconceivable that the mythic underpinnings were only recognized gradually, after the euphoria of viewing the spectacle *SW* had abated. Yet Kaminski's arguments are particularly unclear at this point. On the one hand, he wants to link *SW* to sources of populist entertainment and deny more intellectual sources. On the other hand, he does note Lucas's study of anthropology, including myths, for two years at college (18). Quite bizarrely this leads to the claim that Lucas's reading of scholarly literature (and this seems to directly contradict his claim that Lucas was not interested in the scholarly materials, but read pulp sci-fi materials) was "more of a personal curiosity" (214). What makes this a particularly peculiar argument is that Kaminski speaks about the unconscious absorption of mythic materials while denying that the same thing happened with Lucas's reading of the "rules" provided by myth scholars of the time.

Even so, the very notion of a collective unconscious works as a hermeneutical argument up to a point, but it definitively makes no sense of Lucas's admission of a conscious hunt for a plot that reflects his passion for many of the texts that themselves embody mythic materials. Also, it underplays the connections he makes between *SW* and his interest in mythological materials, whether as a child watching *Flash Gordon* and Westerns or as a college student reading anthropological and cultural studies. Most disastrously for his argument, Kaminski himself cites without comment elsewhere in his book Lucas's claim: "About the time I was doing the third draft I read *The Hero with a Thousand Faces*, and I started to realize I was following those rules unconsciously. So I said, I'll make it fit more into that classic mold" (104). This shows that Lucas had indeed read Campbell before completing the final version of the script. Moreover, while it does suggest an unconscious following of the rules of mythic storytelling, it also makes explicit the notion that Lucas then followed and edited the script when it did not "fit . . . into that classic mold."

Fourth, it was only later, Kaminski argues, that connections between *SW* and myths began to appear. Kaminski believes that Lucas did not adapt the *SW* script with Campbell in mind and that the appeal to the scholar's work on mythologies only comes later. "Word of Lucas's interest in fairy tales and mythology got out and soon the film's perception began to change" (213). Kaminski questions the way the scripts developed without reference to high culture or scholarly literature, and that the references to those works came only later as Lucas and fans attempted to make *SW* sound more culturally and intellectually significant than it really is. This, according to Kaminski, was largely the work of "the intelligentsia," comparing it to the classical Homeric myths in *Ulysses* and *The Odyssey*. "The truth is much simpler—Lucas liked a bunch of cheesy sci-fi serials and comic books and was blessed with an innate sense of storytelling that, like all great natural storytellers, tapped into the same collective unconsciousness that all of mankind's greatest myths do" (214). Only after it became successful was the "fairy-tale-like aspect . . . pushed to the forefront." Yet this is a strange thing to argue, when Lucas had clearly made an *explicit* and quite *conscious* fairy-tale reference with the opening text "A long time ago . . ." in the fourth-draft summary of January 1, 1976 (216). If Kaminski is merely speaking of Lucas's *intentions* then that is one thing. (Lucas sought to entertain, pure and simple—although that has been contested above.) But if the argument is that the later myth-theorizing on *SW* is peculiar and inappropriate, since it is actually just an entertaining piece, then this falls into a sort of genetic fallacy—because *SW*'s sources are those of popular entertainment (and this claim itself has been contested above) this work cannot be of mythological significance—and it does not take seriously Kaminski's own argument about Lucas's *unconscious* influences.

Fifth, and finally, Kaminski claims that Lucas himself bought into this intellectualization of his stories, using Campbell's name in order to give "him proper scholastic backing for his 'mythic' B-movie" (215). "It would not look good for this developing new-age entertainment-religion," Kaminski continues, to be revealed to be of such lowly origins as comic books, pulp fiction, and B-movies, what the intelligentsia would consider juvenile schlock—Lucas's insecurities about his story were well justified" (216). This may or may not be true, but Kaminski is guessing without evidence, and the argument looks odd when compared with Lucas's conscious connection of *SW* and pulp science-fiction, especially *Flash Gordon*, and Lucas's feeling no need to intellectually justify *American Graffiti*. Furthermore, Kaminski makes no mention of Lucas's having been impressed by Stanley Kubrick's direction of *2001 Space Odyssey* or of Lucas's own avant-garde sci-fi dystopia *THX 1138*. Moreover, it is an odd argument given that Lucas remains quite happy to admit the pulp inspiration for much of the concept of *SW* and the fact that he never felt the same need to make grand self-justifying claims for his fun movie *American Graffiti*. Perhaps most damningly, Kaminski has failed to note Lucas's reference to the fairy tale and myth in his interview for *American Film* with Stephen Zito, published in April 1977 *before* the cinematic release of *SW* on May 25, 1977.

Whether Lucas's use of mythological motifs and principles was conscious or not (and Kaminski's arguments are unfortunately logically impoverished, very confused, and distinctly eccentric, as well as evidentially weak), not only scholars of myth but Campbell himself have acclaimed overlaps, and thus a mythological substructure, to Lucas's cinematic vision.

12. Robert A. Segal, *Joseph Campbell: An Introduction* (New York: Garland, 1987), 137.

13. Ibid., 137f.

14. Lucas, cited in Rinzler, 14. The second draft of Lucas's script even opens with a prophecy of a savior (in Rinzler, 361).

15. Lucas, in Laurent Bouzereau, *The Annotated Screenplays* (New York: Ballantine Books, 1997), 6.

16. Rinzler, 15.

17. Lucas, in Sally Kline, ed., *George Lucas: Interviews* (Jackson: University Press of Mississippi, 1999), 89.

18. Rinzler, 4.

19. Dan Rubey, "Not So Long Ago Nor Far Away: New Variations on Old Themes and Questioning *Star Wars*' Revival of Heroic Archetypes," in Douglas Brode and Leah Deyneka, eds., *Myth, Media, and Culture in Star Wars* (Lanham, Toronto, Plymouth: The Scarecrow Press, 2012), 47–64 (53).

20. See Biskind, 344.

21. "What we had in common is we grew up in the '60s, protesting the Vietnam War" (Lucas, in Biskind, 317).

22. Lucas, cited in Rinzler, *The Making of The Empire Strikes Back*, 23. Cf. J. W. Rinzler, *The Making of Return of the Jedi: The Definitive Story* (London: Aurum Press, 2013), 69: the Emperor "was a politician. Richard M. Nixon was his name. He subverted the senate and finally took over and became an imperial guy and he was really evil. But he pretended to be a really nice guy. He sucked Luke's father into the dark side."

23. See Rinzler, 15, 26f; Michael Kaminski, *The Secret History of Star Wars: The Art of Storytelling and the Making of a Modern Epic* (Kingston, ON: Legacy Books Press, 2008), 67. The Vietcong versus imperial America subtext becomes played out again in *Return of the Jedi* (Biskind, 342).

24. Lucas, cited in Taylor, 88.

25. Cited in Taylor, 110. Lucas apparently pointed out to the Palpatine's actor Ian McDiarmid that the Emperor's chamber on the second Death Star is an oval office (see Taylor, 281). *ESB* concept designer Joe Johnston's inspiration for the AT-AT or Imperial Walker, accord-

ing to Chris Taylor, came from a concept developed by General Electric in 1968 called the Cybernetic Anthropomorphous Machine. This was a walking tank commissioned by the army for possible use in Vietnam. "Intentionally or otherwise, Lucas and Johnston were continuing the analogy between the Empire's fight against the rebellion and America's fight in Vietnam" (Taylor, 236). Lucas, however, provides a different account, at least from his end: "The walkers were inspired by *War of the Worlds* more than anything else" (cited in Rinzler, *The Making of The Empire Strikes Back*, 32). A further political reference may be present in the development of *ROTJ*'s Ewoks, if Taylor's reading is sound. "Ewok, whatever its spelling, was mostly inspired by the Miwok Indians, native to Marin" (Taylor, 261).

26. Lucas, cited in Rinzler, *The Making of Return of the Jedi*, 11. Cf. Rinzler, *The Making of Star Wars*, 11f, 129.

27. Lucas, in Kline, 53.

28. Ibid.

29. Lucas, in Rinzler, 5f.

30. Ibid. R. Albert Mohler bitterly complains that Lucas seems "absolutely agog over the power of myth and convinced that modern secular Americans need new myths to replace the tired old 'myths' of religion, including biblical Christianity" ("Faith vs. the Force," *World Magazine* 21, no. 1 (December 31, 2005), http://www.worldmag.com/mohler/mohler .cfm?id=5923, consulted 26-05-05). This, however, is a serious misreading of Lucas's use of old myths and of his understanding of the relation of them to his own mythic creation. So, for instance, he claims that he attempted to find, explore, and present something of "the common threads through all the mythologies and all the religions" (Lucas, interviewed by Bill Moyers, in *The Mythology of Star Wars* [May 1999]). He attempts to make clear that he did not intend to create a new religion but was interested in "telling the old myths in a new way," for a particular time and place. *SW* is an updating of "ancient mythological motifs."

31. Lucas, "Of Myth and Men," cited in Muriel Verbeeck, "Campbell, Star Wars and the Myth," http://archive.li/WpZ2G, consulted 12-02-17.

32. "When I started out making the movies, I was working toward making it modern mythology. I had studied anthropology in college, and social sciences was my major before I got into film. So, I'd taken a class in mythology and read some of his stuff there. I did more research before I wrote the screenplay for *Star Wars*. I read and reread *Heroes of a Thousand Faces* and a few other things he did. That was the extent of the influence he had on me" (Lucas, in an interview from May 1999, cited in Kaminski, 215).

33. Cited in Phil Cousineau, *The Hero's Journey: The World of Joseph Campbell* (San Francisco: Harper & Row, 1990), 180. "It was the first time that I really began to focus. Once I read that book I said to myself, this is what I've been doing. . . . It was all right there and had been there for thousands and thousands of years, as Dr. Campbell pointed out."

34. Lucas, in Kaminski, 215.

35. "Later, after I did Jedi, someone gave me a tape of one of his lectures, and I was just blown away by it. He was much more powerful as a speaker than he was as a writer. Shortly thereafter, we became friends. I met him, and we were friends for a period until his death. In that time, he was a mentor. He was an amazing scholar and an amazing person, and I was privileged to be around him. That was later on, in my so-called 'hiatus period'" (Lucas, in an interview from May 1999, cited in Kaminski, 215).

36. Scott Bukatman, "Zooming Out: The End of Offscreen Space," in Jon Lewis, ed., *The New American Cinema* (Durham and London: Duke University Press, 1998), 248–72 (248).

37. Campbell, 4.

38. Segal, 137f.

39. John Lyden, 'The Apocalyptic Cosmology of *Star Wars*," *The Journal of Religion and Film* 4, no. 1 (2000): 6f.

40. Segal, 64.

41. Campbell, 30.

42. Joseph Campbell with Bill Moyers, *The Power of Myth* (New York: Doubleday, 1988), 148.

43. John Lyden, "The Apocalyptic Cosmology of *Star Wars*," *The Journal of Religion and Film* 4, no. 1 (2000): 7. Campbell claims that his *Hero* is merely observational and descriptive (39 n43). And yet he is obviously *evaluating* and privileging a controversial unifying perspective on myths. After all, with WWII fresh in his mind, he claims that the establishment of essential similarities among myths can aid world peace, demonstrating that all peoples are at heart the same (vii). Campbell does recognize that there are differences between myths but problematically regards these as secondary [viii]. His later *The Masks of God* does at least differentiate myths according to four categories: Primitive, Oriental, Occidental, and Creative. The dominating interpretative tool is Jungian psychoanalysis (*Masks of God: Creative Mythology* [New York: Arkana Penguin Books, 1968]).

44. Lyden, 7.

45. Lucas, cited in Baxter, 166.

46. Roy M. Anker, *Catching Light: Looking for God at the Movies* (Grand Rapids: William B. Eerdmans, 2004), 225.

47. George Lucas, *Star Wars: From the Adventures of Luke Skywalker* (London: Sphere Books, 1977), 20.

48. Lucas, "Of Myth and Men," 94.

49. Campbell, *The Hero with a Thousand Faces*, 11.

50. Robert Segal, interviewed by Rachel Kohn, in 'Myth Is Stranger than Fiction," *The Spirit of Things* on *Radio National* (January 17, 1999).

51. Jeffrey Grupp, "The Force: The Science, Religion and Philosophy of Star Wars," The Force Holocron, January 12, 2007, https://setiishadim.wordpress.com/2007/01/12/the-force-the-science-religion-and-philosophy-of-star-wars/, consulted 12-02-17.

52. David Sandner, "Joy Beyond the Walls of the World: The Secondary World-Making of J. R. R. Tolkien and C. S. Lewis," in George Clark and Daniel Timmons, eds., *J. R. R. Tolkien and His Literary Resonances: Views of Middle-Earth* (London: Greenwood, 2000), 137.

53. Jonathan Rosenbaum, *Movies as Politics* (Berkeley, Los Angeles, London: University of California Press, 1997), 105.

54. Lucas, cited in Baxter, 157.

55. Claude Levi-Strauss, "The Structural Study of Myth," in Robert A. Segal, ed., *Theories of Myth* (Lancaster: Garland Series, 1996), 120.

56. Rudolf Bultmann, in Hans-Werner Bartsch, ed., *Kerygma and Myth*, trans. Reginald H. Fuller (London: SCM, 1953), 10f.

57. This is a disastrous mistake made by Caleb Grimes more recently: "Mythology is concerned with archetypal spiritual truths reported in and by their fictional stories" (*Star Wars Jesus: A Spiritual Commentary on the Reality of the Force* [Columbia: Winepress Publishers, 2007], 36).

58. Rubey, 53.

59. Mark Allan Powell, *What Is Narrative Criticism?* (Minneapolis: Fortress Press, 1990), 94.

60. The phrase is Robert K. Johnston's (*Reel Spirituality: Theology and Film in Dialogue* [Grand Rapids: Baker Academic, 2000], 106).

61. Lucas, "Of Myth and Men," cited in David Wilkinson, *The Power of the Force: The Spirituality of the Star Wars* (Oxford: Lion, 2000), 75.

62. Campbell, *The Hero with a Thousand Faces*, 121.

63. Charles Champlin, *George Lucas: The Creative Impulse*, rev. ed. (London: Virgin, 1997), 124.

64. Clarence Walhout, in *The Promise of Hermeneutics* (Grand Rapids: William B. Eerdmans, 1999), 65–131 (83).

65. Kevin J. Wetmore Jr., *The Empire Triumphant: Race, Religion and Rebellion in the Star Wars Films* (Jefferson, NC, and London: McFarland & Company, 2005), 95.

66. Veronica A. Wilson, "Seduced by the Dark Side of the Force: Gender, Sexuality, and Moral Agency in George Lucas's *Star Wars* Universe," in Carl Silvio and Tony M. Vinci, eds., *Culture, Identities and Technology in the* Star Wars *Films: Essays on the Two Trilogies* (Jefferson, NC: McFarland and Company Inc., 2007), 134–52 (136).

67. Carl Silvio and Tony M. Vinci, "Moving Away from Myth: *Star Wars* as Cultural Artifact," in Silvio and Vinci, 1–8 (1).

68. Lucas, cited in Pollock, 209.

69. Bruno Bettelheim, *The Uses of Enchantment* (Harmondsworth: Penguin, 1976), 8.

70. Bukatman, 268.

Chapter 2: The Force of the Divine

1. Staub, *Christian Wisdom of the Jedi Masters*, 104.

2. Mohler, "Faith vs. the Force."

3. Lucas, "Of Myth and Men."

4. John D. Caputo, *On Religion* (London and New York: Routledge, 2001), 79.

5. Lucas, "Of Myth and Men."

6. Ibid.

7. Henderson, *Star Wars: The Magic of Myth*, 44.

8. Pollock, *Skywalking*, 139.

9. Campbell, cited in Tom Snyder, "Myth Perceptions, Joseph Campbell's Power of Deceit," http://answers.org/cultsandreligions/campbell.html, consulted 26-05-05.

10. Cited in Baxter, *George Lucas*, 165.

11. Campbell, cited in Snyder, "Myth Perceptions."

12. Pollock, *Skywalking*, 139f.

13. Caputo, *On Religion*, 83.

14. Cf. Num. 13:33; Deut. 2:10; 9:2.

15. William O. Stephens, "Stoicism in the Stars: Yoda, the Emperor, and the Force," in Decker and Eberl, *Star Wars and Philosophy*, 16–28.

16. Pollock, *Skywalking*, 140.

17. John Milbank, "The End of Dialogue," in Gavin D'Costa, ed., *Christian Uniqueness Reconsidered: The Myth of a Pluralistic Theology of Religions* (New York: Orbis, 1990), 174–91 (177).

18. Maurice Friedman, "Why Joseph Campbell's Psychologizing of Myth Precludes the Holocaust as Touchstone of Reality," *Journal of the American Academy of Religion* 66, no. 2 (1998): 385–401 (395).

19. Milbank, "The End of Dialogue," 181.

20. Ibid., 177f.

21. Kenneth Surin, "A 'Politics of Speech,'" in D'Costa, ed., *Christian Uniqueness*, 192–212 (200).

22. Volf, *Exclusion and Embrace*, 44.

23. John Brosnan, *The Primal Screen: A History of Science Fiction Film* (London: Orbit, 1991), 181.

24. Jason Wardley has observed that at this stage in the *SW* mythos this particular commanding trooper was understood as being a conscript rather than a clone, and Obi-Wan's subtle influence had a liberating effect on him according to Expanded Universe material—a short story depicts this Imperial individual coming to question his society's values and join the Rebellion.

25. McKee, *The Gospel according to Science Fiction: Forging the Faith of the Future* (Louisville, KY: Westminster John Knox Press, 2007), 17.

26. Anker, *Catching Light*, 228f.

27. However, the ambiguity of Christian practice through the centuries has itself been shockingly stark. Christians sound disturbingly absent-minded when they complain about *SW* characters' ability to manipulate the Force.

28. Campbell, *The Hero*, 156–59.

29. Cited in Robert Jewett and John Shelton Lawrence, *Captain America and the Crusade against Evil: The Dilemma of Zealous Nationalism* (Grand Rapids: Eerdmans, 2003), 26.

30. Kathryn Tanner, *The Politics of God* (Minneapolis: Fortress, 1992), 69.

31. Stover, *Star Wars Episode III*, 233.

32. Stone, *Faith and the Film*, 135.

33. George S. Hendry, "On Being a Creature," *Theology Today* 38, no. 1 (1981): 60–72 (63f.).

34. Augustine, *City of God*, trans. Henry Bettenson (Harmondsworth: Penguin Books, 1972), 11.24.457.

35. Rowan Williams, *On Christian Theology* (Oxford: Blackwell, 2000), 74.

36. See Lynn White Jr., "The Historical Roots of Our Ecological Crisis," *Science* 155 (1967): 1203–7.

37. Michael Welker, "What Is Creation? Rereading Genesis 1 and 2," *Theology Today* 48, no. 1 (1991): 56–71 (64).

38. Hendry, "On Being a Creature," 62.

39. Michael Welker, "The Holy Spirit," *Theology Today* 46, no. 1 (1989): 5–20 (18f.).

40. Stone, *Faith and the Film*, 137.

41. Stover, *Star Wars Episode III*, 233.

42. Augustine, *City of God*, 8.17.324.

43. Pseudo-Dionysius, "The Divine Names," in *Pseudo-Dionysius: The Complete Works*, trans. Colm Luibheid and Paul Rorem (New York: Paulist Press, 1987), chap. 1.1, 588B; 1.1, 588A, 593B.

44. C. S. Lewis, *Mere Christianity* (Glasgow: Collins, 1952), 137.

45. Herbert McCabe, *God Matters* (London: Geoffrey Chapman, 1987), 8f.

46. St. John of the Cross, *The Ascent of Mount Carmel*, trans. Allison Peers (Garden City, NY: Image Books, 1962), 1.12.5.

47. St. John of the Cross, *The Ascent of Mount Carmel*, 2.3.1, available at http://www.ccel.org/ccel/john_cross/dark_night.html, consulted 26-05-05.

48. Pseudo-Dionysius, *The Divine Names*, 7.2, 869A. This type of approach enables Pseudo-Dionysius to argue that it is not a case that God has no names but many names—in fact, an excessively inexhaustible range of names drawn from all things caused by God (1.5, 596A-1.7, 597B).

49. Interview with Kerry O'Quinn, cited in Michelle Kinnucan, "What Star Wars Teaches Us," Common Dreams.org, May 10, 2002, http://www-personal.umich.edu/~lormand /agenda/0205/kinnucan.htm, consulted 12-02-17.

50. Baxter, *George Lucas*, 165.

51. Lucas, cited in Salewicz, *George Lucas Close Up*, 47.

52. Robert M. Bowman Jr., "The Gospel according to George Lucas, Part 1. Fantasy Movies or Phantom Menace?" http://www.wfial.org/index.cfm?fuseaction=artNewAge.article_4, consulted 26-05-05 (site discontinued); Lucas, "Of Myth and Men."

53. Lucas, cited in Baxter, *George Lucas*, 164.

54. Pollock, *Skywalking*, 139.

55. Ibid., 139f.

56. Orson Scott Card, "No Faith in This Force," http://www.beliefnet.com/story/167 /story_16700_1.html, consulted 30-05-05.

57. Jeffrey Overstreet, "Star Wars: Episode III—Revenge of the Sith," *Christianity Today*, May 19, 2005, http://www.christianitytoday.com/ct/2005/mayweb-only/starwars3.html, consulted 12-02-17.

Chapter 3: Evil Strikes Back

1. Augustine, *The Enchiridion*, trans. J. F. Shaw, in *Nicene and Post-Nicene Fathers of the Christian Church—First Series*, vol. 3, ed. Philip Schaff (Edinburgh: T. & T. Clark, 1890), 16; available at http://www.ccel.org/ccel/schaff/npnf103.html, consulted 26-05-05.

2. Campbell, *The Hero*, 44.

3. Lucas, in Laurent Bouzereau, *Star Wars: The Annotated Screenplays* (New York: Ballantine, 1997), 180.

4. Cited in Michelle Kinnucan, "What Star Wars Teaches Us," Common Dreams.org, May 10, 2002, http://www-personal.umich.edu/~lormand/agenda/0205/kinnucan.htm, consulted 12-02-17.

5. Ian McDiarmid, *Empire*, June 2005, 94.

6. Rowlands, *The Philosopher*, 209.

7. Stover, *Star Wars Episode III*, 213.

8. Michael Gelven, *This Side of Evil* (Milwaukee: Marquette University Press, 1998), 24. So, according to Frank Castle in *The Punisher*, "Those who do evil to others [are] the killers, the rapists, psychos, sadists" (*The Punisher*, dir. Jonathan Hensleigh [Columbia Tristar, 2004]).

9. Cited by Hannah Pok, "The *Star Wars* Trilogy: Fantasy, Narcissism and Fear of the Other in Reagan's America," http://hannahpok.com/deepfieldspace/framesrc2c.html, consulted 18-05-05 (site discontinued).

10. Orson Scott Card, "'*Star Wars*' Our Public Religion," *USA Today*, March 17, 1997, 13a.

11. Lucas, "The Beginning: The Making of Episode I," in *Star Wars Episode I: The Phantom Menace*, DVD Disc 2 (Lucasfilm Ltd., 1999).

12. Augustine, *The Enchiridion*, 96.

13. Christopher M. Brown, "'A Wretched Hive of Scum and Villainy': *Star Wars* and the Problem of Evil," in Decker and Eberl, eds., *Star Wars and Philosophy*, 69–79 (79).

14. Lucas, in "The Chosen One" featurette, *Star Wars Episode III: The Revenge of the Sith*, DVD Disc 2 (Lucasfilm Ltd., 2005).

15. Ian McDiarmid, *Empire*, June 2005, 94.

16. See "Sith Order," http://en.wikipedia.org/wiki/Sith_Order, consulted 14-06-05.

17. Hanson and Kay, *Star Wars: The New Myth*, 405.

18. Stover, *Star Wars Episode III*, 282. Cf. Luceno, *Star Wars: Labyrinth of Evil*, 167.

19. Alistair McFadyen, *Bound to Sin: Abuse, Holocaust and the Christian Doctrine of Sin* (Cambridge: Cambridge University Press, 2000), 135f.

20. John Milbank, *Being Reconciled: Ontology and Pardon* (London: Routledge, 2003), 18, 25.

21. Hanson and Kay, *Star Wars: The New Myth*, 278.

22. Lucas, "Of Myth and Men."

23. David West Reynolds, *Star Wars Episode I: The Visual Dictionary* (London: Dorling Kindersley, 1999), 16.

24. Citation from *ROTS*'s opening scroll.

25. Luceno, *Star Wars: Dark Lord,* 54.

26. Wink, *Engaging the Powers,* 17.

27. Luceno, *Star Wars: Dark Lord*, 135.

28. Ibid., 304.

29. Luceno, *Star Wars: Revenge of the Sith*, 13.

30. Ibid.

31. "Mace Windu," http://en.wikipedia.org/wiki/Mace_Windu, consulted 14-06-05.

32. Richard Hanley, "Send in the Clones: The Ethics of Future Wars," in Decker and Eberl, eds., *Star Wars and Philosophy*, 93–103 (94).

33. See Ryder Windham, *Star Wars: Revenge of the Sith Scrapbook* (London: Scholastic, 2005), 13.

34. See "Sifo-Dyas," http://en.wikipedia.org/wiki/Sifo-Dyas, consulted 14-06-05.

35. The shuttle version can be found in Luceno, *Star Wars: Revenge of the Sith*, 23; the troop carrier version is in Abel G. Pena, "Unknown Soldier: The Story of General Grievous," *Star Wars 1*, no. 63 (May–June 2006): 53–59 (57).

36. Ralph C. Wood, *The Gospel according to Tolkien: Visions of the Kingdom in Middle Earth* (Louisville, KY: Westminster John Knox Press, 2003), 51.

37. Robert W. Jenson, "Introduction: Much Ado about Nothingness," in Carl E. Braaten and Robert W. Jenson, eds., *Sin, Death, and the Devil* (Grand Rapids: Eerdmans, 2000), 1–6 (2).

38. The long-standing anti-Semitism in central Europe devastatingly intensified in the 1930s, largely in response to the German feeling of betrayal at the hands of the Allied powers over the Versailles Treaty (1919), the postwar economic catastrophes (late 1920s–early 1930s), the Nazi drive to determine Germany's future, and the shape of World War II in the early 1940s.

39. Milbank, *Being Reconciled*, 2.

40. Luceno, *Star Wars: Dark Lord*, 53, 122.

41. "Palpatine," http://www.starwars.com/databank/character/palpatine/, consulted 05-04-06.

42. Augustine, *Confessions*, trans. S. R. Pine-Coffin (Harmondsworth: Penguin, 1961), V.10.103.

43. Campbell, *The Hero*, 238.

44. Citation from Augustine, *The Enchiridion*, 18.

45. Citation from ibid., 17.

46. The person of Jesus the Christ, as the very incarnated presence of God's Word, is a different case altogether.

47. McFadyen, *Bound to Sin*, 37.

48. *Mississippi Burning*, dir. Alan Parker (MGM, 1988).

49. *Se7en*, dir. David Fincher (New Line Cinema, 1997).

50. Boethius, *The Consolation of Philosophy*, trans. W. V. Cooper (London: J. M. Dent & Co., 1902), book III, 68.29: available at http://www.ccel.org/ccel/boethius/consolation.html, consulted 26-05-05.

51. Boethius, book IV, 109.48.

52. Ibid., 114.50.

53. Gelven, *This Side of Evil*, 43.

54. Augustine, *The Enchiridon*, 17.

55. Roald Dahl, *The Twits* (London: Puffin Books, 1980), 7.

56. Lord Sidious "was a gnarled, ancient man with pale skin, searing, sickly yellow eyes. He wore a heavy dark cloak, . . . and carried glossy black cane, leaning heavily on it to create an illusion of weakness" ("Palpatine," *Wookieepedia,* http://starwars.wikia.com/wiki/Palpatine, consulted 12-02-17).

57. Luceno, *Star Wars: Dark Lord,* 133.

58. Jerold J. Abrams, "A Technological Galaxy: Heidegger and the Philosophy of Technology in Star Wars," in Decker and Eberl, eds., *Star Wars and Philosophy,* 107–19 (118).

59. Rowlands, *The Philosopher,* 219f.

60. Luceno, *Star Wars: Dark Lord,* 56.

61. Ibid., 57, 60, 76.

Chapter 4: Beware the Dark Side Within

1. Lucas, in "The Chosen One" featurette, *Star Wars Episode III: The Revenge of the Sith,* DVD Disc 2 (Lucasfilms Ltd., 2005).

2. Pollock, *Skywalking,* 189.

3. Aristotle, *The Poetics of Aristotle: Translation and Commentary*, Stephen Halliwell (London: Duckworth), esp. chap. 14.

4. Peter T. Chattaway, "*Star Wars: Episode III—Revenge of the Sith,*" http://www.patheos.com/blogs/filmchat/2005/05/review-star-wars-episode-iii-revenge-of-the-sith-dir-george-lucas.html, consulted 12-02-17.

5. Carl Jung, "On the Nature of Dreams," in *The Collected Works of C. G. Jung,* ed. Herbert Read et al. (London: Routledge & Kegan Paul, 1960), 8:293.

6. Lucas, in Hugh Hart, "Flaws in a Good Heart," LosAngelesTimes.com, January 20, 2002, http://articles.latimes.com/2002/jan/20/entertainment/ca-hart20, consulted 12-02-17.

7. "George Lucas Interview—The Story Comes First," January 15, 2002, http://www.starwars.com/episode-ii/bts/profile/f20020115/indexp2.html; Lucas, "Flaws in a Good Heart."

8. Lucas, "Story," in *Star Wars Episode II: Attack of the Clones,* DVD Disc 2 (Twentieth Century Fox, 2002).

9. Lucas, in *Time,* cited http://boards.theforce.net/The_Star_Wars_Saga/b104556/13106765/p2, consulted 08-05-05 (site discontinued).

10. Lucas, cited in http://boards.theforce.net/The_Star_Wars_Saga/b104556/13106765/p2, consulted 08-05-05 (site discontinued).

11. "George Lucas: Mapping the Mythology," *CNN,* May 8, 2002, http://edition.cnn .com/2002/SHOWBIZ/Movies/05/07/ca.s02.george.lucas/, consulted 12-02-17.

12. Henry Sheehan, "Star Wars: Episode III Revenge of the Sith," http://id3481.securedata .net/henrysheehan/reviews/stuv/star-wars-3.html, consulted 12-02-17.

13. Hayden Christensen, in *Empire,* June 2005, 88.

14. Ian McDiarmid, in "The Chosen One."

15. Stover, *Star Wars Episode III,* 175.

16. See ibid., 202f.

17. Ibid., 214, 215.

18. Ibid., 224.

19. In an early scene in Stover's novelization of *ROTS,* Padmé greets her returning husband with the words that things between them have changed, which Anakin promptly misunderstands. He forcefully grabs her by the shoulders and in a thunderous rage accuses her of having *someone else* (164). In the movie, despite his evident love for Obi-Wan earlier, Anakin's second shown dream of Padmé suffering contains Obi-Wan sitting by her urging her not to give up. At this point Anakin announces to his wife that "Obi-Wan and the Council don't trust me."

20. Terry Christensen, *Reel Movies: American Political Movies from* The Birth of a Nation *to* Platoon (New York and Oxford: Basil Blackwell, 1987), 213.

21. Lucas, in "The Chosen One."

22. Hayden Christensen, in "The Chosen One."

23. Stover, *Star Wars Episode III,* 207.

24. Will Brooker, *Batman Unmasked: Analyzing a Cultural Icon* (New York and London: Continuum, 2001), 64f.

25. Jeffrey Overstreet, "Star Wars: Episode III—Revenge of the Sith," *Christianity Today,* May 18, 2005, http://www.patheos.com/blogs/lookingcloser/2008/04/star-wars-episode -three-revenge-of-the-sith-2005/, consulted 12-02-17.

26. William Shakespeare, *King Lear,* ed. G. K. Hunter, New Penguin Shakespeare (Harmondsworth: Penguin Books, 1972), III.ii.59.

27. Lucas, in "The Chosen One."

28. Ibid.

29. John Kekes, *Facing Evil* (Princeton, NJ: Princeton University Press, 1990), 26.

Chapter 5: The Politics of Evil

1. See Anne Lancashire, "*Attack of the Clones* and the Politics of *Star Wars,*" *Dalhousie Review* 82, no. 2 (Summer 2002): 235–53.

2. Karl Barth, *Church Dogmatics,* vol. III, *The Doctrine of Creation,* part 4, ed. G. W. Bromiley and T. F. Torrance (Edinburgh: T. & T. Clark, 1961), 513.

3. Caputo, *On Religion,* 85, 87.

4. Terry Christensen, *Reel Movies: American Movies from* The Birth of a Nation *to* Platoon (New York and Oxford: Basil Blackwell, 1987), 146.

5. See *Jump Cut* (Aug. 18, 1978), cited in Christensen, *Reel Movies,* 146; Karen Winter, "The Politics of Star Wars," http://belladonna.org/Karen/politicsofstarwars.html, consulted 30-05-05.

6. Peter Lev, "Whose Future? Star Wars, Alien, and Blade Runner," *Literature/Film Quarterly* 26, no. 1 (1998): 30–37 (34).

7. David West Reynolds, *Star Wars: Attack of the Clones. The Visual Dictionary* (London: Dorling Kindersley, 2002), 10.

8. Ibid, 10.

9. See, e.g., John Harlow, "And Now, the End Is Near . . . ," *Sunday Times Culture*, May 8, 2005, 10–11 (11).

10. Hanson and Kay, *Star Wars: The New Myth*, 382.

11. Reynolds, *Star Wars: Attack of the Clones*, 39.

12. Lucas, cited in Pollock, *Skywalking*, 165.

13. Segal, *Joseph Campbell*, 14.

14. Martin M. Winkler, "*Star Wars* and the Roman Empire," in Martin M. Winkler, ed., *Classical Myth and Culture in the Cinema* (Oxford and New York: Oxford University Press, 2001), 272–90 (289).

15. Ian Nathan, "R2D2, Where Are You?" *Times Review*, May 14, 2005, 14.

16. Pollock, *Skywalking*, 143.

17. Christensen, *Reel Movies*, 199.

18. See, e.g., Frederick Meek, *Manifest Destiny and Mission in American History: A Reinterpretation* (New York: Alfred A. Knopf, 1963), and Robert Jewett and John Shelton Lawrence, *Captain America and the Crusade against Evil: The Dilemma of Zealous Nationalism* (Grand Rapids: Eerdmans, 2003).

19. John Fousek, cited in Trevor McCrisken and Andrew Pepper, *American History and Contemporary Hollywood Film* (Edinburgh: Edinburgh University Press, 2005), 120; H. W. Brands, cited in McCrisken and Pepper, *American History*, 89. Similarly, see Wink, *Engaging the Powers*, chap. 1.

20. George W. Bush, "President Holds Prime Time News Conference," Oct. 11, 2001, cited in Jewett and Lawrence, *Captain America*, 15.

21. Wink, *Engaging the Powers*, 42.

22. Jewett and Lawrence, *Captain America*, 41f.

23. Donald McDonald, "Militarism in America," *Center Magazine* 3, no. 1 (1970): 29.

24. Jewett and Lawrence, *Captain America*, xv.

25. Lev, "Whose Future?" 31f.

26. Lucas, cited in Pollock, *Skywalking*, 269.

27. Pollock, *Skywalking*, xii.

28. Nathan, "R2D2, Where Are You?" 14.

29. Rohan Gowland, "The Phantom Menace of Idealism: Film Review," *Guardian*, June 16, 1999, http://www.cpa.org.au/z-archive/g1999/958star.htm, consulted 12-02-17.

30. Mark Thornton, "Star Wars," May 30, 1999, http://www.mises.org/story/232, consulted 08-06-05.

31. Lucas, "Of Myth and Men."

32. On this see, e.g., John Milbank, *Theology and Social Theory: Beyond Secular Reason* (Oxford: Basil Blackwell, 1990).

33. Lucas, cited in Tim Rayment, "Master of the Universe," *Sunday Times Magazine*, May 16, 1999, 20.

34. Hanson and Kay, *Star Wars: The New Myth*, 33.

35. Cited in Jack Nelson-Pallmeyer, *Saving Christianity from Empire* (New York and London: Continuum, 2005), 33.

36. Gore Vidal, *Perpetual War for Perpetual Peace: How We Got to Be So Hated* (New York: Thunder's Mouth Press/Nation's Books, 2002), x.

37. Jewett and Lawrence, *Captain America*, 68.

38. Stover, *Star Wars Episode III*, 175.

39. Campbell, *The Power of Myth*, 144.

40. Lucas, at Cannes film festival 2005. See Charlotte Higgins, "Final Star Wars Bears Message for America," *Guardian*, May 16, 2005, http://film.guardian.co.uk/cannes2005 story/0,15927,1484795,00.html#article_continue, consulted 26-05-05.

41. Jonathan V. Last, "The Case for the Empire: Everything You Know about Star Wars Is Wrong," *Daily Standard*, May 16, 2002; http://www.weeklystandard.com/the-case-for-the-empire/article/2540, consulted 12-02-17.

42. Michael Ignatieff, *Empire Lite: Nation-Building in Bosnia, Kosovo and Afghanistan* (London: Vintage, 2003).

43. Ibid., 21. Similarly, according to Deepak Lal, the United States can take "over from the British the burden of maintaining a Pax to allow free trade and commerce to flourish" (Deepak Lal, *In Praise of Empires: Globalization and Order* [New York: Palgrave Macmillan, 2004], 63).

44. Claes G. Ryn, *America the Virtuous* (New Brunswick, NJ: Transaction, 2003), 4.

45. John Ostrander, "Dead Ends," in *Star Wars Clone Wars Volume 5: The Best Blades* (Milwaukee: Dark Horse Comics, 2004).

46. Jürgen Moltmann, *On Human Dignity: Political Theology and Ethics* (London: SCM Press, 1984), 99.

47. Ibid., 111.

48. Volf, *Exclusion and Embrace*, 84.

49. John Lyden, "The Apocalyptic Cosmology of *Star Wars*," *Journal of Religion and Film* 4, no. 1 (2000): 27, http://www.unomaha.edu/jrf/LydenStWars.htm, consulted 15-05-05.

50. Christensen, *Reel Movies*, 199.

Chapter 6: Rebelling against Evil

1. Kathryn Tanner, *The Politics of God* (Minneapolis: Fortress, 1992), 124.

2. Lucas, in Salewicz, *George Lucas Close Up*, 40.

3. Thomas Horn, "Lucas' Star Wars Depicts New Age Messiah," http://www.siriustwins.com/watcher/starwarsmessiah.html, consulted 12-02-17.

4. Pollock, *Skywalking*, 211.

5. Lucas, "Of Myth and Men," cited in Hanson and Kay, *Star Wars: The New Myth*, 213.

6. Lucas, "The Making of Episode I," in *Star Wars Episode I: The Phantom Menace*, DVD Disc 2 (Lucasfilms Ltd., 1999).

7. Several more can be found in Alice Alfonsi, *Star Wars: The Skywalker Family Album* (London: Scholastic, 2002).

8. Rowlands, *The Philosopher*, 213.

9. Mohler, "Faith vs. the Force," *World Magazine* 21, no. 1 (December 31, 2005).

10. This would suggest that Luke's anti-Imperial action is undertaken not as a resolve for revenge. He simply makes no mention of his aunt and uncle later in the movie.

11. Anker, *Catching Light*, 225.

12. Citation from Campbell, *The Hero*, 82.

13. Wilkinson, *The Power of the Force*, 104.

14. Campbell, *The Hero*, 69.

15. Stanley Hauerwas, *The Peaceable Kingdom: A Primer in Christian Ethics* (London: SCM Press, 1983), 14.

16. Campbell, *The Hero*, 90, 91.

17. Matthew Bortolin, *The Dharma of Star Wars* (Boston: Wisdom Publications, 2005), 64.

18. Anker, *Catching Light*, 230.

19. Martin Luther King Jr., *Strength to Love* (London: Collins Fontana, 1969), 31.

20. In his weblog Jason Salas cites a Christian who admitted that while she prevented her children from watching screened sexual activity, she would, without a second thought, allow them to witness screened violence ("On Piety, Star Wars, and Raising Your Children to Be Morally Aware," http://www.jasonsalas.com/2005/11/on-piety-star-wars-and-raising-your.html, consulted 12-02-17).

21. Wink, *Engaging the Powers*, 13.

22. Robert Jewett and John Shelton Lawrence, *Captain America and the Crusade against Evil: The Dilemma of Zealous Nationalism* (Grand Rapids: Eerdmans, 2003), xiii.

23. Jonathan Rosenbaum, *Movies as Politics* (Berkeley, Los Angeles, London: University of California Press, 1997), 107.

24. Michelle Kinnucan, "What Star Wars Teaches Us," Common Dreams.org, May 10, 2002, http://www-personal.umich.edu/~lormand/agenda/0205/kinnucan.htm, consulted 12-02-17.

25. Stone, *Faith and the Film*, 139.

26. Citation from George W. Bush, "President Holds Prime Time News Conference," October 11, 2001, cited in Jewett and Lawrence, *Captain America*, 15.

27. Citation from Peter Lev, "Whose Future? Star Wars, Aliens, and Blade Runner," *Literature/Film Quarterly* 26, no. 1 (1998): 31f.; Ian Nathan, "R2D2, Where Are You?" *Times Review*, May 14, 2005, 14.

28. Campbell, *The Hero*, cited in Walter Wink, *The Powers That Be: A Theology for the New Millennium* (New York and London: Doubleday, 1998).

29. Wink, *Engaging the Powers*, 19.

30. James B. Jordan, "Pacifism and the Old Testament," in Gary North, ed., *The Theology of Christian Resistance* (Tyler, TX: Geneva Divinity School Press, 1983), 92.

31. Lucas, *Star Wars Episode IV: A New Hope*, DVD commentary (Lucasfilm Ltd., 2004).

32. Chapter 31, cited in John Porter, *The Tao of Star Wars* (Atlanta: Humanics, 2003), 68.

33. Citation from Barth, *Church Dogmatics*, 460.

34. Citation from ibid., 398.

35. Cited in Pollock, *Skywalking*, 57. Cf. John Sutherland, "George Lucas Could Be Messing with Your Head," *Guardian*, May 23, 2005.

36. Hauerwas, *The Peaceable Kingdom*, 111.

37. Augustine, *City of God*, 19.11.866.

38. Luceno, *Star Wars: Dark Lord*, 199.

39. Cited in "Palpatine," http://starwars.wikia.com/wiki/Palpatine, consulted 12-02-17.

40. Citation from Walter Wink, *Jesus and Nonviolence: A Third Way* (Minneapolis: Fortress, 2003), 4.

41. Ibid., 72.

42. Campbell, *The Hero*, 353.

43. Lucas, commentary on DVD of *ESB* (2004).

44. Anker, *Catching Light*, 235.

45. Citations from King, *Strength to Love*, 152.

46. *Catechism of the Catholic Church* (1997), § 2304, cited in James Turner Johnson, "Just War, as It Was and Is," *First Things* 149 (2005): 14–24.

47. Cited in Jack Nelson-Pallmeyer, *Saving Christianity from Empire* (New York and London: Continuum, 2005), 1.

Chapter 7: Feeling the Force

1. Nigel Wright, *The Radical Evangelical: Seeking a Place to Stand* (London: SPCK, 1996), 37.

2. Cited in Wilkinson, *The Power of the Force*, 63.

3. Cited in Pollock, *Skywalking*, 144.

4. Ibid., 271.

5. Augustine, *The Enchiridion*, 18, 22.

6. Shanti Fader, "'A Certain Point of View': Lying Jedi, Honest Sith, and the Viewers Who Love Them," in Decker and Eberl, *Star Wars and Philosophy*, 192–204 (202, 204).

7. George Lucas, *Star Wars: From the Adventures of Luke Skywalker* (London: Sphere Books, 1997), 1.

8. Campbell, *The Hero*, 382f.

9. Hanson and Kay, *Star Wars: The New Myth*, 220.

10. Ian Nathan, in "Star Wars: A Celebration," *Empire*, June 2005, 6.

11. Richard J. Foster, *Freedom of Simplicity* (London: Triangle, 1981), 88.

12. Martin Luther King Jr., *Strength to Love* (London: Collins Fontana, 1969), 44.

13. Ibid., 43.

14. Lucas, *Star Wars Episode V: The Empire Strikes Back*, DVD commentary (Lucasfilm Ltd., 2004).

15. Harrison Ford, cited in Baxter, *George Lucas*, 331.

16. Richard H. Dees, "Moral Ambiguity in a Black-and-White Universe," in Decker and Eberl, eds., *Star Wars and Philosophy*, 39–53 (42).

17. Ibid., 45f.

18. Ibid., 46.

19. *ESB* DVD commentary.

20. Will Brooker, *Using the Force: Creativity, Community and Star Wars Fans* (New York and London: Continuum, 2002), 4.

21. Hanson and Kay, *Star Wars: The New Myth*, 320.

22. Luceno, *Star Wars: Dark Lord*, 125.

23. Augustine, *City of God*, 8.8.310f.

24. Boethius, book III, 68.29. Palpatine "ruled with power, and was finally ruled by power. He was a man who saw all, and knew much, and yet was totally blind, and knew nothing, when it mattered the most" ("Palpatine," http://starwars.wikia.com/wiki/Palpatine, consulted 05-04-06).

25. Herbert McCabe, *God Still Matters* (London and New York: Continuum, 2002), 173f.

26. Lucas, *Star Wars: From the Adventures of Luke Skywalker*, 1.

27. Bortolin, *The Dharma of Star Wars*, 82.

28. Teresa of Avila, *The Way of Perfection*, trans. E. Allison Peers (Garden City, NY: Image Books, 1964), 36f.

29. King, *Strength to Love*, 153.

30. James Lawler, "The Force Is with *Us*: Hegel's Philosophy of Spirit Strikes Back at the Empire," in Decker and Eberl, eds., *Star Wars and Philosophy*, 144–56 (155).

31. St. John of the Cross, *The Ascent of Mount Carmel*, trans. Allison Peers (Garden City, NY: Image Books, 1962), 1.3.4.

32. Ibid., 1.5.6.

33. Foster, *Freedom of Simplicity*, 58.

34. Augustine, *City of God*, 9.20.366.

35. See Jonathan Rosenbaum, *Movies as Politics* (Berkeley, Los Angeles, London: University of California Press, 1997), 108.

36. Hanson and Kay, *Star Wars: The New Myth*, 320.

37. Jerome Donnelly, "Humanizing Technology: Flesh and Machine in Aristotle and *The Empire Strikes Back*," in Decker and Eberl, eds., *Star Wars and Philosophy*, 181–91 (187f., 190f.).

38. Mark Hamill, cited in Pollock, *Skywalking*, 163.

39. Pollock, *Skywalking*, 163.

40. Cited in ibid., 138.

41. Lyden, "The Apocalyptic Cosmology of *Star Wars*," *Journal of Religion and Film* 4, no. 1 (2000), "Abstract.

42. Cf. Hanson and Kay, *Star Wars: The New Myth*, 282.

43. See Pollock, *Skywalking*, 160.

44. See "Palpatine," http://starwars.wikia.com/wiki/Palpatine, consulted 12-02-17.

45. "Palpatine," http://www.starwars.com/databank/character/palpatine/, consulted 05-04-06.

46. Lucas, "Of Myth and Men."

47. Lucas, in "The Chosen One," featurette, *Star Wars Episode III: The Revenge of the Sith*, DVD Disc 2 (Lucasfilms Ltd., 2005).

48. Caputo, *On Religion*, 82.

Chapter 8: A New Hope

1. Henderson, cited in Michelle Kinnucan, "What Star Wars Teaches Us," Common Dreams.org, May 10, 2002, http://www-personal.umich.edu/~lormand/agenda/0205/kinnucan.htm, consulted 12-02-17.

2. Christopher M. Brown, "'A Wretched Hive of Scum and Villainy': *Star Wars* and the Problem of Evil," in Decker and Eberl, eds., *Star Wars and Philosophy*, 78.

3. Lucas, cited in Salewicz, *George Lucas Close Up*, 101.

4. Wilkinson, *The Power of the Force*, 91, my emphasis.

5. Lucas, "The Making of Episode I," in *Star Wars Episode I: The Phantom Menace*, DVD Disc 2 (Lucasfilms Ltd., 1999). The relation of questions of causal determinism in *SW* to medieval Christian accounts of divine providence, such as we find in Jason T. Eberl's article, are misleading, however ("'You Cannot Escape Your Destiny' (or Can You?)," in Decker and Eberl, eds., *Star Wars and Philosophy*, 3–15). He badly reads Augustine and Thomas Aquinas as envisioning God's agency as on the same plane as creaturely agency, and therefore God as an agent like other agents, but having more power and control than others.

6. Wink, *Engaging the Powers*, 19.

7. Kahn, *Star Wars Episode VI: Return of the Jedi*, 64.

8. Augustine, *City of God*, 14.6, 556.

9. Anker, *Catching Light*, 236f.

10. Barth, *Church Dogmatics*, 507.

11. Anker, *Catching Light*, 235.

12. Volf, *Exclusion and Embrace*, 85, 153.

13. Anker, *Catching Light*, 238.

14. Hanson and Kay, *Star Wars: The New Myth*, 370.

15. George Steiner, *Death of Tragedy* (New York: Oxford University Press, 1961), 332.

16. Hanson and Kay, *Star Wars: The New Myth*, 126.

17. Nicholas Lash, *The Beginning and End of Religion* (Cambridge: Cambridge University Press, 1996), 207.

18. William F. Lynch, *Images of Hope: Imagination as Healer of the Hopeless* (Notre Dame and London: University of Notre Dame Press, 1965), 21.

19. Merold Westphal, *Suspicion and Faith: The Religious Uses of Modern Atheism* (Grand Rapids: Eerdmans, 1993), 8.

20. R. W. Hepburn, "Optimism, Finitude and the Meaning of Life," in *The Philosophical Frontiers of Christian Theology: Essays Presented to D. M. MacKinnon*, ed. Brian Hebblethwaite and Stewart Sutherland (Cambridge: Cambridge University Press, 1982), 134.

Chapter 9: Whose Force Awakens?

1. Jack Shepherd, "Star Wars The Force Awakens: J. J. Abrams Responds to Criticism about the Film Being a New Hope 'Rip Off,'" *The Independent* (January 10, 2016), http://www.independent.co.uk/arts-entertainment/films/news/jj-abrams-criticism-star-wars -the-force-awakens-a-new-hope-rip-off-a6804546.html, consulted 12-05-2016.

2. Cited in Shepherd.

3. For an interesting and insightful video suggesting the latter, see Nicholas Spargo, "Why *Star Wars The Force Awakens* Is a Massive Disappointment," https://www.youtube .com/watch?v=FNAy7yCMyBw, consulted 11-05-2016. The 2010 anti-prequel movie *The People vs. George Lucas* has inspired "The People vs. J. J. Abrams," https://www.youtube .com/watch?v=GTyLvY3FX_s, consulted 18-04-2016.

4. It is startling, and deeply problematic in the continuity of the *SW* movies' universe, that the planet of Jakku, as well as others in *TFA* such as D'Qar, Takodana, and Hosnian Prime, never appeared on any of the galactic maps prior to J. J. Abrams and Lawrence Kasdan's writing involvement. Even Ryder Windham and Dan Wallace's updated and expanded edition of *Star Wars: The Ultimate Visual Guide*, which was published as late as 2015, misses these planets in its galaxy ([London: Dorling Kindersley, 2015], 14). Jakku is close to the "core" worlds, so it is quite a stretch of the imagination to justify its *sudden appearance* on *TFA*'s galactic map.

5. See Lucas, cited in Rinzler, *The Making of Star Wars*, 191; Taylor, 151.

6. Pablo Hidalgo, *Star Wars, The Force Awakens: The Visual Dictionary* (London: Dorling Kindersley, 2015), 25.

7. George Lucas, https://www.youtube.com/watch?v=VEIrQUXm_hY, consulted 11-05 -2016. The full interview can be found at https://www.youtube.com/watch?v=6jWtbJxzGpQ, consulted 11-05-2016.

8. Lucas announces at the various premieres, "I think the fans are going to love it. It's very much the kind of movie they've been looking for." (See "George Lucas Thinks The Force Awakens Is Too 'Retro,' Calls Disney 'White Slavers,'" *Telegraph Film*, December 31, 2015, http://www.telegraph.co.uk/film/star-wars-the-force-awakens/george-lucas-disney-criticism/, consulted 11-05-2016.)

9. "Abrams keeps talking about wanting to evoke the feel of the originals rather than the prequels—in the *Vanity Fair* story, he says he considered putting Jar Jar Binks's bones in the background of a *Force Awakens* scene" (Bruce Handy, "The Daring Genesis of J. J. Abrams's *Star Wars: The Force Awakens*," *Vanity Fair* (June 2015), http://www.vanityfair.com /hollywood/2015/05/star-wars-the-force-awakens-vanity-fair-cover, consulted 11-05-2016; Spencer Kornhaber, "The *Star Wars* Sequel Lucas Didn't Get to Make," *The Atlantic* (May

7, 2015), http://www.theatlantic.com/entertainment/archive/2015/05/star-wars-vanity-fair-the -force-awakens/392669/, consulted 11-05-2016.

10. Three recent critical studies of gender issues in *SW* are Cole Bowman, "Pregnant Padmé and Slave Leia: *Star Wars'* Female Role Models," in Jason T. Eberl and Kevin S. Decker, eds., *The Ultimate Star Wars and Philosophy: You Must Unlearn What You Have Learned* (Malden, Oxford and Chichester: John Wiley & Sons Ltd., 2016), 161–71; Jennifer L. McMahon, "Docile Bodies and a Viscous Force: Fear of the Flesh in *Return of the Jedi*," in Eberl and Decker, 172–82; Mara Wood, "Feminist Icons Wanted: Damsels in Distress Need Not Apply," in Peter W. Lee, ed., *A Galaxy Here and Now: Historical and Cultural Readings of Star Wars* (Jefferson, NC: McFarland Press, 2016), 62–83. For a sustained criticism of similar readings see McDowell, *Identity Politics in George Lucas' Star Wars*, chap. 3. Unless attentive to the context, the criticisms of "slave-Leia" as a sexist representation, with the Princess being reduced to eye candy, are very disturbing. After all, the reduction of Leia to a sex object is precisely *what Jabba imposes upon her*, and *ROTJ*'s sympathies are certainly not with him. It has been too easy for the commentators to miss this through their confusion of the movie's scene with the titillated response from many of the male members of the audience. Similarly, the criticisms of the reduction of Padmé in *ROTS* to the destroyed lover is not simply a matter of removing the scenes involving political discussion for pacing purposes but also a feature of the *tragic nature of her story*. Chris Taylor suggests that there was another reason: "Unfortunately, [Natalie] Portman [the actress] was increasingly difficult to deal with on set—some of the crew say she made several actresses playing her handmaidens, including Keira Knightly . . . cry in the previous prequels, allegedly for the crime of talking to her without permission. According to some Lucasfilm insiders, many of her lines were cut from *ROTS* for that reason. She had little left to do but to be barefoot and pregnant with the Skywalker twins" (Taylor, 343).

11. Cited in Taylor, 106.

12. See Rinzler, *The Making of Star Wars*, 47.

13. Lucas, cited in Rinzler, *The Making of The Empire Strikes Back*, 21.

14. Hidalgo, 56.

15. Hidalgo, 30.

16. Lucas, cited in Rinzler, *The Making of Star Wars*, 441.

17. Lucas, cited in ibid.

18. Lucas, cited in ibid., 442.

19. For example, see Kline, 69.

20. Finn's ability to hold off Kylo Ren (even if Ren is injured) for a period with a lightsaber and deliver a cutting blow is equally little more than a problematic plot device.

21. There is a possible explanation through some Expanded Universe depictions of the Kyber Crystals' connection with the Force. But given that this has appeared nowhere in the *SW* movies to date, *TFA* needs to better explain why the lightsaber called out to Rey without slipping into yet another superficial plot-device element. The closest the movies have come to it is the connection of the Force and the dark side intensively with certain places such as the cave on Dagobah.

22. *The Ultimate Visual Guide* contains the following claims: "Under Palpatine's rule, the Academy becomes the Imperial Naval Academy, where students are fed propaganda to

believe that all alien species are inferior beings"; and "[Grand Moff] Tarkin believes that humans are superior to aliens," 96 and 102, respectively).

23. Hidalgo, 29.

24. Hidalgo, 22.

25. A further example of this tendency can be seen in Alan Dean Foster's novelization. In Leia's conversation with Han about their fallen son she claims that "he was born with equal potential for good and evil" (*Star Wars: The Force Awakens* [London: Century, 2016], 197).

26. The depiction of the Nemoidians in terms of a biological acquisition-imperative might echo the *Star Trek* universe's Ferengi, but it nevertheless provides a biological essentialism, and accordingly there is no sense of redemption of a whole people in the prequels. The species' very essence runs counter to the proper demands of the good life as Lucas conceives it. There is an even more politically disturbing essentialism that takes place with the depiction of the Tuskens. For a provocative critical reading of this, see Paul Charbel, "Deconstructing the Desert: The Bedouin Ideal and the True Children of Tatooine," in Peter W. Lee, ed., *A Galaxy Here and Now: Historical and Cultural Readings of Star Wars* (Jefferson, NC: McFarland Press, 2016), 138–61. The very name of *Tatooine* was developed from a transliteration of the Arabic name of a Tunisian city called Tataouine (see Taylor, 151).

27. See Lucas, cited in Rinzler, *The Making of Star Wars*, 290.

28. Henry A. Giroux, *The Mouse That Roared: Disney and the End of Innocence* (Lanham, Boulder, New York and Oxford: Rowman & Littlefield Publishers, Inc., 1999), 141.

29. Gregory E. Rutledge, "Jedi Knights and Epic Performance: Is the Force a Form of Western-African Epic Mimicry?" in Lee, 106–37 (130).

30. Hidalgo, 21.

31. Hidalgo, 20.

32. The numbering of the character "FN-2187" provides a reference to Lipsett's short movie and from there a further reference to Lucas's *SW*.

33. Elizabeth A. Kus and Janina Scarlet, "The Intergalactic Guide to Girls and Gender Psychology," in Travis Langley, ed., *Star Wars Psychology: Dark Side of the Mind* (New York: Sterling, 2015), 84–94 (89).

34. On a different note, it is odd and very poorly scripted for a weapon to charge itself by draining the sun of its energy "until it disappears." How could the planet, and the Starkiller base built on it, survive such a star-extinguishing event?

35. Leonidas Donskis, in Leonidas Donskis and Zygmunt Bauman, *Moral Blindness: The Loss of Sensitivity in Liquid Modernity* (Cambridge and Malden: Polity, 2013), 39.

36. Cited in Rob van Scheers, *Paul Verhoeven*, trans. Aletta Stevens (London: Faber and Faber, 1997), xiii.

37. Terry Eagleton, *Holy Terror* (Oxford and New York: Oxford University Press, 2005), 106.

38. Ibid., 131.

39. Taylor, 267.

40. Alan Dean Foster, cited in Taylor, 267.

41. The cracked Kyber Crystal and subsequently unstable lightsaber reflects the instability of his characterization.

42. Missing the complications of the good-evil motif, the connection of Palpatine and Nixon, the Ewoks and the Vietcong, and the prequel allusions to American and British foreign

policy through the line "if you're not with me you're my enemy" makes Peter W. Lee's reading a distinctly misplaced and eccentric one: "[*SW*'s] good/bad narrative valorized Americanism with a celebratory portrayal of continual progress and—despite Lucas's claims of a mystical Force overcoming monstrous technological terrors—American mechanical prowess" ("Periodizing a Civil War: Reaffirming an American Empire of Dreams," in Lee, 162–88 [163]). He does admit that Lucas claimed *SW*'s "anti-Nam message" later in the paper, but Lee does not follow through on the political implications for rereading *SW* in this light [177].

43. Lucas, cited in Taylor, 88.

44. Lucas, cited in ibid., 301. Taylor explains that when Lucas began composing *TPM* in 1994 the government "started pushing its tax-cutting, regulation-slashing 'Contract with America'" [ibid.]. "It was perhaps no coincidence, then, that Lucas started writing about a 'Trade Federation,' aided and emboldened by corrupt politicians, embroiled in some sort of dispute over the taxing of trade to the outlying star systems." The name of the Trade Federation's leader, Nute Gunray, is an echo to Newt Gingrich, the House Speaker; and the name of its senator, Lott Dod, is a reference to the GOP Senate leader Trent Lott. As Taylor comments, "We're a long way from the subtlety of his Vietnam metaphor here" [ibid.].

45. Ibid., 342.

46. Lucas, cited in ibid.

47. Foster, *Star Wars: The Force Awakens*, 173.

48. Giroux, *The Mouse That Roared*, 86.

49. Hidalgo, 56.

50. Foster, *Star Wars: The Force Awakens*, 256.

51. "The New Republic, with what First Order admirals mock as typical shortsightedness, was so thorough in its galactic disarmament that the First Order's secret fleet of Star Destroyers now stands almost unchallenged" (Hidalgo, 42).

52. See John C. McDowell, *Identity Politics in George Lucas' Star Wars* (Jefferson, NC: McFarland Press, 2016), chapters 1–2.

53. George A. Dunn, 'Why the Force Must Have a Dark Side," in Jason T. Eberl and Kevin S. Decker, eds., *The Ultimate Star Wars and Philosophy: You Must Unlearn What You Have Learned* (Malden, Oxford and Chichester: John Wiley & Sons Ltd., 2016), 195–207 (202).

54. Lee, 165.

55. Taylor, 44.

56. Lucas, cited in ibid., 58.

57. J. J. Abrams, cited in Josh Dickey, "There's a 'Light Side'? Star Wars Used to Just Have 'The Force' and 'The Dark Side'" (December 8, 2015), http://mashable.com/2015/12/08/star-wars-calendar-8/#8Nj_WkHansql, consulted 09/05/2016.

58. Stephen J. Sansweet, Pablo Hidalgo, Bob Vitas, and Daniel Wallace, with Chris Cassidy, Mary Franklin, and Josh Kushins, *The Complete Star Wars Encyclopedia*, Volume 1 (London: Titan Books, 2008), 285.

59. Lucas, cited in Taylor, 194.

60. Rinzler, *The Making of Return of the Jedi*, 40.

61. George Lucas, https://www.youtube.com/watch?v=O8hQVlRgFlU, consulted 11-05-2016. (The full interview can be found at https://www.youtube.com/watch?v=6jWtbJxzGpQ, consulted 11-05-2016.) A little later he apologized for the analogy and admitted that he had had long-lasting respect for the corporation. See Daniel Kreps, "George Lucas Apologizes

Over 'Force Awakens' Criticisms," *Rolling Stone* (January 1, 2016), http://www.rollingstone.com/movies/news/george-lucas-apologizes-over-force-awakens-criticisms-20160101, consulted 11-05-2016.

62. Lucas admits to Charlie Rose, "They [viz., the people at Disney] looked at the stories, and they said, 'We want to make something for the fans.' . . . They decided they didn't want to use those stories, they decided they were going to do their own thing. . . . They weren't that keen to have me involved anyway—but if I get in there, I'm just going to cause trouble, because they're not going to do what I want them to do. And I don't have the control to do that anymore, and all I would do is muck everything up. And so I said, 'Okay, I will go my way, and I'll let them go their way.'"

63. Ben Child, "Attack of the Moans: George Lucas Hits Out at 'Retro' Star Wars: The Force Awakens," *The Guardian* (December 31, 2015), http://www.theguardian.com/film/2015/dec/31/george-lucas-attacks-retro-star-wars-the-force-awakens, consulted 11-05-2016.

64. Lucas, cited in J. W. Rinzler, *The Making of The Empire Strikes Back: The Definitive Story* (New York: Ballantine, 2010), 13.

65. Giroux, *The Mouse That Roared*, 89.

66. Ibid.

67. Neil Postman, *Amusing Ourselves to Death: Public Discourse in the Age of Show Business* (New York: Penguin Books, 1985), 108.

68. Giroux, *The Mouse That Roared*, 114.

69. Brad Evans and Henry A. Giroux, *Disposable Futures: The Seduction of Violence in the Age of Spectacle* (San Francisco: City Lights Books, 2015), 10.

70. Walter Brueggemann, *Journey to the Common Good* (Louisville, KY: Westminster John Knox Press, 2010), 1.

Afterword

1. S. Brent Plate, *Religion and Film: Cinema and the Re-Creation of the World* (London and New York: Wallflower, 2008), 1.

2. George Lucas, in John Seabrook, "Why Is the Force Still with Us?" *The New Yorker* 72, no. 41 (January 6, 1997): 48.

3. Ursula K. Le Guin, cited in Kevin J. Wetmore Jr., *The Empire Triumphant: Race, Religion and Rebellion in the* Star Wars *Films* (Jefferson, NC, and London: McFarland & Co., 2005), 10. Cf. Lucas, in Kline, 143.

4. Neil Postman, *Amusing Ourselves to Death: Public Discourse in the Age of Show Business* (New York: Viking Penguin, 1985), 160.

5. Ibid., 161.

6. Ibid., 163.

7. Lucas, cited in Andrew Bank, "May the Force Be with Jew: The Jedi-Hebraic Connection," in Douglas Brode and Leah Deyneka, eds., *Sex, Politics, and Religion in Star Wars: An Anthology* (Lanham, Toronto, Plymouth: The Scarecrow Press, 2012), 47–53 (50). Accordingly Michael Pye and Linda Myles were badly off the target when in their 1979 article they claimed that *SW* "offers the ultimate escape, withdrawal from complex questions of morality. . . . It is a holiday from thought" (in Kline, 85).

8. Rutledge, 132.

9. Lucas, cited in Taylor, 72.

10. Lucas, cited in Rinzler, *The Making of The Empire Strikes Back*, 20.

11. See Lucas, in Rinzler, *The Making of Star Wars*, 436.

12. Lucas, cited in Bank, 51.

13. J. P. Telotte, *Science Fiction Film* (Cambridge: CUP, 2001), 128.

14. Lucas in "The Chosen One." As chapters 4–6 should have made clear, a claim that Christianity sees good and evil "in black-and-white terms," such as that made by Julien Fielding, is a distinct misreading of the Christian traditions (Julien Fielding, "Beyond Judeo-Christianity: *Star Wars* and the Great Eastern Religions," in Douglas Brode and Leah Deyneka, eds., *Sex, Politics, and Religion in Star Wars: An Anthology* [Lanham, Toronto, Plymouth: The Scarecrow Press, 2012], 25–46 [36]).

15. Lucas, cited in Rinzler, *The Making of The Empire Strikes Back*, 24; and in Rinzler, *The Making of Return of the Jedi*, 70, respectively. Cf. *The Making of Return of the Jedi*, 277.

16. Lucas, cited in Rinzler, *The Making of Star Wars*, 126.

17. Kazanjian, cited in Rinzler, *Making of Return of the Jedi*, 7.

18. Card, "No Faith in This Force."

19. Cited in Jenkins, 195.

20. Citation from Anker, 220f.

21. Ralph C. Wood, *The Gospel according to Tolkien*, 163.

22. St. John of the Cross, 2.7.5, 2.7.12.

23. Kathryn Tanner, *The Politics of God: Christian Theologies and Social Justice* (Minneapolis: Fortress Press, 1992), vii. One otherwise sympathetic blog reviewer of the first edition of my book was worried that I was a little too harsh about the abuses of the church. I find it difficult not to be driven by the injunction to "test the spirits" (1 John 4:1) in the light not only of the success narratives of Acts of the Apostles but the form of betrayals of the Gospel that constantly tempt us and that are witnessed to throughout the New Testament itself (for instance, in the letters to the seven churches in Revelation). To cite Tanner again, "the Christian theological tradition is likely to be vitiated or many people by the recorded history of its uses" (3). Hope in the Gospel does emerge from the ability to read saintly stories or identify success narratives rather than texts of terror. Rather, it has its ground in the constancy of God's faithfulness to even an unfaithful people.

24. Alex Langley, "These Archetypes You're Looking For," in Travis Langley, ed., *Star Wars Psychology: Dark Side of the Mind* (New York: Sterling, 2015), 111–22 (121). Cf. Charles Champlin, cited in Rinzler, *The Making of The Empire Strikes Back*, 333.

Select Bibliography

Primary Sources

Cinematography

(1977) *Star Wars Episode IV: A New Hope*, directed by George Lucas
(1980) *Star Wars Episode V: The Empire Strikes Back*, directed by Irvin Kershner
(1983) *Star Wars Episode VI: Return of the Jedi*, directed by Richard Marquand
(1999) *Star Wars Episode I: The Phantom Menace*, directed by George Lucas
(2002) *Star Wars Episode II: Attack of the Clones*, directed by George Lucas
(2004-5) *Star Wars: Clone Wars*, 25 episodes
(2005) *Star Wars Episode III: Revenge of the Sith*, directed by George Lucas
(2015) *Star Wars Episode VII: The Force Awakens*, directed by J. J. Abrams

Novelizations

Star Wars: From the Adventures of Luke Skywalker. George Lucas. London: Sphere Books, 1977.
Star Wars: The Empire Strikes Back. Donald F. Glut. London: Sphere Books, 1980.
Star Wars: Return of the Jedi. James Kahn. London & Sydney: Futura, 1983.
Star Wars Episode I: The Phantom Menace. Terry Brooks. London: Century, 1999.
Star Wars Episode II: Attack of the Clones. R. A. Salvatore. London: Century, 2002.
Star Wars: Revenge of the Sith. Matthew Stover. London: Century, 2005.
Star Wars: The Force Awakens. Alan Dean Foster. London: Century, 2016.

Other Materials

Alfonsi, Alice. *Star Wars: The Skywalker Family Album*. London: Scholastic, 2002.
Barr, Patricia, and Adam Bray, Daniel Wallace, and Ryder Windham, *Ultimate Star Wars*. London: Dorling Kindersley, 2015.
Bouzereau, Laurent. *Star Wars: The Annotated Screenplays*. New York: Ballantine, 1997.
Feinberg, Scott, and J. J. Abrams. "'Awards Chatter' Podcast—J. J. Abrams ('Star Wars: The Force Awakens.'" *The Hollywood Reporter*. January 8, 2016. http://www.hollywoodreporter.com/race/awards-chatter-podcast-jj-abrams-853171, consulted 12-05-2016.
Fry, Jason. *Star Wars The Clone Wars: The Visual Dictionary*. New York: Dorling Kindersley, 2008.

Hidalgo, Pablo. *Star Wars, The Force Awakens: The Visual Dictionary*. London: Dorling Kindersley, 2015.

Kline, Sally, ed. *George Lucas: Interviews*. Jackson, MI: University Press of Mississippi, 1999.

Lucas, George. Interview with Bill Moyers. "Of Myth and Men: A conversation between Bill Moyer and George Lucas on the Meaning of the Force and the True Theology of *Star* Wars." *Time* 153, no. 16 (April 26, 1999). https://www.youtube.com/watch?v=YpiEk42_O_Q, consulted 11-05-2016.

———. Interview with Senator Bill Bradley. "American Voices—George Lucas Special." https://soundcloud.com/billbradley/american-voices-george-lucas-special, consulted 14-05-2016.

Luceno, James. *Star Wars: Dark Lord. The Rise of Darth Vader*. London: Century, 2005.

———. *Star Wars: The Labyrinth of Evil*. New York: Del Ray, 2005.

———. *Star Wars: Revenge of the Sith. The Visual Dictionary*. London: Dorling Kindersley, 2005.

Reynolds, David West. *Star Wars: Attack of the Clones. The Visual Dictionary*. London: Dorling Kindersley, 2002.

———. *Star Wars Episode I: The Visual Dictionary*. London: Dorling Kindersley, 1999.

Reynolds, David West, James Luceno and Ryder Windham. *Star Wars: The Complete Visual Dictionary*. London: Dorling Kindersley, 2006.

Rinzler, J. W. *The Making of Return of the Jedi: The Definitive Story*. London: Aurum Press, 2013.

———. *The Making of Star Wars: The Definitive Story Behind the Original Film*. Ebury Press, 2008.

———. *The Making of The Empire Strikes Back: The Definitive Story*. New York: Ballantine, 2010.

Sansweet, Stephen J., Pablo Hidalgo, Bob Vitas, and Daniel Wallace, with Chris Cassidy, Mary Franklin, and Josh Kushins. *The Complete Star Wars Encyclopedia*, 3 Volumes. London: Titan Books, 2008.

Windham, Ryder. *Star Wars: Revenge of the Sith Scrapbook*. London: Scholastic, 2005.

———. *Star Wars: The Ultimate Visual Guide*. London and Camberwell: Dorling Kindersley, 2005.

Windham, Ryder, and Dan Wallace. *Star Wars: The Ultimate Visual Guide*. Updated and expanded ed. London: Dorling Kindersley, 2015.

Windham, Ryder, and Peter Vilmus. *Star Wars: The Complete Vader*. London: Simon and Schuster, 2009.

Secondary Sources

Baxter, John. *George Lucas: A Biography*. London: Harper Collins, 1999.

Bortolin, Matthew. *The Dharma of Star Wars*. Boston: Wisdom Publications, 2005.

Brin, David, and Matthew Woodring Stover, eds. *Star Wars on Trial: Science Fiction and Fantasy Writers Debate the Most Popular Science Fiction Films of All Time*. Dallas: Benbella Books, 2006.

Brode, Douglas, and Leah Deyneka, eds. *Myth, Media, and Culture in Star Wars: An Anthology*. Lanham, Toronto, Plymouth: The Scarecrow Press, 2012.

————. *Sex, Politics, and Religion in Star Wars: An Anthology*. Lanham, Toronto, Plymouth: The Scarecrow Press, 2012.

Brooker, Will. *Star Wars*. London: Palgrave Macmillan, 2009.

————. *Using the Force: Creativity, Community and Star Wars Fans*. New York and London: Continuum, 2002.

Champlin, Charles. *George Lucas: The Creative Impulse*. Rev. ed. London: Virgin, 1997.

Colebatch, Hal G. P. *Return of the Heroes: The Lord of the Rings, Star Wars, Harry Potter, and Social Conflict*. 2nd ed. Christchurch, NZ: Cybereditions Corporation, 2003.

Dalton, Russell W. *Faith Journey through Fantasy Lands: A Christian Dialogue with Harry Potter, Star Wars, and the Lord of the Rings*. Minneapolis: Augsburg Books, 2003.

Decker, Kevin S., and Jason T. Eberl, eds. *Star Wars and Philosophy: More Powerful Than You Can Possibly Imagine*. Chicago and LaSalle, IL: Open Court, 2005.

Eberl, Jason T., and Kevin S. Decker, eds. *The Ultimate Star Wars and Philosophy: You Must Unlearn What You Have Learned*. Malden, Oxford and Chichester: John Wiley & Sons Ltd., 2016.

Frankel, Valerie Estelle. *A Rey of Hope: The Unauthorized Guide to Feminism, Symbolism and Hidden Gems in Star Wars The Force Awakens*. LitCrit Press, 2016.

Gordon, Andrew. "*Star Wars*: A Myth for Our Time." *Literature/Film Quarterly* 6, no. 4 (1978): 320–25.

Grimes, Caleb. *Star Wars Jesus* (Enumclaw, WA: Winepress, 2007).

Hanson, Michael J., and Max S. Kay. *Star Wars: The New Myth*. Xlibris, 2001.

Henderson, Mary. *Star Wars: The Magic of Myth*. New York: Bantam, 1997.

Jenkins, Garry. *Empire Building: The Remarkable Real Life Story of Star Wars*. London: Simon & Schuster, 1997.

Kaminski, Michael. *The Secret History of Star Wars: The Art of Storytelling and the Making of a Modern Epic*. Kingston, Ontario: Legacy Books Press, 2008.

Kapell, Matthew Wilhelm, and John Shelton Lawrence, eds. *Finding the Force of the Star Wars Franchise: Fans, Merchandise, and Critics*. New York: Peter Lang, 2006.

Lee, Peter W., ed. *A Galaxy Here and Now: Historical and Cultural Readings of Star Wars*. Jefferson, NC: McFarland Press, 2016.

Lyden, John. 'The Apocalyptic Cosmology of *Star Wars*', *The Journal of Religion and Film* 4, no. 1 (2000), 7, http://www.unomaha.edu/jrf/LydenStWars.htm.

Maxford, Howard. *George Lucas Companion*. London: B. T. Batsford, 1999.

McDowell, John C. "From Sky-Walking to the Dark Knight of the Soul: George Lucas' *Star Wars* Turns to Tragic Drama." In Douglas Brode and Leah Deyneka, eds. *Myth, Media, and Culture in Star Wars: An Anthology*. Lanham, Toronto, Plymouth: The Scarecrow Press, 2012, 65-82.

————. *Identity Politics in George Lucas' Star Wars*. Jefferson, NC: McFarland Press, 2016.

————. *The Politics of Big Fantasy: The Ideologies of Star Wars, The Matrix, and The Avengers*. Jefferson, NC: McFarland Press, 2014.

————. "*Star Wars*' Saving Return." *Journal of Religion and Film* 13, no. 1. April, 2009, http://www.unomaha.edu/jrf/vol13.no1/StarWars.htm.

————. "'Unlearn What You Have Learned' [Yoda]: The Critical Study of the Myth of *Star Wars*." In Terry R. Ryan and Dan W. Clayton, eds. *Understanding Religion and Popular Culture*. London: Routledge, 2012, 104–17.

Pollock, Dale. *Skywalking: The Life and Films of George Lucas, the Creator of Star Wars*. Hollywood, New York, London, Toronto: Samuel French, 1990.

Porter, John. *The Tao of Star Wars*. Atlanta: Humanics, 2003.

Rowlands, Mark. *The Philosopher at the End of the Universe*. London: Ebury Press, 2003.

Salewicz, Chris. *George Lucas Close Up: The Making of His Movies*. London: Orion, 1998.

Silvio, Carl, and Tony M. Vinci, eds. *Culture, Identities and Technology in the Star Wars Films: Essays on the Two Trilogies*. Jefferson, NC, and London: McFarland & Company, 2007.

Staub, Dick. *Christian Wisdom of the Jedi Masters*. San Francisco: Jossey-Bass, 2005.

Taylor, Chris. *How Star Wars Conquered the Universe: The Past, Present, and Future of a Multibillion Dollar Franchise* (New York: Basic Books, 2014).

Wetmore, Kevin J., Jr. *The Empire Triumphant: Race, Religion and Rebellion in the Star Wars Films*. Jefferson, NC, and London: McFarland & Company, 2005.

Wilkinson, David. *The Power of the Force: The Spirituality of the* Star Wars. Oxford: Lion, 2000.

Winkler, Martin M. "*Star Wars* and the Roman Empire." In Martin M. Winkler, ed. *Classical Myth and Culture in the Cinema*. Oxford and New York: Oxford University Press, 2001, 272–90.

Selected Websites

https://en.wikipedia.org/wiki/Star_Wars

http://www.starwars.com

http://starwars.wikia.com/wiki/Main_Page

Other Materials

Adorno, Theodor. *The Culture Industry: Selected Essays on Mass Culture*. J. M. Bernstein, ed. London and New York: Routledge, 1991.

Anker, Roy M. *Catching Light: Looking for God at the Movies*. Grand Rapids: William B. Eerdmans, 2004.

Augustine. *City of God*. Henry Bettenson, trans. London: Penguin Books, 1972.

Barth, Karl. *Church Dogmatics*, volume 3, *The Doctrine of Creation,* part 4. Ed. G. W. Bromiley and T. F. Torrance. Edinburgh: T. & T. Clark, 1961.

Bauman, Zygmat, and Leonides Donskis. *Moral Blindness: The Loss of Sensitivity in Liquid Modernity*. Cambridge and Malden: Polity Press, 2013.

Beaudoin, Tom. *Virtual Faith: The Irreverent Spiritual Quest of Generation X*. San Francisco: Jossey-Bass, 1998.

Biskind, Peter. *Easy Riders, Raging Bulls: Sex-Drugs-and-Rock 'n' Roll Generation Saved Hollywood*. New York: Touchstone, 1998.

Booker, M Keith. *Alternate Americas: Science Fiction Film and American Culture*. Westport: Praeger, 2006.

Campbell, Joseph. *The Hero with a Thousand Faces*. New York: Princeton University Press, 1949.

———. *Masks of God: Creative Mythology*. New York: Arkana Penguin Books, 1968.

Caputo, John D. *On Religion*. London and New York: Routledge, 2001.

Cartmell, Deborah, and I. Q. Hunter, Heidi Kaye, and Imelda Whelehan, eds. *Alien Identities: Exploring Difference in Film and Fiction*. London: Pluto Press, 1999.

Christensen, Terry. *Reel Movies: American Political Movies from The Birth of a Nation to Platoon*. New York and Oxford: Basil Blackwell, 1987.

Cornea, Christine. *Science Fiction Cinema*. Edinburgh: Edinburgh University Press, 2007.

Evans, Brad, and Henry A. Giroux *Disposable Futures: The Seduction of Violence in the Age of Spectacle*. San Francisco: City Lights Books, 2015.

Foucault, Michel. In *Michel Foucault: Power*. James D. Faubion, ed. New York: The New Press, 2000.

Giroux, Henry. *Breaking in to the Movies: Film and the Culture of Politics*. Malden and Oxford: Wiley-Blackwell, 2001.

———. *The Mouse That Roared: Disney and the End of Innocence*. Lanham, Boulder, New York and Oxford: Rowman & Littlefield Publishers, Inc., 1999.

Good, Howard. *Media Ethics Goes to the Movies*. Westport, CN: Greenwood Press, 2002.

Gorringe, Timothy J. *Furthering Humanity: A Theology of Culture*. Surrey: Ashgate, 2004.

———. *The Education of Desire: Towards a Theology of the Senses*. London: SCM, 2001.

Hauerwas, Stanley, and William H. Willimon. *Resident Aliens: Life in the Christian Colony*. Nashville: Abingdon Press, 1989.

Jantzen, Grace M. *Death and the Displacement of Beauty. Volume One: Foundations of Violence*. London: Routledge, 2004.

Johnston, Robert K. *Reel Spirituality: Theology and Film in Dialogue*. Grand Rapids: Baker Academic, 2000.

Kaveney, Roz. *From Alien to the Matrix: Reading Science Fiction and Film*. London and New York: I. B. Taurus, 2005.

King, Martin Luther, Jr. *Strength to Love*. London and Glasgow: Collins, 1963.

Kuhn, Annette, ed. *Alien Zone: Cultural Theory and Science Fiction Cinema*. London and New York: Verso, 1990.

Kupfer, Joseph. *Feminist Ethics in Film: Reconfiguring Care through Cinema*. Bristol and Chicago: Intellect Ltd., 2012.

Lasch, Christopher. *The Culture of Narcissism: American Life in an Age of Diminishing Expectations*. New York and London: W. W. Norton & Company, 1979.

———. *The Minimal Self: Psychic Survival in Troubled Times*. New York and London: W. W. Norton & Company, 1984.

Lev, Peter. *American Films of the 70s: Conflicting Visions*. Austin: University of Texas Press, 2000.

Martin, Joel W., and Conrad E. Ostwalt, eds. *Screening the Sacred: Religion, Myth, and Ideology in Popular American Film*. Boulder, San Francisco, and Oxford: Westview Press, 1995.

McKee, Gabriel. *The Gospel according to Science Fiction: Forging the Faith of the Future*. Louisville, KY: Westminster John Knox Press, 2007.

Milbank, John. *The Word Made Strange: Theology, Language, Culture*. Malden and Oxford: Blackwell, 1997.

Miles, Margaret R. *Seeing and Believing: Religion and Values in the Movies*. Boston: Beacon, 1996.

Postman, Neil. *Amusing Ourselves to Death: Public Discourse in the Age of Show Business*. New York: Viking Penguin, 1985.

Ryan, Michael, and Douglas Kellner, eds. *Camera Politica: The Politics and Ideology of Contemporary Hollywood Film*. Bloomington and Indianapolis: Indiana University Press, 1988.

Segal, Robert A. *Joseph Campbell: An Introduction* (New York: Garland, 1987).

———. *Myth: A Very Short Introduction* (Oxford and New York: Oxford University Press, 2004).

Stone, Bryan P. *Faith and the Film: Theological Themes at the Cinema*. St. Louis: Chalice Press, 2000.

Telotte, J. P. *Science Fiction Film*. Cambridge and New York: Cambridge University Press, 2001.

Volf, Miroslav. *Exclusion and Embrace: A Theological Exploration of Identity, Otherness, and Reconciliation*. Nashville: Abingdon Press, 1996.

Williams, Rowan. *Faith in the Public Square*. London, et al.: Bloomsbury, 2012.

———. *In Christian Theology*. Oxford: Blackwell, 2000.

———. *Writing in the Dust after September 11*. Grand Rapids: William B. Eerdmans Publishing Company, 2002.

Wink, Walter. *Engaging the Powers: Discernment and Resistance in a World of Domination*. Minneapolis: Fortress, 1992.

———. *Jesus and Nonviolence: A Third Way*. Minneapolis: Fortress, 2003.

Wood, Ralph C. *The Gospel according to Tolkien: Visions of the Kingdom in Middle-Earth*. Louisville, KY: Westminster John Knox Press, 2003.

Index